MW01596676

THE DIARY
OF AN OFFALY
SCHOOLBOY
1858-59

1. *Opposite Title page: Emmet Square, Birr with the bow-fronted shop of Francis Shields to the right of the Cumberland monument (courtesy of the National Library of Ireland)*

THE DIARY OF AN OFFALY SCHOOLBOY 1858-59

WILLIAM DAVIS

Edited by
Sandra Robinson

ESKER PRESS

FOR

OFFALY HISTORICAL AND ARCHAEOLOGICAL SOCIETY

TULLAMORE

2010

Published by Esker Press, Tullamore

for Offaly Historical and Archaeological Society

Bury Quay, Tullamore, Ireland

00353 5793 21421

www.offalyhistory.com

info@offalyhistory.com

© Sandra Robinson 2010

1SBN 978-0-9548720-2-1 (HB)

1SBN 978-0-9548720-3-8 (SB)

All rights reserved.

Without limiting the rights under copyright reserved alone, no part of this publication
may be reproduced, stored in or introduced into a retrieval system, or transmitted,
in any form or by any means (electronic, mechanical, photocopying, recording or
otherwise), without the prior written permission of both the copyright owner and
publisher of this book.

Printed in Ireland

Foreword

The Offaly Historical and Archaeological Society is pleased to have been given the opportunity to present this diary to the public and congratulates its editor, Sandra Robinson, for saving the diary for posterity and for her painstaking work in editing a difficult manuscript and providing helpful annotations to allow us better understand the mindset of its young teenage author, William Davis.

Diaries describing life in nineteenth-century County Offaly (formerly King's County) are not plentiful. One thinks of the diary of Robert Goodbody, the well-known Quaker entrepreneur, who died in 1860 and that of his daughter-in-law, Lydia Goodbody. But there is nothing to match the Davis diary for its description of events at family and parish level that at the same time offers comment on affairs of the moment, both local and national.

The Davis diary has some interesting observations on the purely local ramifications of the 1859 general election with trouble in Fivealley where the views of the parish priest did not coincide with others in the county and, as a consequence, Eglish secured its own item of news in the only King's County newspaper of the period, the Birr or Parsonstown-based, *King's County Chronicle*. Another local newspaper, the *Central Weekly Times*, had commenced in Tullamore in 1859 and painted in its early issues a rosy picture of Tullamore and the progress the town had made in the previous ten years. This new local newspaper lasted no more than six months with the well-established Birr-based *Chronicle* launching an undercutting competitor in Tullamore to kill off the *Central Weekly Times*.

The Famine of 1845-49 was well over and did not get even a passing reference in the Davis diary. Agriculture was improving and new fairs had been fixed for Birr in July 1857 that would harness the benefit of the improved access by rail to the Dublin markets. It was the age of the railways with the connection to Tullamore from Dublin completed in 1854 and that to Athlone in October 1859. The Birr to Roscrea line had been completed in 1858.

William Davis, the father of the diarist died in 1854 and was succeeded in his position as rate collector by his brother James who also served as guardian to the disinherited young William. William had a constant need of money as is clear from the diary and yet he could be extravagant as, for example, in his purchase of a photograph of himself when such new inventions were still expensive. William had been sent to second-level school in Birr at a time when such opportunities were scarce and beyond reach for most of the population. His dream of obtaining a commission in the army occupies many of his entries in this diary with his elderly mentor and father-figure, Abraham Whitfield, urging him on with colourful stories and yarns of army life in the far-flung British Empire. William was an avid reader of both the local and national newspapers and was able to connect some of Whitfield's yarns with the newspaper stories of the time.

This all too short diary offers a window on an age now long gone, but in which one can see the seeds of modernisation in post-Famine Ireland. The interaction between town and country is much evident in this commentary. Eglish barony, comprised of the parishes of Drumcullen and Eglish, had no large town and the nearest centres were Kilcormac and Birr. Birr was a most respectable town presided over by the third earl of Rosse, the 'astronomer-earl' and after 1854 a body of town commissioners comprised of the senior property owners. The British Association for the Advancement of Science visited Birr in 1857 and were shown over the great telescope or 'Leviathan of Parsonstown' and paid a call to see the museum of local historian and solicitor, Thomas Lalor Cooke. At the time that William Davis was writing the well-to-do of the town and district were preparing for an opera evening in the meeting rooms above the printing office of the *King's County Chronicle* in Cumberland (now Emmet) Street. Soon the town would have gas-lighting and a model school.

The seeds of modernisation in midlands Ireland are laid bare in this all to brief record of the concerns of a young man about to embark on life and not sure of his footing. It is a familiar theme but greatly enhanced here by the intimate portrait of rural Protestant Ireland, then seemingly strong, but actually in decline. The powerful third earl of Rosse, who influenced so much of the character of Birr, died in 1867. By that time our young diarist had, like so many others, taken the boat to England and was almost certainly at work in the prosaic world of the Liverpool post office. Perhaps his task in the sorting office allowed him to dream of far off places and his early ambitions to see the world as an officer in the British army. His work for the empire carried him no further than Liverpool. The year 1869 would mark the Disestablishment of the Church of Ireland and soon after came the first of many land acts that would change the proprietorial landscape of Ireland. It was only in the new century that William Davis returned to Ireland to live with some of his family, not in Eglish but in Dublin where they survived on a small business in the then increasingly fashionable suburb of Rathgar. William Davis died in 1921 as the years of British rule in Ireland were drawing to a close.

Michael Byrne

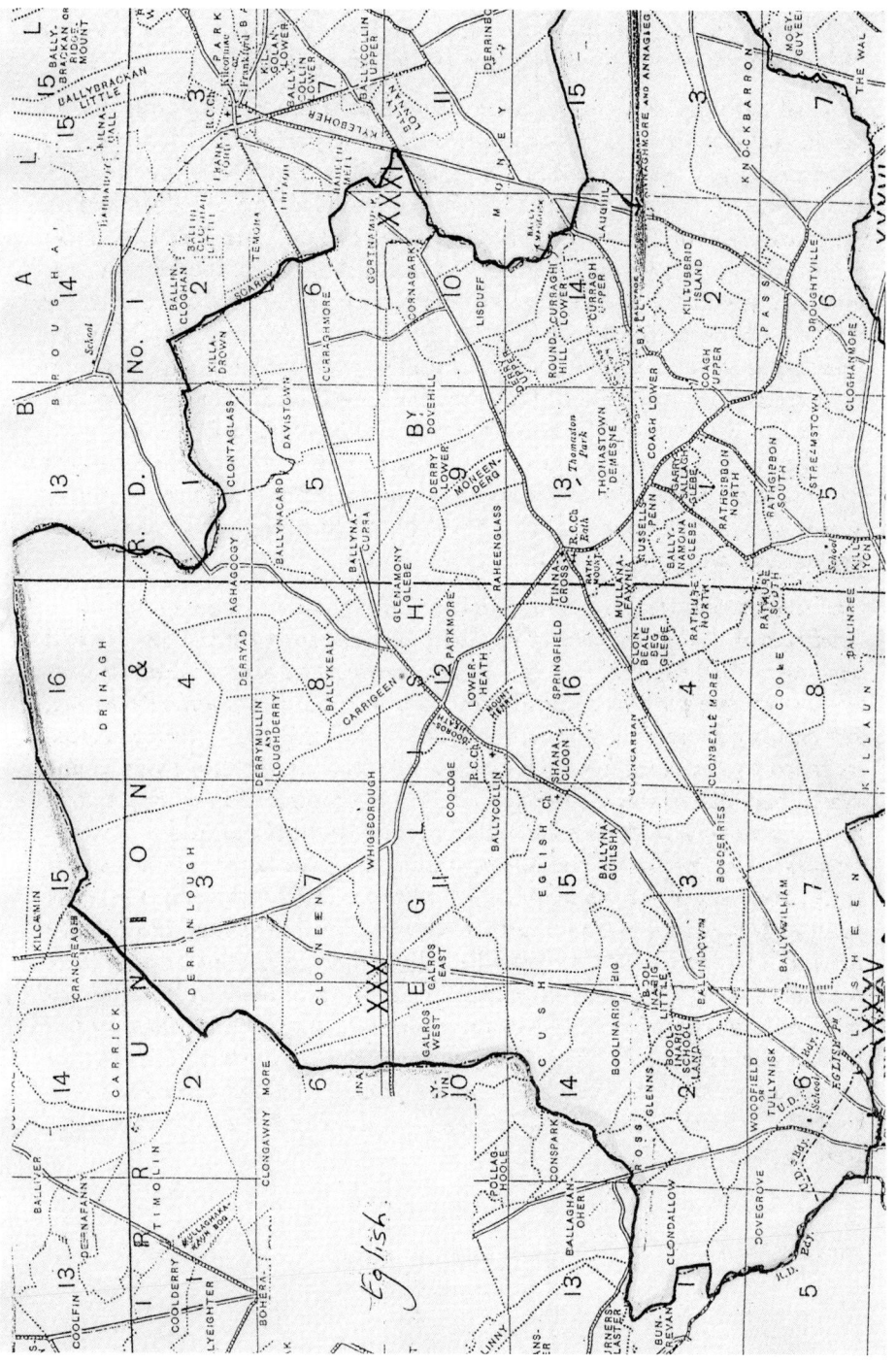

2.   *The townlands of the Eglish district about 1900*

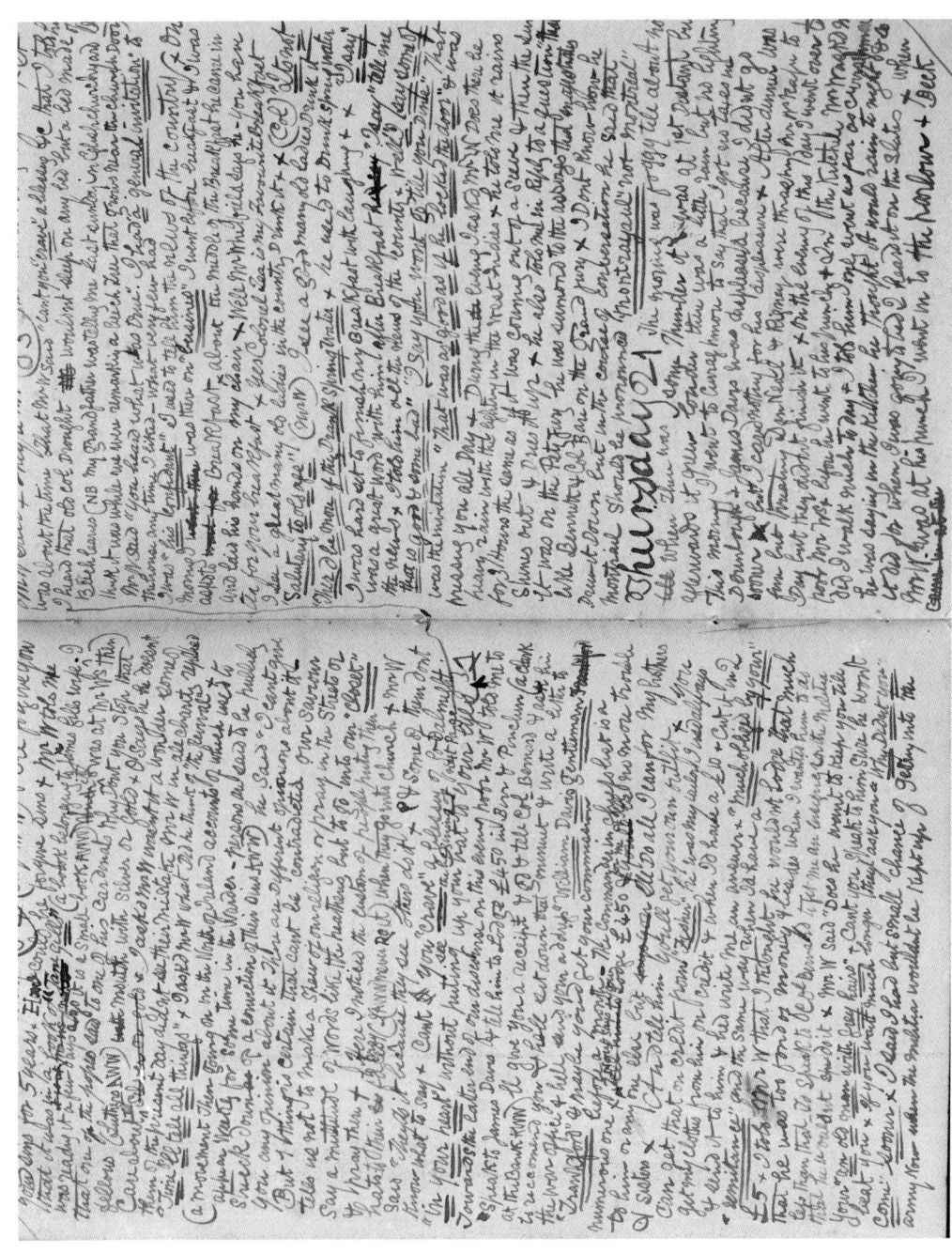

3.   *The original manuscript of the Davis diary of 1858-59, ff 84-85*

Preface

The lives of the living rarely intertwine with those of the dead, particularly those long passed before our arrival into the world. We may hear their names from time to time around the family table, however more often than not, little more than the surname, family relationship and some anecdotal stories are recalled.

The same could have been said of William Davis but for the fortunate survival, from a domestic bonfire in the 1980s, of his diary covering the years 1858-59. The survival of the diary has allowed a long deceased man to provide an intimate portrait of the lives of two people in mid-nineteenth century King's County (since 1920 known as County Offaly). They were William Davis, the brother of my great grandfather, and William's neighbour, Abraham Whitfield, both of whom resided in the vicinity of Frankford (now Kilcormac), King's County, for a large part of their lives.

William's diary is not just a record of his daily observations and interactions with people around him, brief as it may be, it also gives an insight into the social, cultural and economic world in which William lived in mid-nineteenth century King's County. Indeed, in the survival of William's diary he has (intentionally or otherwise) left us today with a very personal view of life, a contrast from that generally gleaned from official administrative records kept largely for and by those in the upper echelons of society during that period. William's surviving diary, though brief, covers nearly two years. In it he records his observations of life often commenting on political and social events on the local and national stage. A constant theme in William's diary is the purchasing, borrowing and reading of newspapers, a clear indication of the importance of newspapers in society during this period and something we take for granted in this age of instant media. References to local elections and the prominent role of priests are of particular interest, while more mundane entries such as 'could not go to church for my shoes were bad', reflect William's perilous enough financial state of affairs.

While William's diary contains a broad spectrum of entries, the core theme revolves around William's friendship with Abraham Whitfield, and it is clear both were an unlikely pairing. William, the author of the diary, was a shy, naïve, sensitive, stubborn sixteen-year old. He was the son of a small farmer/tax collector whose widowed family clung increasingly desperately to the lower middle class rung of the social ladder. William, born 1842, was the eldest son of William Davis (senior) and his third wife Jane Davis nee Watkins. At the age of eleven William was disinherited by his father William (senior), who altered his will shortly before he died in 1854. William (senior) left his brother James Davis as his executer and his second son Richard, born 1846, as heir to his property. For William and those about him, his father's actions must have appeared harsh and indeed one can only wonder how his father's decision influenced William's view of the world, his expectant place in it and subsequent relationships with his siblings. It is clear from William's diary that he felt an outsider among his kin.

Abraham Whitfield was a retired army officer in his early sixties. Abraham was generous, obstinate, gregarious and firmly camped in the middle class. Their families, while of the same Protestant faith, would have had little to do with one another socially. Abraham Whitfield's military background and class would have given him an entrée into the drawing rooms of the upper class, but no such opportunities would have been open to the family of William Davis. However, each filled a gap in the other's life. William found in Abraham a sympathetic listener and confidante. Abraham found in William a patient and willing audience for his endless trove of army stories. He was interested in William's future and proffered advice. Each offered the other companionship at a time when they were both in need of it. William had no close friends and felt something of an outsider among his family, while Abraham rarely left his house, probably due to failing health. Abraham Whitfield died in February 1860, only four months, to the very day, after the last entry in this diary.

Their conversations came to form a large part of the diary that William had started in 1858. Initially he wrote the day's events on any old scraps of paper that came to hand. These he later transcribed into a small, plain, unlined notebook. He wrote with an ink pen, in writing that oscillates between small and miniscule. There are often 765 words to an 11cm x 17cm page – about half the size of A5. The first one third of the 1858-59 diary is written in a shorthand which I believe to be Odell's. This journal was the first in a series, but none of the others survived. The year 1858 is covered intermittently with brief entries. The entries for 1859 are much more frequent and comprehensive.

Chapter one of this book is William's own introduction to the diary which he wrote as an afterthought, squeezing it into the last six pages of the notebook. The diary appears as William wrote it although some editing was necessary. William was a diligent record taker and if Abraham told him a story three times, William recorded it three times. Here versions two and three of such entries are omitted. Spelling mistakes have been corrected and it was necessary to insert numerous full stops, which appear to have been a concept alien to William. The round brackets which appear in William's diary text are William's own punctuation. The square brackets in the diary text indicate my comments which were added later for the purpose of explanation. A brief introduction written by myself precedes each chapter. The year 1858 is covered in one chapter. The diary entries for that year were short and infrequent. Thereafter each chapter spans one calendar month.

Sandra Robinson

4.   *The home of William Davis, the diarist as now much improved.*

5.   *Ballincard House, 2009 (courtesy of Mr Ger Murphy)*

Contents

William added this introduction to the diary as a postscript, which he then squeezed into the last pages of the notebook. I have brought it to the front of the diary. This chapter includes-

William's early childhood and chaotic schooling, the robbing of Mrs Burriss, the tragic death of William's father with its unfortunate legacy and William's confirmation.

William's diary started with brief and occasional entries covering the year of 1858. These now follow in chapter two and include- A neighbour packs for London, a coursing meeting, a narrow escape from death at the threshing, and Mr Whitfield (Mr W) tells of fire fighting in Liverpool.

Each following chapter contains the entries for one month. This chapter includes controversy in Birr about the Crimean gun, preparations for a hunt, newspaper wars in Offaly, a Birr banknote, a shopping trip, family tensions and a trudge through the snow to Clonaslee.

William despairs of school, a photographer comes to Birr, sad tales of illness and death, haggling over the hay, a rare glimpse of Mrs Whitfield, a scathing summary of some relatives, a nutting foray, William and little brother James succumb to temptation, Captain Young offers advice, uncle Francis has a terrible injury, aunt Sally loses her mind and the court-martial of Sergeant Tremble of Kinnitty.

An American circus comes to Birr, Mr Whitfield meets the governor of Barbados, black soldiers in the army, a Canadian walks on water?, Wesley's visit to Offaly, John Philpot Curran and the Emmets, brother Richard's schooling ends abruptly, William tracks down Mr Whitfield's old army comrade.

Appendices

To my parents
Henry Robinson and Emma Fitzroy

Acknowledgements

This book would never have been realised without the enormous help I have received from many people since I first obtained the diary of William Davis. I am very grateful to everyone for their courtesy, generosity and encouragement in my undertaking to edit, expand on and contextualise that part of William's life which he recorded while living in mid-nineteenth century King's County.

I am particularly grateful to Offaly Centre for Independent Living and my carers- Sylvia Farrell, Veronica Hall, Geraldine Clancy, Pauline Murphy, Valerie Flynn, Anne Newman, Mary Egan and Bernie Kenny. They have enabled me to live my life as fully as possible within the constraints of my illness. This book would never have been completed without their help. A very particular thank you to my sister, Glynis, who never flagged in her support and practical help throughout this long project.

I must thank Anne Coughlan (the former county librarian), Mary Butler and all the staff at Offaly County Library, Tullamore, who were of great assistance with research. My local librarians, Anne Ryan and Mary Hynes of Banagher library and Maura O'Rourke of Ferbane library were also always ready to help in any way possible.

I am very grateful to Michael Byrne of the Offaly Historical and Archaeological Society who has been a great encouragement to me and has been a great help in getting the project to the publishing stage. I also wish to thank Mr Ger Murphy for his interest and assistance with comments and photographs. Members and staff of OHAS were of enormous help in the research stage and in the final publishing, particularly Margaret White Mulligan and John Kearney.

Fiona Clarke and Eleanor Wallace, Cliona O'Brien, and Paul Voorheis were a great help with any computer problems that arose. Thanks are also due to Ron Robinson for making the diary available to me, Natalie and Jonathan Voorheis, Maureen and William Kidd, Mr and Mrs Davis of Davis Lodge, Mountbolus, Mr Derrick Davis, Mountbolus, Mr Dick Watkins, Tadgh Pey & Brian Pey.

I wish to express my thanks to the staff of the Representative Church Body Library, Dublin and of the Royal Ulster Rifles, Museum, Belfast.

The following businesses kindly gave donations towards research costs.

Gerard Browne, Birr

Tom Enright, Birr

Fayles Hardware, Birr

Loughnane Concrete, Birr

Brendan Mannion, Birr

John Ryan, Birr

List of Illustrations

Front Cover:

The main street of Birr about 1900 with the 1747 column commemorating the victory of the duke of Cumberland at Culloden in the foreground

Back Cover:

Eglish barony in 1837 (from Samuel Lewis, *A topographical dictionary of Ireland*)

Endpapers:

The Eglish district from the Bog Survey map of 1810 prepared by John Longfield (courtesy of Mr Michael Byrne)

1. Opposite Title page: Emmet Square, Birr with the bow-fronted shop of Francis Shields to the right of the Cumberland monument (courtesy of the National Library of Ireland)

2. The townlands of the Eglish district about 1900

3. The original manuscript of the Davis diary of 1858-59, ff 84-85

4. The home of William Davis, the diarist as now much improved.

5. Ballincard House, 2009 (courtesy of Mr Ger Murphy)

6. Watkin's house at Ballynaguilsha, Eglish, 2009 (courtesy of Mr Ger Murphy)

7. Birr workhouse about 1960

8. Eglish Church of Ireland church in 2009 (courtesy of Mr Ger Murphy)

9. The Birr Telescope c. 1858 with (left to right) Clere and Randal Parsons with Miss Knox and at their feet, Charles Parsons (from David H. Davison, *Impressions of an Irish Countess: the photographs of Mary countess of Rosse, 1813-1888*. Birr, 1989, p. 28). Reproduced by kind permission of the earl of Rosse.

10. A view of Castle Street, Birr, c. 1856 from the ramparts of Birr Castle at Castle Street showing the Woods' brewery (formerly the Robinson distillery) in the foreground to the right and a market at Castle Street in the background (from David H. Davison *Impressions of an Irish Countess: the photographs of Mary countess of Rosse, 1813-1888*. Birr, 1989, p. 27). Reproduced by kind permission of the earl of Rosse.

11. John's Place, Birr in the 1890s (courtesy of the National Library of Ireland)

12. John's Place, Birr in the late 1890s with a view of the monument to the third earl of Rosse, died 1867 (courtesy of the National Library of Ireland)

13. The Mercy convent at Birr completed in the mid-1850s by architect, Augustus Welby Pugin (courtesy of the National Library of Ireland)

14. The Roman Catholic chapel at Birr completed in 1817 (courtesy of the National Library of Ireland)

15. Oxmantown Mall, Birr in the 1890s with the Church of Ireland church in the background (courtesy of the National Library of Ireland)

16. The interior of St Brendan's Church of Ireland church, Birr in the 1890s (courtesy of the National Library of Ireland)

17. The old bridge at Birr in the 1890s (courtesy of the National Library of Ireland)

18. A military parade at Crinkle Barracks in the late 1890s

19. The camp outside the walls of Crinkle Barracks in the 1890s (courtesy of the National Library of Ireland)

20. A view of Crinkle barracks in the 1890s

21. The hunt at Gloster House near Birr in the 1870s (from the Magan Collection, courtesy of the Offaly Historical and Archaeological Society)

22. Cannon on show at Emmet Square, Birr in the 1890s (courtesy of the Offaly Historical and Archaeological Society)

23. The Crimean gun trophy now situate at John's Place, Birr with the Greek temple of 1833 in memory of the young John Clere Parsons in the background (courtesy of Mr Ger Murphy)

24. Thomas Lalor Cooke, Birr solicitor and historian, died 1869 (courtesy of the Offaly Historical and Archaeological Society). Cooke objected to the Crimean war trophy being placed in Birr Castle demesne.

25.   The Willis printing shop at Charleville (now O'Connor) Square, Tullamore in the 1830s (courtesy of the Irish Architectural Archive). It was from here that the *King's County Chronicle* was distributed in the Tullamore district.

26.   Cumberland (now Emmet) Square, Birr about 1910 (courtesy of the National Library of Ireland)

27.   Birr courthouse in the mid-1820s (courtesy of the Offaly Historical and Archaeological Society)

28.   William, third earl of Rosse, died 1867

29.   Sir John Pope Hennessy, MP for King's County, 1859-65 (courtesy of the Offaly Historical and Archaeological Society)

30.   Emmet Square, Birr with Dooly's Hotel in the background in the 1890s (courtesy of the National Library of Ireland)

31.   A label describing Dooly's Royal Arms Hotel, Birr in the mid-1800s (courtesy of Mr Michael Byrne)

32.   Emmet Square in the 1890s with the King's County and Ormond Club (founded 1859) to the left and Dooly's Hotel to the right

33.   Whigsborough House in the early 1900s (from the Magan Collection, courtesy of the Offaly Historical and Archaeological Society)

34.   A steamer on the River Shannon at Banagher in the 1890s

35.   Ballyboy former Church of Ireland church in ruins in the 1980s

36.   Castle Bernard, Kinnitty in the early 1900s

37.   Hunt meet at Syngefield House in the early 1900s (courtesy of the Offaly Historical and Archaeological Society)

38.   The ruins of Garrycastle at Banagher from a drawing by George Petrie from *Excursions through Ireland*, vol. i, Leinster (Dublin, 1821)

39.   The fair at Banagher in the 1890s

40.   Dermody's shop at Fivealley in the 1980s

41.   The meeting rooms on the first floor of the *King's County Chronicle* printing offices at Emmet Street (formerly Cumberland Street) erected in the 1850s and damaged by fire in 1903 (courtesy of Mr Michael Byrne)

42.   John Wesley, the founder of Methodism and a frequent visitor to Ireland over the period of the 1740s to the 1780s

43.   Kinnitty village in the early 1900s

44.   Birr Castle about 1900 (courtesy of the National Library of Ireland)

45.   Eglish Castle in the 1970s (courtesy of Mr Michael Byrne)

46.   Eglish Lodge, 2009 (courtesy of Mr Ger Murphy)

47.   The Birr telescope in the 1880s

48.   The town of Banagher in the early 1900s

49.   The town of Ferbane about 1930

50.   The town of Kilcormac about 1900

51.   James Davis (brother of the diarist William) and his wife Ann nee McBride c. 1915.

52.   The Davis family Dublin home at 14 Rathgar Road, Dublin (courtesy of Ms Natalie Voorheis)

53.   The Davis memorial in Mount Jerome cemetery, Dublin (courtesy of Ms Natalie Voorheis)

Book and newspaper inserts:

(a)   A description of Eglish parish in 1837 (from Samuel Lewis, *A topographical dictionary of Ireland*, London, 1837)

(b)   A description of Drumcullen parish in 1837(from Samuel Lewis, *A topographical dictionary of Ireland*, London, 1837)

(c)   Advertisement from the *King's County Chronicle* of 16 June 1858 for the Frankford Wool Stores

(d)   Advertisements from the *King's County Chronicle* of 6 June 1858

(e)   Notice for the Brady school from the *King's County Chronicle*, 11 January 1860

(f)   Notice of the departure of James Weir from Birr from the *King's County Chronicle* of 2 November 1859

(g)   Notice and report of the sale of the Davis, Curraghmore farm, in June 1879 from the *King's County Chronicle*

Abbreviations

GV   *Griffith's General Valuation of Ireland*

KCC   *King's County Chronicle*

NE   *National Encyclopaedia*

OCL   Offaly County Library

OHAS   Offaly Historical and Archaeological Society

PLU   Poor Law Union

RCB   Representative Church Body Library

SD   *Slater's Directory*

6.   Watkin's house at Ballynaguilsha, Eglish, 2009 (courtesy of Mr Ger Murphy)

Principal dates in William Davis's life

1842	William Davis born on 19 March.
1848	William starts school.
1851	He is almost killed in a traffic accident in Birr.
1854	His father, also William, dies on 27 February.
1854	The dead man's brother, James Davis, replaces him as cess or tax Collector.
1856	William starts school with Weir in Birr.
1857	William is confirmed.
1857	He begins to visit his elderly neighbour Mr Whitfield.
1858	William begins keeping a journal.
1860	Mr Whitfield dies on 22 February aged 64.
1873	William's grandfather Watkins dies, aged 98.
1876	William is appointed as an overseer at the Liverpool Post Office
1888	Uncle James dies. He had retired as rate collector in 1880 after 27 years and was succeeded by William's brother, James.
1905	William returns to Ireland about this time after a long career in the Post Office, probably all in Liverpool.
1911	William is living with his sister Charlotte in Rathgar, Dublin.
1915	Charlotte dies of pneumonia in April aged 64.
1921	William dies in Dublin after an accident, aged 79.

Editor's Introduction

Family Origins

The origins of the Davis family of Davistown, Frankford, King's County, (now Kilcormac, County Offaly), are uncertain due to the common occurrence of the name Davis in the King's County in the nineteenth century and the duplication of first names amongst those families. The Protestant branch of the Davis family, the subject of this diary, was probably located in the Drumcullen/Eglish area since at least 1802. In that year a Davis family of Ballywilliam is listed amongst the Protestant parishioners of Drumcullen.[1]

In 1826 Richard Davis - probably William's grandfather, - had a holding of forty-five acres at Curraghmore.[2] William's father, also William, (referred to here as William senior to avoid confusion), was born circa 1806. He was the eldest in a family of at least twelve children. Our first official glimpse of him is in July 1826 when he was listed as cess collector for the Barony of Eglish.[3] The cess was a local tax for the maintenance of roads, services, and public buildings in the county. This position carried some financial risk, as any uncollected cess had to be met by the collector unless he could prove that it was irrecoverable.[4] William (senior) was twenty years old at this time and continued in this occupation for the next twenty-eight years until his death in 1854.

Circa 1828 he married his cousin, Miss Davis of Rathrobin, Killoughy.[5] Their daughter, Sarah, was born on 2 August 1829. By 1835 Sarah's mother was dead and William senior remarried. His second wife was Maria Bulfin, a Roman Catholic. The marriage took place in the Roman Catholic Church in Eglish in May 1835. She was probably a daughter of Edward Bulfin and his wife Ellen (nee Mohan) of nearby Derrinlough House.

Shortly after their son Ned was born in 1837 tragedy struck again when Maria died. Following his mother's death his Davis grandparents reared Ned in Curraghmore. Sarah was probably reared by her mother's brother Richard Davis of Corbally, near Clonaslee. She was married from that house in November 1853[6] when she wed Henry Kenny of Feirmore Cottage[7], near Eyrecourt, Co. Galway.

---

1   See C.C. Ellison, 'Early 19th century lists of Protestant parishioners in the diocese of Meath' in *Irish Ancestor* (no. 2, 1973), pp 113-26.

2   Tithe applotment book, King's County, National Archives of Ireland (N.A.I).

3   [Wright, John]. *The King's County directory* (Birr, 1890, reprinted as *Offaly one hundred years ago*. Tullamore 1989), p. 237.

4   *Offaly one hundred years ago*, p. 237.

5   Daughter of James Davis of Rathrobin, in the nearby parish of Killoughy. Descendants of that James Davis still live in Davis Lodge, Rathrobin, today.

6   The marriage was performed in Clonaslee Church by Rev. John Baldwin.Source: *King's County Chronicle*, 30 November 1853 (hereafter *KCC)*

7   Feirmore, as it appears in newspaper records of the time, is probably a misspelling of the placename Fenmore which is near Eyrecourt.

On 5 June 1839 William senior, now aged thirty-three and twice widowed, married for the third time at Whigsborough, near Birr. His bride, Jane Watkins, was seventeen. She was the daughter of James and Sarah Watkins of Ballynaguilsha, Eglish. The Watkins lived in a small two-storey house and rented thirty-eight acres from Cassidy of Killyon.[8] In contrast to her two predecessors, Jane was to outlive her husband by fifty-one years.[9] William Davis (senior) and Jane Watkins had seven children - Lizzy b. 1840, William b. 1842 (the author of the diary), Margaret b. 1844, Richard b. 1846, James b. 1848, Charlotte b. 1850 and Tom b. 1852.

Eglish and Drumcullen district.

William Davis (senior) and family lived somewhere in Davistown townland from at least the early 1840s. In September 1846 they moved into a two-storey, slate roofed house, also in Davistown. It faced south-east towards the Slieve Bloom Mountains eight miles away and was reached by a long laneway, which wound through some acres of tillage from the main Birr/ Frankford road. Behind the house were pasture and a large area of furze. This led to the Silver River and an extensive area of bog. It may have been merely a coincidence that the name of the townland was Davistown. It does not seem to have been named after this Davis family.[10] Davistown House, the residence of Mr Abraham Whitfield, was only a few yards away to the east of the Davis home. Between the two houses lay a large shallow pond and a small orchard.

To the west of Davistown was Ballincard, the residence of Robert Maxwell. Most of his farm of 343 acres surrounded his large house, which stood on top of a small hill surrounded by trees.[11] Curraghmore, the home of grandmother Davis was a half-mile away to the south-east in Curraghmore townland. It was a small house encircled by poor quality wet moory ground.

The district around Davistown comprising the parishes of Eglish and Drumcullen was predominantly flat and low-lying with extensive areas of bog and scrub. Valuation summaries for the civil parishes at the census of 1851 show the region around the parishes of Eglish and Drumcullen to have one of the lowest valuations in the county. Only Clonmacnoise to the north

---

8   Probably John Valentine Cassidy who succeeded his father Robert in 1858, *Offaly one hundred years ago*, p. 324

9   There had been Watkins in Eglish parish since at least 1690 when Joseph Watkins had a house at 'Ballydown'. James Watkins's family are listed among the Protestant parishioners of Eglish in 1802, at Ballydown in the 1824-25 landholders, and as farmers of Ballindown in the 1840 census of Eglish and Drumcullen parishes.

10   See Mr Whitfield's comments below and see Brian Pey (ed.), *Eglish and Drumcullen: a parish in Firceall* (Birr, 2004), pp 333.

11   He also leased 100 acres in assorted lots to others in the immediate vicinity. Source: Richard Griffith, *King's County: valuation of the several tenements in the Union of Parsonstown situate in the county above named.* (1854) pp 6, 25 (commonly known as Griffith's valuation, hereafter GV)

had a lower valuation[12]. The land quality in Eglish and Drumcullen varied greatly from townland to townland. Pockets of good pasture and tillage sat interspersed with areas of poor tillage, bog, furze and scrub. Some ground was subject to flooding. Farm holdings were small. Most were less than fifty acres and many were below ten acres.[13]

Farming was a mixture of arable and pasture. Crops consisted of oats, barley, wheat, potatoes, turnips, mangles and cabbage. Some peas, beans and rape were also grown together with small amounts of flax and rye.[14] The pasture supported large numbers of sheep that were bought in from the west to be bred or fattened. The biggest centre of the sheep trade at the time was Ballinasloe Fair in neighbouring County Galway. Cattle were also usually bought in from the west to be fattened for a year before being sold on to the Meath graziers. Horses were plentiful and mules and donkeys were also kept. Nearly everyone had fowl and at least one pig.

The Famine Years

On 24 February 1844 William Davis (senior) became collector of the poor rates for the districts of Eglish and Drumcullen in the Parsonstown poor law union area. The poor rate was a tax for the maintenance of the poor relief system in each poor law union area. He also continued in his position as barony cess collector, a position he had held for at least eighteen years previously. The onset of potato blight in the mid 1840s and its return in subsequent years brought great distress to Offaly. The parishes of Eglish and Drumcullen were no exception. The Church of Ireland curate of Eglish and Drumcullen, Mr Healy,[15] whom we meet later in William's diary, wrote to the Society of Friends on May 13 1847 saying;

> *'Fever is alarmingly prevalent all around me and I could not attempt describing the innumerable cases of violent dysentery that are presenting themselves before me daily. ...... almost all flock to me, and from an early hour in the morning until late at night I am occupied (except when duty calls me away) giving out medicine or food. I implore you if you can at all, grant me a little more help.'[16]*

12 Grainne C. Breen, 'Landlordism in King's County in the mid-nineteenth century', in William Nolan and Timothy P. O'Neill (eds) *Offaly history and society* (1998) p. 630.

13 See table in Appendix 6.

14 Grainne C. Breen, 'Landlordism in King's County in the mid-nineteenth Century', in William Nolan, and Timothy P. O'Neill (eds) *Offaly history and society*, (1998) p. 655.

15 Robert Healy 1818-1879. Established Church. Born in Dublin, son of Robert Healy M.D. Entered Trinity College 1 July 1834 aged 16. B. A. 1840. Perpetual Curate Eglish 1842 – 1860. Rector Clonfadforan 1860 – 1864. Rector , Newtownfertullagh 1864 – 1865. Vicar Kilcleagh 1865 – 73. Died at the Parsonage, Female Orphan Homes, Clontarf, 5 October 1879. His wife Annie died at the rectory, 2 Moate, March 1869. Source: Representative Church Body Library, (hereafter RCB).

16 See appendix 1.

7.   *Birr workhouse about 1960*

Some idea of the harsh conditions can be gained by examining the census figures[17] for the area. These show that the population of Drumcullen parish fell by 25.7% between 1841 and 1851. Eglish suffered a fall of 34.3%. This population decline continued into the following decade with Drumcullen losing another 35% and Eglish losing 30.4% between 1851 and 1861. In twenty years both parishes had each lost over 50 % of their inhabitants. The number of houses recorded in the census makes for equally startling reading. The occupants of class four houses[18] fared the worst. In Drumcullen parish the number of class four houses fell from 114 in 1841 to 35 in 1851, a drop of 69.2%. In Eglish class four houses declined from 209 in 1841 to 38 in 1851, a drop of 81.8%. Almost all of these houses disappeared totally from the landscape during those ten years. They are not even recorded as uninhabited in 1851. Occupants of class three houses[19] fared a little better. Their numbers in Drumcullen and Eglish parishes fell by 23.4% and 14.2% respectively between 1841 and 1851.

17   Courtesy Offaly County Library, Tullamore (hereafter OCL).

18   One-roomed hovel or cabin.

19   Home with two – four rooms with windows inhabited by cottiers and small farmers.

EGLISH, a parish, partly in the barony of LOWER OR-
MOND, county of TIPPERARY, and province of MUNSTER,
but chiefly in that of EGLISH, or FIRCAL, KING's county,
and province of LEINSTER, 3 miles (N.E.) from Parsonstown,
on the road to Tullamore; containing 3290 inhabitants. This
parish is six miles in length by four in breadth, and comprises
7722 statute acres there is a great deal of bog, and some limestone for building and burning. Eglish Castle is the residence
of Capt. English; Tullinisky, of Handy Dynelly, Esq., Whigsborough, of R. Drought, Esq.; and here is the residence of the
Rev. W. Parsons. The living is a vicarage, in the diocese of
Meath, forming part of the union of Fireall; the rectory is impropriate in the Marquess of Downshire. The tithes amount
to £148.12.3., of which £96.18.5. is payable to the impropriator, and the remainder to the vicar: the glebe comprises 116a.
2r. 38p., the annual value of which is £99.8. The church is a
very old building. In the R.C. divisions the parish is the head
of a union or district, comprising also Drumcullin parish, in
each of which is a chapel. There are six private schools, in
which about 240 children are instructed.

(A)   A description of Eglish parish in 1837 (from Samuel Lewis, *A
topographical dictionary of Ireland*, London, 1837)

DRUMCULLIN, a parish, in the barony of EGLISH, or FIR-
CALL, KING's county, and province of LEINSTER, 5 miles (S.
W. by S.) from Frankford, on the road to Parsonstown; containing 3,113 inhabitants. At a very early period, a religious
establishment existed here of which St. Barrindeus was abbot
about the year 590. Nearly one-half of the parish is bog, but
the land near Droughtville is considered some of the best pasture ground in the barony. A spacious lake covers an extensive
flat at the foot of a range of thickly planted hills. Contiguous
to it is a castle, which can at pleasure be insulated by its waters: it was reduced to its present state of ruin by Cromwell's
forces. There are limestone quarries near, in which the fossil
remains are abundant and nearly perfect. There are two fairs
at Killion; and petty sessions are held at Thomastown every
second Thursday. The seats are Droughtville, the principal
residence of the Drought family, in a demesne comprising pe-
culiar groups of conical hills, which form a picturesque and
pleasing scene; Thomastown, of Capt. Bennett; Dove Grove,
of J. Berry, Esq; Dove Hill, of Holmes, Esq.; Clonbela, of -

Moloy, Esq.; and Killion, of R. Cassiday, Esq. The parish is in the diocese of Meath; the rectory is impropriate in the Marquess of Downshire, and the vicarage forms part of the union of Fircall. The tithes amount to £228.18.5., of which £147.13.10. is payable to the impropriator, and the remainder to the vicar: there is a glebe of 216a.3r.6p., valued at £180.1. per annum. In the R. C. divisions it forms part of the union or district of Eglish; the chapel, situated at Rath, is a large plain building. There is a school at Killion, which has a house and an acre of land, rent-free, from Mr. Cassiday, and in which are about 40 boys and 25 girls: Mrs. Holmes maintains one at Dove Hill: there are also four pay schools one of which at Thomastown, has a house rent-free from Mr. Bennett, and in which about 130 children are educated. Adjoining Droughtville, are the remains of the old church of Drumcullin, having a fine entrance arch of curious workmanship. Near Pallis Inn, in this vicinity, are the ruins of a castle; and, towards Frankford, are four other fortified places in a similar state of decay. The plains around are supposed to have been the scene of different sanguinary encounters as within a spade's depth, vast quantities of human bones have been found: each surrounding height has vestiges of ancient fortifications; and on a very strong rath, which commands the whole district, there is an entire fort, most difficult of access, defended by a regular and double course of works, still in good preservation: this rath, being now planted, presents a very striking appearance. At Ballincar is a spa, of the same nature as that of Castleconnell, near Limerick; the water is of a yellow hue, and famous for healing scorbutic ulcers: another spa of the same kind is at Clonbela.

(B) A description of Drumcullen parish in 1837 (from Samuel Lewis, *A topographical dictionary of Ireland*, London, 1837)

In Davistown townland the population dropped from 73 in 1841 to 24 in 1851. The number of houses fell from 13 to 4. By 1861 the population was still 24 with three houses remaining.

As the 1840s progressed the distress in the county increased. In 1849 Birr workhouse was overwhelmed by the numbers seeking assistance and shelter. Originally built to accommodate 800[20], there were frequently over 2,000 people housed in a combination of the original workhouse, an additional workhouse, temporary buildings and a fever hospital. In the week ending 5 May 1849 there were 3,007 people present. In that week alone 520 people were admitted and 59 died. Two weeks later 101 people died within a seven-day period.[21] At a meeting of the Birr Board of Poor Law Guardians in February 1849 Doctor Baker, who was alarmed at conditions in the workhouse, described how dysentery and diarrhoea were prevalent among the able-bodied inmates. He said the broken down emaciated look of the paupers as they entered the workhouse was appalling. He attributed the very poor state of health of these people to the absence of outdoor relief in Birr union. He also drew the attention of the guardians to the high mortality rate in the workhouse and the inadequacy of the nursery, which accommodated 136 infants and nurses in a room 21 feet by 50 feet. He suggested another room more suitable for holding infants be built over the dining hall. The guardians then discussed these matters for some time but could not come to any decisions at that meeting. One guardian J. Persse Grome,[22] 'Considered it was truly ridiculous to be wasting so much of their valuable time in talking over such unimportant matters. It was all sympathy for paupers and beggars [sic] brats, and in what way they were to be made comfortable, as if they had not been used to cabins and hovels of the meanest and filthiest kind from their birth; such talk was really monstrous and absurd, to a degree of his greatest indignation, and while all this pity was felt for the beggars, there was no sympathy at all for the Landlords,[sic] and gentlemen of the country, at whose expense these persons were to be fed sumptuously, and get in addition Nutmeg Whey, [sic] and all these luxuries to be provided by a heavy taxation, laid upon the gentry of the country, and to have their time taken up with such subjects, and he hoped he would hear no more of it.'[23] It was not uncommon for people to collapse and die of starvation in the street or on the roadway. In April 1849 the schoolmaster of Birr workhouse, Mr Fallon, came upon an emaciated John Killileigh dying on the roadside near Syngefield.[24] Also in that month Henry Davis, while driving towards Kinnitty, came upon Laurence Dolan in a similar state of distress lying by the road about a mile from Birr.[25] Both men

---

20   Source: John O'Connor, *Workhouses of Ireland.* (1995), p. 238.

21   Poor law union minute books for Birr union, 1849 (hereafter PLU).

22   J. Persse Grome, J.P., Cumberland Square, *Slater's Directory 1846 (hereafter SD)*

23   *KCC,* 21-2-49.

24   *KCC,* 28-4-49.

25   *KCC,* 28-4-49.

died shortly after being found. The following month the body of a man who had died of starvation in a wood near Sharavogue was found when local dogs returned home with pieces of the body. The unfortunate man had been calling at houses along the way, begging for food. At one he had snatched up a few cabbage leaves lying in a window[26]. In that year 756 people died in Birr Fever Hospital. Barrack Street in Cork was the only Fever Hospital in Ireland that had a higher death rate than Birr.[27]

There had been general unrest in the district of Eglish and Drumcullen for some time previously. Theft of livestock, especially sheep, was common. Sometimes the animals were killed and butchered on the spot.[28] A heifer belonging to Mr Abraham Whitfield, (who features frequently in the diary), was killed and taken away from Davistown in March 1847.[29] In January of that year sheep belonging to Charles Burriss, who is also mentioned in the diary, were taken away.[30] Robbery with violence occurred frequently and travellers on the road were waylaid even during daylight hours.[31]

> 'The plunder of cattle and sheep is enormous...... Some stringent measures for the protection of property must be speedily adopted..... Landlords find it an utter impossibility to procure their rents, or even a small portion of the large arrears due them. They cannot exercise their rights without being threatened with death. We know of more than one proprietor who are obliged daily to appear well armed, in order to preserve themselves from assassination.'[32]

In 1851 sheep belonging to William Davis (senior) were killed.[33] During the spring of the previous year a cow belonging to his brother James had been poisoned.[34] His role as collector of county cess and the poor rate made William Davis (senior) apprehensive about his safety. Sometimes he was accompanied through his collection district by a large body of police.[35]

26   *KCC*, 2-5-49.

27   T. P. O'Neill, 'The Famine in Offaly' in William Nolan and Timothy P. O'Neill (eds) *Offaly history and society*, (1998) p.724.

28   *KCC*, 4-1849.

29   *KCC*, 31-3-1847.

30   *KCC*, 27-1-1847.

31   *KCC*, 1849.

32   *KCC*, 21-3-1849.

33   He was awarded one pound and ten shillings in malicious damages for sheep killed at the summer assizes. Source: Record of the Summer Assizes contained in *Grand Jury presentment book* , 1851 in Offaly County Library.

34   James Davis was awarded £7 in a malicious injuries claim for a cow poisoned. Source: Record of the Lent Assizes 1850 contained in *Grand Jury presentment book* , 1850.

35   *KCC*, 15 December 1847.

Two policemen lived with the family for their protection between 1848 and 1852. In such circumstances it was very difficult to get in the poor rate. William Davis's collection of the poor rates was sporadic and from time to time he was admonished by the Birr board of guardians who believed that *'He has not used the diligence he ought to have done or his collection would have been better.'*[36] However, at the end of most years there was only a small amount outstanding in the area covered by him. In 1849 his collecting was very erratic and £36-6- ¼ remained due out of a total of £778-18-1¾. The board of guardians found it very difficult to maintain a steady flow of funds and in May of that year £6,000[37] in poor rates was still outstanding across all districts in the Birr poor law union.[38]

There were similar difficulties with the collection of the county cess and in July 1849 the poundage paid to the barony cess collectors was raised from nine pence per pound collected to one shilling in an effort to encourage collection of the cess.[39]

From time to time William (senior) seized property in lieu of outstanding rates or cess. It was his practice to lodge the full amount from the sale of goods seized in lieu of poor rate to the account of the Birr poor law union even if it exceeded the amount due. This was an unpopular practice with all other parties concerned. It played havoc with the poor law union accounts and the unfortunate defaulter was left at the loss of the excess which would be credited to him against future rates.[40] In January 1849 a seizure of property in lieu of unpaid county cess resulted in a court case where William and Eliza McNamara were each sentenced to three months imprisonment for rescuing a cow seized by William Davis.[41] Despite repeated reminders from the board of guardians to the collectors of the poor rates 'Of the necessity of making every possible exertion to get in the rate',[42] collection remained erratic leading to the exasperation of the board.[43] William Davis's inconsistent rate collection and the headaches he provided for the accountant probably contributed to the loss of his position in December 1849. In late 1849 he was one of a number of poor rate collectors who opposed the proposed poundage of 9d per pound collected for 1850. The poundage

36   PLU records, 10 November 1849.

37   *KCC*, 2-5-1849.

38   'Each workhouse was to be administered by a board of guardians consisting of
        representative ratepayers of the union. Each union was rated for the number of poor
        which it sent to the workhouse; half was to be paid by the tenants and half by the
        landlords. When the burden of paying the rate became too heavy for the tenants
        an amendment exempted those rated at £4 or less' Source: Hickey & Doherty, *A
        dictionary of Irish history since 1800*, (1980)

39   *Offaly one hundred years ago*, p. 237.

40   PLU 20-10-49 and 4-1-1850.

41   *KCC*, January 1849.

42   *KCC*, January 1849.

43   *KCC*, January 1849.

for the previous year appears to have been one shilling. As a result of this resistance the positions of collectors for some districts were advertised by the board. William Davis and two others applied for the district of Eglish and Drumcullen. In his anxiety to obtain the position Mark Guinan offered to accept 8d per pound collected. He received two votes, George Dooley eight votes and William Davis six votes. Guinan was eliminated whereupon his supporters declared for Dooley who was duly elected.

By 1854 William Davis (senior) seems to have been renting 112 acres of mixed quality land at Davistown from the Woods family, 43 acres of poor land in the neighbouring townland of Clontyglass from William Longworth and 62 acres of good land from John Drought at Knockbarron.[44] William Davis (senior) had been suffering from consumption for some years. His health deteriorated in 1853 and by the end of that year he was bedridden. A will had originally been made in favour of William (junior), who was the eldest son of his marriage to Jane Watkins. But now a new will was made. It left the family affairs in the hands of William senior's brother James until such time as William senior and Jane's second son, Richard, reached maturity.

William senior died on 27 February 1854, aged forty-eight.

Uncle James Davis, usually referred to as 'The Lame Fellow' in the diary, was at this time unmarried and lived at Lelaghmore, about a half-mile south east of Curraghmore. In 1852 he had commenced collection of the poor rates for the district of Ballyboy in place of William Manifold who was murdered on 19 October of that year near the Blue Ball, Tullamore. In 1854 James replaced his brother William as cess collector for the barony of Eglish. At that time James seems to have been renting a total of 141 acres[45] from others in the area surrounding Curraghmore. The largest portion of land was an area of 79 acres in Gortnamuck which also contained his house of Lelaghmore.[46] In 1858 James narrowly escaped death when he became entangled around the shaft of a threshing machine on his farm.[47] Prompt action by some workmen saved his life. It is unclear if his permanent limp was a result of this accident. He spoke with a pronounced stutter. It remained difficult for the Birr poor law guardians to ensure regular collection of the poor rates and James incurred their wrath from time to time as his brother had done.[48] In an effort to remedy the situation the board initiated a remuneration of one shilling per pound collected before 1 March and six pence per pound collected thereafter.[49] In January and February 1860

---

44   Valuations of approximately £45, £20, and £52 respectively. *GV* pp 6-34.

45   Total valuation of land which James rented was approximately £84, *GV* pp 5-41.

46   Land valuation £44-15-10. House valuation £3-5-0, *GV* p. 41.

47   *KCC*, 31 March 1858.

48   PLU 8-1-1859.

49   PLU 24-9-1859.

James collected £402-5-11 which yielded income of approximately £20. Collection of £278-8-5 after 1 March was worth approximately £7 to him. His earnings for that year from the county cess were £35-13-9. Income from tax collection varied from year to year depending on the poundage for the year (amount paid to the collector per pound collected), and the rate struck (amount per pound valuation, which the taxpayer paid). James Davis in 1859 earned a total of £47-8-0 from the cess and poor rate collection. In 1860 he earned a total of £62-13-9 from cess and poor rate collection. The former converts to €4,855 in today's money. The latter converts to €6,198 approximately in 2003 money.[50]

The collection of the cess and poor rates gave him an income substantially above that earned by the majority of his neighbours. There would have been additional income from his farming. However, I do not have any information on his outgoings, debts owed by him, or debts owed to him, and so it is impossible to get an accurate idea of his wealth and standard of living. The diary certainly gives the impression that he had to be frugal with money. His income had to support himself, his deceased brother's widow and her seven children, probably his mother and his sister, keep three houses, and pay several employees. James Davis was prominent in the local woollen business in the 1850s to the 1870s and advertisements appeared in the local newspaper for his business in partnership with others in those decades. He held his position as a tax collector until his retirement in 1880 when he was succeeded by his nephew, also James. Both were members of the select vestry and comfortable farmers. James Davis sold his virtually freehold farm of 155 acres at Curraghmore to the solicitor, Adam Mitchell, in June 1879.

The sum of £450 necessary for the purchase of an ensigncy in the army, which Mr Whitfield constantly urges William, the diarist, to lodge in the bank for that purpose, was completely beyond the finances of uncle James Davis. The sum of £450 was equivalent to more than nine years of James Davis's income at that time.

---

50   These conversions were calculated using Table 1, Composite Price Index 1750 to 2003 from the Office of National Statistics, U.K. and for further comparisons see appendix nine.

8.   *Eglish Church of Ireland church in 2009 (courtesy of Mr Ger Murphy)*

Abraham Whitfield

Abraham Whitfield of Davistown House, who will be found throughout the diary, was born in 1796 in the townland of Lowerheath, near Fivealley, Birr. He was among the youngest of nine brothers and sisters.[51] In 1815 he followed his brother William Whitfield into the army as an ensign.[52] He chose the 8th West Indian Regiment but this was soon to be disbanded and consequently Abraham spent the next few months kicking his heels in the depot on the Isle of Wight. In 1816 he was sent home on half-pay of £0-2-7½ daily. He appears to have remained in Ireland on half-pay for the next ten years.

In 1817 he married Martha Jane Mitchell in the Protestant church at Ballyboy. We lose sight of him for the next ten years except for a brief glimpse in 1824 when he is listed among the landholders of Offaly. At that time he held 25 acres in Tullow, Kinnitty.

He was restored to full pay (£0-5-3 per day) in 1827 when he went to Newry to join the 86th Regiment as ensign[53] He spent most of the next five years on foreign service, first in Barbados and then in Jamaica. While in Barbados in 1830 he was promoted to lieutenant and he returned to England.

He joined the 33rd in Burnley, Lancashire, but he was soon off again to the Caribbean, this time to Jamaica. Service in the Caribbean was extremely harsh on both the officers and other ranks.[54] Both the climate and the terrain made for difficult living conditions and at times the death rate from disease was greater than losses experienced under war conditions.[55] Consequently tropical postings were unpopular with many men. The more affluent and well connected officers could sometimes avoid such foreign service. Officers with less means and the enlisted men were not so fortunate. Abraham Whitefield was understandably irate when he was sent to Jamaica instead of one Rolers who had gone on half-pay rather than submit himself to service in Jamaica.

However, colonial service did have some advantages for an officer. The cost of living was less expensive than in Europe and the high rates of death and disablement due to the unhealthy climate and living conditions offered better promotion opportunities. These considerations made tropical service a more attractive option for the officer of limited means. The purchase of

---

51   William, John, George, Martha, Ann, Mary, Margaret and Sarah. His father's name was probably George. See C.C. Ellison, 'Early 19th century lists of Protestant parishioners in the diocese of Meath' in *Irish Ancestor* (no. 2, 1973), p. 115.

52   The lowest rank of commissioned officer in the British Infantry.

53   Royal County Down Regiment.

54   *Journal of the Society for Army Historical Research*, vol. 12, no. 48, p. 218.

55   Ibid., vol. 58, 1980, p. 227

an officer's uniform and mess made considerable inroads into what may at first seem to be relatively generous pay. Nevertheless, the life of even a lowly ensign was much more comfortable than that of the enlisted men, especially in peacetime. Army life was not always as romantic as the picture Abraham presents. He spent the last four years of his army career serving in the British Isles before retiring in 1836 at forty years of age. The sale of his commission should have raised approximately £700[56], thereby providing him with a pension. By the late 1830s he was living with his wife in Davistown House.[57] He was involved in a local mill, possibly the adjoining corn mill,[58] just east of Davistown townland. He also farmed eighty eight acres around Davistown House.[59] The house and land were rented from the Woods sisters.

His marriage to Martha Jane Mitchell disintegrated and the couple separated. She moved to Kinnitty. Abraham rarely mentioned his wife so we are left with only an intriguing glimpse of this woman. They do not seem to have had any children. It is unclear how he was related to the many other Whitfield families living in the vicinity. William refers to him as Mr W throughout the diary.

Towns and Villages

The towns and villages that played an important part in the lives of the Davises and their neighbours were Birr, Frankford (now Kilcormac) and Ballyboy.

Birr

Birr or Parsonstown, is situated eighty-six miles west of Dublin, and was a substantial market and post town with a population of 5,401 in 1861.[60] The population had reached its nineteenth-century peak of 7,151 in 1851.[61] Thereafter there was a slow but consistent fall in the town's population.

---

56   Source: From Capt. W. Miles, , 'When promotion was slower still' in *The Journal of the Society for Army Historical Research*, vol. 12, no. 48, p. 216.

57   Source: Ordnance survey field name books of the King's County 1837-40, published in typescript form in the 1930s and now available in the Offaly County Library, volume 1, p. 227.

58   Source: Griffith's Valuation Map.

59   GV, p. 6 and see Pey, *Eglish and Drumcullen*, p. 331. The mill was used four months of the year in 1850.

60   Source: *SD*, 1870.

61   *SD*, 1856.

9.   *The Birr Telescope c. 1858 with (left to right) Clere and Randal Parsons with Miss Knox and at their feet, Charles Parsons (from David H. Davison, Impressions of an Irish Countess: the photographs of Mary countess of Rosse, 1813-1888. Birr, 1989, p. 28). Reproduced by kind permission of the earl of Rosse.*

By 1891 the town had 4,313 inhabitants.[62] Markets were held every Saturday. Corn, flour, vegetables, dairy produce, livestock, drapery, groceries, coal, iron, timber and spirits were among the many items bought and sold.[63] Fairs were held four times a year in February, May, August and December.[64] The town's gas lighting had been installed in 1855.[65] The railway extension from Ballybrophy to the town was completed in 1858 bringing an improvement in the transport of goods and produce.

There were at least four schools in Birr and two others in the village of Crinkle about a mile away to the south.[66] Birr was dominated by two prominent features. The first was Birr Castle and its demesne, the home of the Parsons family, which hugged the west side of the town. The second

---

62   *SD*, 1894; 1991 Census figures for Birr urban district were 3,280 and environs 776, total 4056, source C.S.O.

63   Source: Michael Byrne, (ed), *An A – Z of Offaly in 1837* (1998) p. 74. This is the Lewis dictionary of 1837 with the Offaly entries reproduced with illustrations.

64   *SD*, 1856.

65   *SD*, 1856.

66   *SD*, 1856.

was a large stone column supporting a statue of the Duke of Cumberland standing at the eastern entrance to the town. This statue commemorated the Battle of Culloden.

Crinkle was the home of a large military barracks was built to accommodate 1,110 men, 48 officers and 15 horse.[67] The barracks made a significant contribution to the commerce of Birr and the surrounding district. There were at least 280 businesses and trades carried on in the town itself with an additional 27 at Crinkle.[68] Other features in the town were a constabulary barracks in Cumberland Square, a bridewell in Cumberland Street, the workhouse near Syngefield, a convent of the Sisters of Mercy at Oxmantown Bridge, the courthouse, three dispensaries and a fever hospital at Connaught St. Five cars left Birr daily. One each travelled to Banagher and Athlone/ Longford. Two travelled to Templemore and one left for Ballybrophy/ Roscrea. The mail coach went to Ballybrophy every evening. A horse-drawn omnibus left Birr for Roscrea and Ballybrophy twice every morning.[69]

Frankford

Frankford, (now Kilcormac), was a small post[70] and market town on the banks of the Silver River, eleven miles east of Birr. Much of the village was built along the main street which was part of the Tullamore/ Birr road. Frankford had a population of 850 in 1861.[71] The population peak had been in 1841 with inhabitants then numbering 1,345.[72] But in the following ten years the number of residents decreased sharply. By 1881 the population was 559.[73] Frankford had a dispensary and an asylum for six elderly widows. One doctor attended the town. There was one national school and a police barracks.[74] The Roman Catholic church stood in the centre of the town. Market was held on Saturday with fairs taking place in April, May, September and November. The town supported nineteen businesses including a distillery and two corn mills. The mail car called daily at the post office at 5 p.m. on its way to Moate.

---

67   *An A – Z of Offaly in 1837*, p. 75

68   *SD*, 1856.

69   *SD*, 1856.

70   Had a main Post Office branch

71   *SD*, 1870.

72   *SD*, 1846.

73   Source: St George Joyce, *The King's County, epitome of its history, topography etc.* (Tullamore 1998) being a reprint of the edition of 1884, p. 56

74   Source: *SD*, 1856.

Ballyboy

The small village of Ballyboy lay about a mile to the east of Frankford. Its population peaked at 348 in 1841[75]. This had declined to 219 by 1851[76] and to less than a hundred by 1891.[77]. At the time the diary was written the village supported six businesses including a flour mill. The Protestant church, built in 1815, dominated the village, which also had a national school. Fairs were held in May, August and December.[78]

10   *A view of Castle Street, Birr, c. 1856 from the ramparts of Birr Castle at Castle Street showing the Woods' brewery (formerly the Robinson distillery) in the foreground to the right and a market at Castle Street in the background (from David H. Davison Impressions of an Irish Countess: the photographs of Mary countess of Rosse, 1813-1888. Birr, 1989, p. 27). Reproduced by kind permission of the earl of Rosse.*

---

75   Source: *SD*, 1846.

76   Source: *SD*, 1856

77   Source: *SD*, 1894.

78   Source: *SD*, 1856.

Chapter 1

William Davis's Introduction, 1842-58

William added this introduction to the diary as a postscript, which he then squeezed into the last pages of the notebook. I have brought it to the front of the diary.

This chapter includes William's early childhood and chaotic schooling, the robbing of Mrs Burriss, the tragic death of William's father with its unfortunate legacy and William's confirmation.

I begin my journal with an account - written from memory - of my school days and incidents which happened before 1858.

I was born at Davistown, March 19th, 1842 at about twelve o'clock on a Saturday. The first schoolmaster I went to (when I was near six years old) was a little young fellow of the name of Tommy Brown to the Eglish church school about the beginning of 1848. I used to stop at my grandfather's[79] and walk a few perch[80] every morning to school. Before and at this time my brother Ned was at school with Brown's father in Cree near Birr as a boarder. My sister Lizzy was at my grandfather's this time also going to Tommy Brown, but it was thought that Brown was no good and we left him and went to Bartley Toole.[81] Toole was a Roman Catholic who kept school on his own account at the Fivealley. While going to him Lizzy and I walked

---

79   Grandfather Watkins's house at Ballynaguilsha, near Eglish.

80   A measure of length the measure of which could differ from locality to locality. Approximately five and a half yards. Source: *National encyclopaedia*, published by Mackenzie, London, circa 1898, (hereafter *NE*), vol. 10, p. 406.

81   Source: in the *National report on education 1826* Bartholomew O'Toole was teacher at Cloncarbin school with fifty pupils. Source: *Cill Laidhain – A window to the past*, p. 18

the three miles from Davistown to the Fivealley every day. Ellen[82] also at this time used to walk from my grandfather's every morning to Bartley's school - as it was called.

After being for some time with Bartley we all three returned to the Eglish church school to a man of the name of Moore who replaced Brown in October 1848. On Moore leaving Eglish Daly came in his place about the middle of 1850. Lizzy, Ellen and I remained at the church school stopping at my grandfather's - Lizzy and I going home on every Friday evening. There used to be no school on Saturdays. Ned also came some of the time to Moore walking the four and a half miles from Davistown every morning. I remember that this time I used to wear a stiff brown bib.

We then left Daly and returned home from my grandfather's. Lizzy and Margaret went to Mrs Ryan of the Frankford girls' church school (called the Preaching House school) and I went to Mr Ryan her husband also in Frankford. I do not think Ned was going any place this time. When Ryan died, Horn, a nephew of Mrs Ryan taught in his stead. I did not go to Horn but after going to the Widow Ryan for a while removed to Connor Guilfoyle's school in Frankford. Lizzy and Margaret continued with the widow Ryan.[83]   Ned also was going to Connor Guilfoyle with me. Here Ned bought a Voster's[84] Arithmetic in Frankford. I got one from Birr. When Mrs Ryan and her nephew soon after removed from Frankford (Mrs Ryan married again), Lizzy and Margaret joined me and Ned at Connor's. Connor was a cripple and used to go on two little hand stools. But Connor unlike the church teachers should be paid. Our money not being forthcoming he summoned for it. My father then gave it to my uncle James Davis but as well as I recollect James Davis kept the money himself. My father had to pay it again. (Until early 1852 my father was guarded by two policemen who lived in our house and for about four years previously). After this Ned went to Birr as a boarder to Brady. I returned alone to Eglish to Daly walking there every day. It was during this time that my eye was cut in the fair of Birr, Feb 11th, 1851 and that Mr Burriss died March 23rd 1851. He was buried in Banagher. I remember I was at his funeral with my father and my uncle William Watkins. Mr Burriss's wife Catherine was my grandfather's sister and my mother's aunt.

---

82   Ellen Watkins, William's aunt.

83   In Griffith's valuation 1854 Connor Kilfoyle is listed as the lessee of a house and offices on Fairgreen Street., Frankford, valuation £1-15-0. Also in 1854 a Cornelius Guilfoyle is listed as the lessee of a house and yard on Melsop Street, Birr, valuation £1.

84   The complete title of this book is : *Arithmetic in whole and broken numbers: digested after a new method and chiefly adapted to the trade of Ireland. To which are added, instructions for book-keeping and advice to a young merchant* by Elias Voster, 'A new edition carefully corrected and revised', 1840, price 2s 6d. Source: List of early printed books in Trinity College Dublin.

11 *John's Place, Birr in the 1890s (courtesy of the National Library of Ireland)*

12 *John's Place, Birr in the late 1890s with a view of the monument to the third earl of Rosse, died 1867 (courtesy of the National Library of Ireland).*

Shortly after this James Davis[85] and his company robbed Mrs Burriss of her property on the pretence that it was for my mother they were doing it. My uncle William Watkins collected a party and got a few cattle and some bacon &c in right of his aunt Mrs Burriss. For this the minister Healy[86] was offended with him and my uncle Richard Watkins and this helped to drive Richard Watkins out of the church. But James Davis did not offend him though he robbed without any right at all. Mr Burriss was my mother's uncle and promised her as a fortune £100 at his death, but he died without making a will. Mrs Burriss came to live to my grandfather's. (About '54 my uncle Richard began to attend mass).

My father began to sink into a decline and I believe Ned returned from Brady's finally. But previous to this when my eye was cut he was at home. I remember he was jealous of all the attention that was paid me. Daly left Eglish and I returned home. I think we all remained at home for some time.

13.   *The Mercy convent at Birr completed in the mid-1850s by architect, Augustus Welby Pugin (courtesy of the National Library of Ireland)*

---

85   William usually refers to his uncle as "The Lame Fellow" throughout the diary. He was a brother of William's father and executor of William's father's will upon his death in 1854.

86   Robert Healy 1818-1879. Established Church. Born in Dublin, son of Robert Healy M.D. Entered Trinity College 1 July 1834 aged 16. B. A. 1840. Perpetual Curate Eglish 1842 – 1860. Rector Clonfadforan 1860 – 1864. Rector Newtownfertullagh 1864 – 1865. Vicar Kilcleagh 1865 – 1873. Died at the Parsonage, Female Orphan Homes, Clontarf, October 5th 1879. His wife Annie died at the rectory, Moate, March 2nd 1869. Source: Representative Church Body Library, (hereafter RCB).

14.   *The Roman Catholic chapel at Birr completed in 1817 (courtesy of the National Library of Ireland)*

15.   *Oxmantown Mall, Birr in the 1890s with the Church of Ireland church in the background (courtesy of the National Library of Ireland)*

I believe this was about 1852 the year that Bland[87] and O'Brien[88] were elected. In the September of this year my father began to grow worse and used to go to consult Dr Hersie of Kinnitty. I saw a prescription of his dated September 9th 1852. On Sept 27th my uncle Wm went to America and my aunt Kate some weeks before him. On Sept 30th Mrs Burriss died and was buried at Eglish. On Nov 15th my brother Tom was born - we had Ballincard this time for I remember that this year at the time of the election I used to sleep at Ballincard sometimes to mind the fruit &c and it was shortly after that Maxwell came there. I believe sometime about '53 Margaret, my brother Richard and I went to Armstrong to the Preaching House school in Frankford (Armstrong was a young fellow from Kinnitty).Before my father died he made a will in my favour but James Davis took advantage of me being wilful and caused another will to be made in my brother Richard's favour. That is in his own, for he wished to have management of the place as long as possible till Dick be of age. James Davis and a lot of the Davises brought together by him were at the making of the will. These were like so many deathbed vultures preying on the substance of us who were soon to be orphans, but they did not come to look after us often since. James Davis was at this time poor enough only that he had the poor rate collecting of Ballyboy in place of Wm. Manifold [89] who was a short time before shot in his gig coming from Tullamore. Dyass[90] escaped although in the gig. No one was punished for this murder.

Before my father died a long time he kept his bed and my wilfulness vexed him. The lame fellow who was hitherto kept at a distance took advantage of me. On account of some disagreement with Armstrong I left him and went to Ballyboy (before my father died) to Cooney who taught the national school there but after going a short time I returned to Armstrong (also before my father died). Margaret and Richard continued going to Armstrong while I was at Ballyboy. On the morning of Monday Feb 27th 1854 my father died.

87   The Honorable Loftus Bland, MP for King's Co. 1852-59. Born Blandsfort House, Queen's Co. 1803. Called to the Irish Bar 1831. Later JP for King's and Queen's Counties. 'He supported George Moore 's party in favour of Tenant's Rights, Free Ballot and Religious equality for all......... considered an excellent landlord, an outstanding farmer and a highly revered judge'. Died January 1862. Source: Patrick Meehan, *The members of parliament for Laois and Offaly 1801-1918.* (1972), pp 131-2.

88   Ibid, p.130. Sir Patrick O'Brien, 2nd Baronet of Borris-in-Ossory was MP for King's County 1852-1885. Born Dublin 1823, called to the Irish Bar in 1844. Became a Liberal MP in 1852 and later a Home Ruler and supporter of Isaac Butt. In 1880 he opposed Parnell and supported William Shaw for leadership of the Home Rule Party. Also J.P. for King's County and Deputy Lieutenant for Dublin. Died,1895.

89   William Manifold was shot dead at Pallas Hill near the Blue Ball , Tullamore on 19 October 1852. Bernard of Kinnitty had lately bought some land through the Encumbered Estates Court. There were large arrears of rent due which Bernard had his agent Manifold pursue. Consequently three tenants were dispossessed and Manifold was shot shortly thereafter. Source: Rev. Andrew Shaw, *History of Ballyboy, Kilcormac and Killoughy,* (1990) p.132. See also *KCC* , 20-10-1852 and 27-10-1852.

90   Mr John Dyass of Frankford. *KCC,* 20-10-1852. This is probably the same Dyass of Frankford who is mentioned several times in William's diary.

16. *The interior of St Brendan's Church of Ireland church, Birr in the 1890s (courtesy of the National Library of Ireland)*

I believe Ned was in Curraghmore at the time and for some time before. Lizzy was on that morning in Birr on some message. I did not see my father nor was I in his room for some weeks before he died for young as I then was I was rejected and despised but I'll not lay blame on the dead. James Davis for his own advantage took every means of turning my father against me - and he got plenty to help him - his mother and his old uncle Willy &c &c. My father smoked and spoke a few minutes before he died. At about 8 he departed at the age of 48 years. When my mother saw him dying she told me and I hurried up to the room. Us two were with him when he was dying. I believe my mother asked would she turn him in the bed and he said his last words 'It's no matter if you put me out on the boards'. Two days after, (Ash Wednesday) March 1st, he was buried in Aghancon churchyard. Richard and I were at the funeral. Then James Davis began to oppress us and grow fat on our oppression. After this event Lizzy went to school to Mrs Ridler[91] in Birr stopping at lodgings. (I believe she first stopped at James Smallman's, a stepbrother of my grandmother's since gone to America and next at an old maid's in Church Lane, Miss Geers, and then at a Mrs Wilkinson in Compton's Row). We all the time continued with Armstrong. Ned went to Australia in the harvest of this year 1854 - it being ordered in the will that he should get means to emigrate. At about this time also Lizzy returned from Birr her school days over.

---

91   Elizia Ann Ridler, Cumberland Sq. Birr, listed under Academies and Schools in *SD*, 1846 and 1856.

The Russian war was at this time and Armstrong left Frankford and joined the militia from which he afterwards volunteered into the line. Previous to this the Rev. Carleton[92] left Frankford and went to Dublin and a fellow of the name of Gordon came in his place. In place of Armstrong, Benson (a little fellow) came to teach school. In the interval before Benson came Richard and I went to Cooney of Ballyboy for a while beginning May 14th 1855. About when I was going to school to Benson, James Davis brought me not much with my consent to his first cousin , Mick Moynan, a draper of Tullamore intending to bind me to him but I took a dislike to Moynan and refused to surrender to him.[93] This displeased James Davis. When Gordon the minister went away soon a man named Nuthill came. He remained a while and then Mr Robinson, a nice man, supplied his place. The master Benson went and Cahill, a married man with a family, came. We went to him for a while till he went mad and left Frankford - I always considered his intellect to be unsound. After he going mad in 1856 Margaret remained at home and James Davis began to talk of sending Margaret to Mrs Ridler and me to Weir[94] who kept a boarding school. I remember on Friday August 1st I was in Birr with James Davis and he called at Weir's to make an agreement with him about me (the July vacation was out at the time) but Weir was not home till next day. James Davis by himself was in Birr that day and settled for my schooling.

On Monday August 4th 1856 I went to Curraghmore & brought down the gig and pony with which Margaret and I on that day began to go to Birr school. I remember James Davis was telling me to be attentive &c and expressed his fear that I would be a disgrace to all belonging to me. We used every evening before leaving Birr in the gig get 1d worth of bread each. After driving the pony and gig for about 6 weeks James Davis bought an ass and got a little blue cart with a seat across in the middle and we drove in that for the remainder of the quarter. Then Margaret stopped and I continued going some days of another quarter in the ass's car. But the days were getting short and it was arranged for me to stop at Weir's (about latter end of 1856) before Christmas. Weir had at this time ten or eleven boarders. The minister, Mr Robinson, soon after left Frankford. Dubourdieu[95] supplied his place. About this time my old teacher Connor Guilfoyle died in Birr whither he

---

92   Rev. Henry Carleton officiated at Ballyboy from 1848 until 1857. Source: Clergy succession list in *History of the diocese of Meath* by John Healy . Published 1908 by The Society For Promoting Christian Knowledge.

93   Michael Moynan, haberdasher, High Street, Tullamore, Source: SD 1856.

94   James Maxwell Weir, graduate of Trinity College Dublin. Sch., 1852, B.A., Aest., 1858. M.A. Aest 1862. Source: George D. Burtchaell and Thomas U. Sadleir, *Alumni Dublinenses*, Trinity College, Dublin published by Thoms , Dublin, 1935,

95   Armand Du Bourdieu, B.A.. Graduated from Trinity College, Dublin 1854, Rector of Ballyboy 1857-75. Lived in Frankford in what is now the Post Office . He was said to never speak or salute those whom he met in the street. Hence the local saying "As proud as Du Burdu". Source: *Alumni Dublinenses* and Reverend Andrew Shaw, *History of Ballyboy, Kilcormac and Killoughy,* (1990) p. 21.

had previously gone to teach. Early in 1857 I left Weir (as boarder) and my bed &c were removed to Muirison's in Townsend St (facing the Fair Green). Margaret and I lodged there and boarded ourselves. I went to Weir as a day scholar and Margaret began with Mrs Ridler again. The family at our lodgings consisted of Mrs Muirison, a widow and her two daughters, dressmakers, and two of her sons, printers. On 30th of June '57 the first of the new fairs was held in Birr. After the July vacation of 1857 James Davis refused to supply us with money necessary to maintain us at Muirison's, our lodgings, so we brought home our little furniture. We stopped at home for the rest of the year.

This autumn the minister Healy was going someplace near Tullamore when a goat on the roadside frightened his horse. The car was upturned and his leg was broke. He was confined to his room for several weeks during which he had to hire others to do his Sunday's preaching &c. While he was laid up in his room I with other youth of the parish attended him to prepare for confirmation. When the Bishop of Meath came to Ballyboy on the 24th of October 1857, I was confirmed. On the Advent Sunday following I received the sacrament from Booth[96] of Birr who helped Healy to officiate.

17. *The old bridge at Birr in the 1890s (courtesy of the National Library of Ireland)*

96   Reverend Thomas Booth, Oxmantown Place, Birr. Source: *SD* 1856.

18.   A military parade at Crinkle Barracks in the late 1890s

CHAPTER 2

1858

William's diary started with brief and occasional entries covering the year 1858. These now follow in chapter two and include: a neighbour packs for London, a coursing meeting, a narrow escape from death at the threshing, and Abraham Whitfield (Mr W) tells of fire fighting in Liverpool.

Journal for the year 1858, occasional and brief, partly from memory and partly from record.

Davistown, Monday, January 25th 1858.

Today Margaret returned to school and I drove her into the lodgings at Muirison's in Birr. Before I came home I bought a caricature - she who had no taste for music was after getting a concertina. It was in ridicule of music that's nothing but pretended music. I wrote on the cover 'The devil has old maids at the last' and posted it to my aunt Mary Anne Davis. It was the first that ever I sent and I hope will be the last. Not long ago I asked Mr W [Whitfield] what he thought of sending caricatures. He said 'It's only foolishness!' Another time we were talking on the subject he said it was an old custom to send them on the 14th of February, [Valentine's Day].

Later he gave me a little brass-barrelled pistol for he knew I was fond of contriving such things. It was for firing corks and the like.

Davistown, Wednesday, January 27th 1858.

Today I heard from Wm. Rigney[97] with deep regret that poor Mr W is going to leave Davistown. He is going to get a situation of what they call storekeeper in London. Mr W said it wouldn't be for a while yet and that he would shortly hear from his brother, George Whitfield, about it. George is a clerk at Somerset House[98] in London. He said he'd have as good a house

---

97   Labourer employed by Mr Whitfield.

98   The home of some government departments.

as Mr Healy and £100 a year, that it was better to work in a public office from ten till three and not in shops where they work from morning till night. Somerset House, is a great building as large as Frankford in a street called The Strand.

Today we were churning out at the back of Mr W's house next the orchard. Mr W brought in a drink of buttermilk and said to me 'Go seven miles for a drink of milk churning day and seven miles from it the day after.' He asked me to go with him to a coursing meeting at Thomastown, [near Birr] next Friday week.

Davistown, Friday, February 5th 1858.

In the morning I was carried with Mr W in his jaunting car to the coursing meeting at Roundhill near Thomastown. There were a great many hares killed and George McBride had the fleetest bitch. We passed by the lame fellow walking on the way home but carried Wm. Conway.

19. *The camp outside the walls of Crinkle Barracks in the 1890s (courtesy of the National Library of Ireland)*

20.   *A view of Crinkle barracks in the 1890s*

Davistown, Saturday, February 6th 1858.

The very minute I went out today Mr W asked me was I sorry for going to the coursing meeting. I said 'No but glad sir.' In the course of chat a while after this I asked him was Ryalls or Crawley esquires. He said no they weren't. 'I'll tell you what Ryalls is', (says Mr W) 'he's a little idiot.'[99]

Davistown, Tuesday, February 23rd 1858.

Today Mr W began to tell me of his school days in Tullamore with a man of the name of Doran. 'He would not on any account', (says Mr W) 'inflict corporal punishment on a boy. But he slept only three hours in the night for he'd be drinking whiskey. He'd come up to our room with a big stick – "Up boys, it's time." Well we'd cover ourselves up and he'd go down to the whiskey. After a time he'd come up again and this time we should get up. There was a very stupid boy there of the name of Jos Manly, he couldn't get him to learn anything.[100] He called him up one day – "Jos, I want to ask you a question. If you bought a knife for 6d and sold it for 8d would you lose or gain?"

---

99   This may refer to George Ryall of Eglish and Joseph Crawley of Dovehill who are recorded in the *GV* of 1854, p. 21 and p. 6 respectively.

100   The Manlys had a number of businesses in Tullamore in 1823. Among these is Joseph Manly, brewer, Market Square who may have been the boy referred to here. Source: Thomas Lalor Cooke, *The early history of the town of Birr or Parsonstown with the particulars of remarkable events there in more recent times also the towns of Nenagh, Roscrea, Banagher, Tullamore, Philipstown, Frankford, Shinrone, Kinnetty and Ballyboy and the ancient septs, princes, and celebrated places of the surrounding country* (Dublin, 1875, reprinted, Tullamore, 1990 with a new introduction and biographical note on Cooke by Margaret Hogan, pp i-xxxi), pp 407-10.

"I'd lose sir."

"That'll do Jos, I'll take no more of your father's money."

There was a dancing master there of the name of Astare. I think he was a Frenchman'.

Davistown, Thursday, April 15th 1858.

Mr W told me that when he was in Barbados he could not go to bed with the heat till it'd be near dark. At daybreak a cannon would be fired and the fife and drums would begin. 'I often thought bad of getting up early. I'd be fast asleep when the cannon would be fired and hardly have time to dress myself before the fife and drums would begin to play. There was a fellow there from the Queen's County [Laois] of the name of Flood and he thought very bad of getting up early. He left the army because of it. When he went home he paid a man for beating a drum under his window every morning the way he could defy it.'

21.   *The hunt at Gloster House near Birr in the 1870s (from the Magan Collection, courtesy of the Offaly Historical and Archaeological Society)*

I asked Mr W what would be done with an officer's effects when he'd die. 'Three days after the officer's death the sergeant auctions off everything belonging to him at the lowest price. The money is sent home to the War Office for anyone belonging to him to claim it. That box there belonged to poor Clark and I bought it.' He pointed to the big black box that was on the kitchen floor. Rebecca[101] had it down putting quilts &c in it before they went off to London. I could see Lieutenant Whitfield on it in white letters. Mr Whitfield told me that box went over the whole world.

---

101   Rebecca Murray, housekeeper to Mr Whitfield. William usually referred to her as Beck.

Davistown, Thursday, May 13th 1858.

I was after going back to school a while before this. Margaret and I had ceased going to school after the July vacation of 1857 for the lame fellow would not get me clothes or give us money to support us in Birr. In January of this year he sent Margaret back. She went first to Mrs Ridler and then to Miss Alley[102]. Charlotte joined her at the lodgings shortly after, going to school to Mrs Marshall's.

During the spring of this year I was rebelling against the lame fellow's authority. I was almost naked for I was without shoes and had only a bad trousers. About Easter he was near being crushed to death in a threshing machine[103]. When he recovered he bought me clothes and I returned to Weir, stopping at Muirison's lodgings with Margaret and Charlotte.

During the July vacation Miss Alley married a gauger[104] stopping at 30 Cumberland Street. This is also the home of my grandmother's brother William Smallman and we removed from Muirison's to his house about midsummer. Margaret and I first went to Birr, she to Mrs Ridler and I to Weir, on Monday 4th August 1856 when she was just 12 years of age.

Today I told Mr W of a fight that happened in the public house at the barracks lately between civilians and soldiers - one soldier's skull was fractured. All Mr W said was 'The dirty Irish can't be quiet'.

Davistown, Sunday, October 10th 1858.

Today when I was out at Mr W's he felt a new trousers I had on (a black one with spots of blue and red threads running closely through it and with a black and orange stripe. It now - November 25th 1859 - is my everyday trousers along with the one I got afterwards at Kelly's in Frankford and it is the one I had on when I had my likeness taken). He went into the parlour bringing out one of his in the piece - a brownish plaid (the one he now wears, November 25th 1859). He said mine was as thick as it. There was no lining for it, he never wore linings in a trousers.

Ned Duffy from Frankford was afterwards there taking his measure for it and I remember they were talking of ships taking fire. 'Liverpool is a terrible place for fires,'(says Mr W). 'There used to be two fires on average in the week. Every night I would put my duds where I could lay my hands on them. Then when there would be a fire the sergeant would throw a handful of gravel again

---

102   Mary Louisa Alley and Louisa Alley, The Green, Birr, listed under Academies and Schools in *SD* 1856.

103   See appendix 4.

104   *Collins English dictionary*: a) A customs officer who inspects bulk merchandise especially liquor casks for excise duties. b) A collector of excise taxes. According to Cecil English, Athlone, it refers to men who went around measuring the specific gravity of spirits to ensure no adulteration had taken place. He says that gaugers did not travel inspecting weights and measures. A set of weights and measures were kept in the town hall where you brought your pint of ale or pound of butter to be checked if you suspected short measure.

the window and call me. A great mob would gather and they'd be striving to make off with something. I'd get up on a bale of cotton where I wouldn't be dirty. Then I'd say to one of them that would be peeping in "make away with that!" He'd put in his hand to reach for something and one of the men would box him back. Then they'd call me names and spit at me.'

22. *Cannon on show at Emmet Square, Birr in the 1890s (courtesy of the Offaly Historical and Archaeological Society)*

23. *The Crimean gun trophy now situate at John's Place, Birr with the Greek temple of 1833 in memory of the young John Clere Parsons in the background (courtesy of Mr Ger Murphy)*

CHAPTER 3

January 1859

This chapter includes: controversy in Birr about the Crimean gun, preparations for a hunt, newspaper wars in Offaly, a Birr banknote, a shopping trip, family tensions and a trudge through the snow to Clonaslee.

Journal for the year 1859 - every day with such reflections and remarks as occurred to me in transcribing the same from original documents, also the weather.

Davistown, Saturday, January 1st 1859.

Today was fine. I stayed up till after twelve o'clock last night to see the old year buried and to witness the entrance into the world of 1859. Richard, James and I went to Eglish where Healy preached. Our grandfather wished me a happy year and said I was growing taller than him. At nightime I went out to Mr W's for our smoothing iron. He said 'The sun shows frost', and told me to push near the fire.

Davistown, Sunday, January 2nd 1859.

Morning frosty and a slight fog. I was at Eglish, Healy preached. In the evening I went out to Mr W's and told him that Biddulph's[105] hounds would be out for a drag hunt on Friday. 'That would be a good hunt', (says Mr W). 'A roasted herring would do to drag along.' I asked him was it not against the law, that I had heard that if they caught you they'd flog you. 'No,' (says Mr W) 'they daren't do that now... the law is too severe. If they touched you, you could destroy them.'

Davistown, Monday, January 3rd 1859.

Morning frosty, day fine. I asked Mr W was what was in the almanacs about the weather true. 'No....how can you or anyone tell whether it will freeze tonight or not?' He then told me how Moore's *Almanac* came into

---

105   Probably Francis W. M. Biddulph J.P. Rathrobin, Mountbolus see *Offaly one hundred years ago*, p. 324.

notice, he said it was by the merest chance. Moore was in company with a friend one day and an apprentice came in to know what weather would be put down for June 4th. Moore did not like to be interrupted and – "put a great shower of snow" says he. It was put down and there chanced to be a great shower of snow that day and then Moore could tell anything.

I said that I thought that slavery was a cruel thing. 'So it is', (says Mr W) 'did you ever read *Uncle Tom's Cabin*?' I said I did not and he told me it would be worth my while to get it. I drew down shorthand saying I'd like to learn it. I afterwards got Odell's shorthand from Wat Keating, a junior assistant at Weir's.

Davistown, Thursday, January 6th or 12th day, 1859.

I saw Mr W today in the field of rape where he was putting some of it in a hand bucket. Last year when he was going to leave for London he gave the place to his nephew George McBride and he sowed this rape. But now Mr W has made up his mind not to leave Davistown.

24. *Thomas Lalor Cooke, Birr solicitor and historian, died 1869 (courtesy of the Offaly Historical and Archaeological Society). Cooke objected to the Crimean war trophy being placed in Birr Castle demesne.*

Davistown, Friday, January 7th 1859.

Morning frosty, day a little wet. This forenoon I was out at Mr W's and he asked me did I hear anything about Cooke and the gun since. This was about the gun that was taken at the Russian War which the government gave to the town of Birr. The town commissioners handed it over to Lord Rosse who put it in his demesne. I saw the gun arrive for we got a half-day from school. It came by the railway which was lately constructed[106] (Mr W once travelled by railway from Liverpool to Manchester. Wm. Davis).

There was a great crowd of people waiting to see the cannon drawn into the town. They were a long time settling it before they could put it in drawing order. At last it was brought to Lord Rosse's demesne in front of the castle escorted by a lot of military from the barracks and a great crowd of people. Colonel Smith made a speech and then delivered it up to Lord Rosse who made a speech. Cooke says the gun should be put in the square beside the Duke for all to see and Mr W is of the same opinion. I had to tell him that it remains in the demesne yet[107].

Davistown, Sunday, January 9th 1859.

Day fine. The Rev. Henry Carleton late of Frankford preached. On my way home the lame fellow and his party overtook me and asked me up to Curraghmore. I declined and came home to eat my dinner. When by and by a gig came down from Curraghmore for my mother and Lizzy to go up none of them would go. Lizzy was lately on a visit to Ballinasloe with a Miss Skerrit and her friends (they keep a bridewell there). Miss Skerrit used to be sometimes at James Whitfield's[108] and she invited Lizzy down for a fortnight. While she was away the lame fellow came down and called her names. He threatened to wear a whip on her when she came home. Now he has the effrontery to send for her. After a time I went up in the gig. I stayed up till after midnight and slept in Lelaghmore with John Bell and the lame fellow. They had a kind of a party among the rest. John Bell was there to mind Biddulph's hounds that came to Curraghmore tonight for the hunt

106   The twenty-two and a half miles from Ballybrophy to Birr were completed in March 1858 by the Great Southern & Western Railway. Source: Tom Middlemass,, *Irish standard gauge railways*, (1981) p. 17.

107   Thomas Lalor Cooke , 1792-1869, solicitor and author. He resigned his seat as a town commissioner as a protest against the gun not being placed in a public area in the town. He refers to this incident in his *History of Birr* pp 125-6. The gun which is now placed in John's Mall was a Russian eighteen-pounder made in 1827. Information from Cornelius F. Smith to Michael Byrne.

108   James Whitfield was married to William's aunt, Elizia Davis. They had at least three children. Francis, married Anne Jane Finnamore in Ballyboy 1/12/1861. Thomas, married Margaret Pratt in Ballyboy 1 January 1875. Source: Ballyboy Church Records in OHAS. Also one daughter, the M.A. Whitfield mentioned several times in the diary. There were probably two other daughters, Sarah and Eleanor. Source: Eglish church records in the care of the Birr rector.

tomorrow. Lelaghmore is a place a few perches from Curraghmore. John, Davy, Mary Anne[109] and his mother live in Curraghmore and he sleeps in Lelaghmore. It formerly belonged to his brother Tom since gone to America with his family. Tom used to write but none of his letters were answered.

Davistown, Monday, January 10th 1859.

This morning the lame fellow sent John Bell and myself up to George Percy's (an uncle of John Bell's who lives in the direction of Munny, about two miles from Lelaghmore WD) for the loan of a saddle for some of them at the hunt. He gave us Biddulph's huntsman's horn to sound in the way that the people would know there was to be a hunt. On our way we had to cross a drain about three or four perches from Lelaghmore. John Bell got safe over it but the very minute I leaped it I lost my balance and fell back into the middle of it and was wet up to the waist. I didn't get cold as I was striding about after the hunt and my trousers dried on me. We got the saddle and carried it back in our turn to Curraghmore. I couldn't sound the horn but John sounded it most of the way and had the whole country in an alarm. I went after the hunt most of the way but was not well able or willing to follow it everywhere on foot. My young brother James is very fond of going to hunts and was at this one. He followed it everywhere in his lightest and easiest dress (his old torn trousers and tunic). When it was over I had my dinner in Curraghmore and then came home. Mr W was at his punch when I went out to get the *Warder*[110] and I did not see him.

Davistown, Tuesday, January 11th 1859.

Day fine. I recollect that I told the lame fellow to get me a school trousers. He was sending some fat cattle to Dublin and I helped to drive them as far as Frankford. There he got me a light coloured Irish tweed trousers which was entered to our account. I left it at Sweeny's to be made and came home. On the way I saw Mr W feeding rape to the sheep from a hand bucket.

He was in the kitchen when I went out to him in the evening. Says he to me 'They hunted bad in Capalohy, I was on the hill and they were at a loss every minute.' I told him I heard that William Whitfield (son of Francis of Harvest Lodge[111]) flung a stick at a hare when she was close pressed by the hounds. 'More rascal he is', (says Mr W) 'to go fling a stick at a hare, he's

---

109   John, Mary Anne and David Davis were siblings of William's father.

110   Published 24 March 1821 until 26 June1880. Continued in different forms until September 1939. Source: *Newsplan Ireland* by James O'Toole B.A. Published by the British Library and the National Library of Ireland ,1992.

111   William's aunt, Sarah Davis, married Francis Whitfield. They had at least six children. William born 1840, died 16/8/1923. Tom born 1845, died 6/1/1905. Dick born 1847, died 3/2/1931. David George born 1851, died 3/4/ 1926. John Drought born 1858, died1/12/1940. Also one daughter. Source: William's Diary and Whitfield gravestone in Ballyboy churchyard.

no sportsman.'

Davistown, Friday, January 14th 1859.

Day fine. In the evening I went out to the orchard where Wm. Rigney was stubbing up the apple trees. I think Mr W was intending to till it but he afterwards changed his mind and did not. After a while I went into Mr W's kitchen and sat down. I told him I saw two hawks the other day after a little bird out in Troy's and they caught it. 'They say', (says Mr W) '- whether it's true or not - that the cuckoo's a hawk.' Then he was telling me of the colour and size of both. He said a hawk was bigger than a cuckoo and of a darker blue (or possibly vice versa WD). 'Another thing the old people used to say', (says Mr W) 'was that the cuckoo used not build any nest for herself but I don't credit it.' Mr W then said these words of the poet John Logan.[112]

25. *The Willis printing shop at Charleville (now O'Connor) Square, Tullamore in the 1830s (courtesy of the Irish Architectural Archive). It was from here that the King's County Chronicle was distributed in the Tullamore district.*

112   John Logan 1748-1788, Scottish clergyman and poet.

"Sweet bird thy bower is ever green
The sky is ever clear
Thou hast no sorrow in thy song
No winter in thy year".

'I was telling Albert a riddle today', (says Mr W) 'and he didn't understand it.' Albert was very fond of riddles this time and I asked Mr W to repeat it. I forgot it at the time but I afterwards cut it out of the paper and here subjoin it.

[It remains attached to the page of the diary. SR]

"This [sword] in a moment brings me to an End;
But this [book] informs me that I will never die:
The Soul, secur'd in her Existence, smiles
At the drawn Dagger, and defies its Point.
The Stars shall fade away, the Sun himself
Grow dim with Age, and Nature sink in Years;
But Thou shall flourish in Immortal Youth,
Unhurt amidst the War of Elements,
The Wreck of Matter and the Crush of Worlds".[113]

(Mr W said this in a very solemn voice WD).

There is a new paper started in Tullamore called *The Central Weekly Times*. It was lately advertised in the *Chronicle*. Mr W thinks that the *Chronicle* is only a very middling paper.

NB. Two brothers Warren, John Gilmore and George Anthony came to Tullamore and started a paper there under the name of the *Leinster Reporter*, the first newspaper I believe that ever was printed in Tullamore. I heard that they claimed the county printing business on the grounds that they were the proprietors of the only paper in the county town. But Shields[114] of Birr (editor of *The King's County Chronicle* &c) started another - *The Central Weekly Times* - publishing it at Willis's printing offices in Charleville Square Tullamore (although printed in Birr), and thus secured the county printing. As the Messrs Warren became disappointed in their expansion and I suppose finding the profits of their paper not enough to live on, in July of this year

113   Cato's soliloquy by Addison published 1713. Joseph Addison, 1672-1719.

114   Francis H. Shields, printer, publisher and proprietor of the *King's County Chronicle*, Cumberland Sq. *SD*, 1856.

the two Tullamore papers were amalgamated. They are now published by Willis in Tullamore under the name *The Leinster Reporter and Central Weekly Times*.[115] I have not heard whether the Warrens are still (December 3rd 1859 WD) in Tullamore,

Davistown, Saturday, January 15th 1859.

Day fine. This morning Richard and I were out in Mr W's orchard getting some of the apple trees that Wm. Rigney rooted up yesterday. We dragged eight apple trees across the pond and stubbed up one on the bank of the pond but out in our own field. This was a little one that Ned planted a long time ago. We planted them in the garden, nine in a line in the following order; five for myself in line with the two along the ditch facing Ballincard and three for Richard in a line facing the high road. Of these three the nearest the house is Ned's apple tree and we planted the last in the little alder grove for James.

Davistown, Sunday, January 16th 1859.

Morning wet, day fine. In the evening out at Mr W's he told me the artillery are drawn up at Berlin with match in hand. He showed me a Birr banknote[116] and said the manager, John Quain[117], wrote his name very plain.

Birr, Monday, January 17th 1859.

Day nearly all wet. Today our Xmas leave was out and I left home for Birr this morning but did not go to school. Richard commenced going to school to Brady stopping in Birr all week and going home on Saturday like Margaret, Charlotte and I. This is the same fellow as Ned went to school with some years ago. He kept a boarding school then but not now.

Birr, Tuesday, January 18th 1859.

Day mostly wet. I was at school for the first time since Christmas.

---

115   Continued from 25 October 1859 – 18 April 1861. Continued as *Leinster Reporter* from 24 April 1861 – 16 January 1930. Source: *Newsplan Ireland*.

116   'Notes were printed in London, numbered and signed by a clerk there, then sent to Dublin to be stamped and dispatched to the branches where they were signed by the manager before issue. They were payable at the issuing branch, and every branch held a stock of gold for this purpose'. Source: G.L. Barrow, *The emergence of the Irish banking system 1820-45*, (1975).

117   John Quain was manager of the Provincial Bank Birr, *KCC*, 12 February 1859.

Davistown, Wednesday, January 19th 1859.

Morning and day generally wet, evening fine. I was at school today in Birr. As we were sitting by the fire this evening in Birr Richard and I were wishing to be at home. When Margaret defied us to go we walked home and slept there. It was a fine moonlight night and we were home near eight.

Birr, Thursday, January 20th 1859.

All day fine. This morning Richard and I walked to Birr. I posted a letter to R. Allen, Long Row, Nottingham and enclosed a four pence piece, three pence of which was for *Plumb's* shorthand and a penny for postage. This is a little book I saw advertised on the cover of poor Richard's almanac of this year.

Birr, Monday, January 24th 1859.

With the exception of a little mist the day was fine. This morning Richard and I walked in from home.

(Note, I did not as yet mention Margaret and Charlotte coming but they used to come in the ass's car driven by James).

This evening the Fivealley post boy (Comerford from Riverstown) called with the shorthand book I sent for last Thursday. It was only a small tract, not nearly so easily learned as Oddel's which I afterwards got. My uncle William used always direct the papers he sent me to Davistown, Fivealley, and this post boy used to call with them to me in Birr in the evenings both when I was at Muirison's and at Marshall's.

Davistown, Saturday, January 29th 1859.

Day generally wet, evening hail. I was at school. During the week the lame fellow came in and told us that he'd bring Margaret and me to Corbally[118] on Sunday. I had nothing better for head wear than a scotch cap I got some time ago and he said when some of them would be in today I could get something better.

My mother was in and after school we went to Paxton's[119] and got a hat on credit. But just as I was coming up the street at John Meara's corner the lame fellow saw me and got it changed for another of the same shape but more expensive - five shillings and nine pence. I also got a necktie and a

---

118 Corbally, a townland approximately one mile east of Clonaslee. It was the home of Richard Davis, a cousin of William's father.

119 William Paxton. Linen & Woollen Drapers, Haberdashers and Hatters, Market Square, Birr. *SD*, 1856.

white handkerchief and six pence to get my hair cut. I went to Finally's[120] and got it cut for three pence.

Afterwards when I was walking home Mrs Mohan and son of Derryadd overtook me a piece this side of the town and gave me a carrying in her car. We soon overtook Wm. Rigney who was coming home from Birr and I was carried in his car the rest of the way. There was a girl (from Birr) of the name of Carten with him coming on a visit to Beck. She is a sister of James Carten who was the fellow workman of Jack Healy when he was at Harbourne's.[121] When I got down at the piers there was a great shower of hailstones. I wore my new hat home.

Corbally, Sunday, January 30th 1859.

Morning snowing, day cold. This morning before daylight Margaret and I went to Curraghmore in order to go from there to Richard Davis's of Corbally. We were there just about the time they were getting up. The old one got in a huff and wanted to know from us when did we get the letter (of invitation). I don't wonder at this for though they live on our money and have lived on it we seldom get so much as a CIVIL WORD from one of them. This morning was wet and before the lame fellow came over from Lelaghmore they were for a long time settling upon who'd go, saying amongst themselves that there was load enough for the car (meaning Margaret and I) and that no one but mad people would go out on a day like this. At last they agreed that John and Mary Anne would go and for Davy to stay at home. They gave me Davy's coat and that along with two of my own kept me pretty comfortable.

John rode while Margaret, the lame fellow, Mary Anne and I went on the car. After getting plenty of snow in our faces we arrived in Corbally about eleven and then the day cleared up. Some of the party including Margaret and I went to prayers in Clonaslee church about half a mile this side of Corbally. The Rev. Baldwin,[122] - an aged man, - preached. I spent tonight at Richard Davis's and stayed up till after midnight. Among the rest of the company there was my stepsister Sarah, her husband Henry Kenny and one or two of their children, her mother in law, her brother in law Richard Kenny (a fellow whom I take to be a dandy) and Sarah and Jane Kenny his two sisters. Also Dick Davis[123] of Munny and his two daughters.

The lame fellow, his brother Dick, Richard Kenny and I slept in the same bed. I and Richard Kenny in the foot and the other two in the head.

---

120   Probably Finlay, hairdresser, Main St Birr. *SD*, 1856.

121   Possibly George Harbourne, Boot and Shoemaker, Bridge St, Birr. *SD*, 1856.

122   Rev. John Baldwin. 1781- 18/12/1859, son of Rev. John Baldwin. Perpetual Curate, Clonaslee, 1814 – 1859. Source: RCB.

123   Probably brother of William's father.

Davistown, Monday, January 31ˢᵗ 1859.

The morning and forenoon snow, evening fine but a little cold. This morning I breakfasted in Corbally and shortly after we set out for home. Margaret, Mary Anne and the lame fellow were on the car. I went in Richard Davis's car for he was going home at the same time. His daughter Elizabeth Anna was with him. I got carried as far as the three roads of Ballyboy where they turned off and I got on the lame fellow's car. He stopped in Frankford and I drove the car from there to Curraghmore, Margaret getting down to go home from Curraghmore lane. The old one sent me over to Lelaghmore to put up the car and didn't as much as ask me to come to the fire although I was nearly wet to the skin over it, for it snowed on us most of the way home.

When I was a little while at home I went out to Mr W's and was telling him of the wetting we got. 'I know Corbally well', (says Mr W) 'there's a place near Clonaslee that belongs to my cousin Freer, he's lame and wears an iron in his shoe.'

While I was abroad Mr W asked me would I read the *Warder*. I said I would and he got it for me. Today Mr W told me an anecdote of the Princess Royal, the circumstances of which happened since she was married to the Prince of Prussia. (I suppose he saw it in the *Warder*.) He said there was some old Duchess of court in Berlin and she saw the Princess Royal (the Queen of Prussia) lifting a chair one day from one part of the room to another and O, the like of that wouldn't be allowed in the Royal family of Prussia. "Do you know", says the Princess Royal "my mother is Queen of England, Ireland and Scotland and I saw her once lifting two chairs, one under each arm, for the children to sit on?"

FRANKFORD WOOL STORES,

May 28th, 1858.

MESSRS. JAMES DAVIS of Curraghmore, and OLIVER GRIFFIN having a commission from

MR. CHARLES C. FARRELL, OF DUBLIN, to buy Wool, are now prepared to give full Market Price, and pay Cash down for all Parcels that may be offered at their Stores as above, or at BIRR or BANAGHER, where they will attend on the respective Market Days.

N.B.—New Wool Bags to hold 120 Fleeces each, on Sale at 4s. 6d. each.

(C) Advertisement from the King's County Chronicle of 16 June 1858 for the Frankford (Kilcormac) Wool Stores

26.   *Cumberland (now Emmet) Square, Birr about 1910 (courtesy of the National Library of Ireland)*

CHAPTER 4

February 1859

This chapter includes the death of Mrs Gaynor, William's close call in Birr, sore feet and bad shoes, herbal remedies, the theft of a pair of boots.

Davistown, Sunday, February 6th 1859.

There was some snow while I was in church and a little rain as I came home. In the evening I went out to Mr W's and read the *Warder*. He said they are going to elect Lever[124] (founder of the American packet[125] station in Galway) member for Galway and 'very worthy he is of it.'

Before I had the paper read some people were coming in and Rebecca said I could read in the parlour. I was strange and ashamed to go in but Mr W told me to go and so I did. While I was there I read a verse that was done in girl's fancy work and framed on the wall. It was headed 'A Summer Evening's Meditation'. At the bottom was 'The Provincial School Mountmellick' and it had the name of one of the Robinsons on it. 'What a little thing lasts longer than oneself', (says Mr W). 'The girl that did that died before she was eighteen. There was eleven of them in it and there's only one of them alive now.'[126]

Before I came in Mr W was showing me a little verse in the form of a valentine which Albert got yesterday from the city of York. I suppose it was from his aunt Mary Anne.

---

124   John Orrell Lever, director of the Atlantic Royal Mail Steam Navigation Company. Stood as Conservative and headed the poll in 1859 chiefly due to his promise to open a Galway - America Packet-ship service. The service failed and Lever was not re-elected in 1865. Source: 'Politics in mid- 19th Century Ireland' by K. Theodore Hoppen in *Studies in Irish history*, edited by Art Cosgrove & Donal McCarthy. Published by University College Dublin, 1979.

125   A boat carrying mail, passengers and goods on a regular route. Source: *Collins English dictionary.*

126   The Provincial School, Mountmellick was a Quaker school founded in 1786. A number of Robinson girls attended – see *One hundred years of Mountmellick School* (Dublin, 1886), pp 77-89.

27. *Birr courthouse in the mid-1820s (courtesy of the Offaly Historical and Archaeological Society)*

Birr, Tuesday, February 8th 1859.

Day some wet. There was at this time a little old fellow at Weir's, a tutor of the name of Gaynor. Today his mother was dead and she is to be buried tomorrow. We are to get the day to ourselves on account of the funeral. This evening I walked home.

Davistown, Wednesday, February 9th 1859.

Day wet, evening hailstones. This forenoon I went out to Mr W's and told him about Gaynor's mother being dead. She was 70 years old and lived at the back of Lord Rosse's demesne at Croghan [near Birr]. I asked him had he the *Warder* yet and he enquired. A Mrs Coughlan had it. I told him there was a thing in it about young Sharpe in Birr getting a whole lot of goods under false pretences in Dublin and there was a trial on it. When I was coming in he said he'd send Frances[127] for the paper in about an hour and it would be there for me to read later.

---

127   Frances Healy, sister of Mr Whitfield's housekeeper, Beck.

Birr, Friday, February 11th 1859 (fair day of Birr).

On this day eight years my eye was cut by accident in Birr. Wallace a drunken drawing master got up in a car in the absence of the owner and drove through the town. I was with the lame fellow when Wallace drove the car against me. I had a narrow escape of my life. I was in Birr for a week in Molloy's Hotel[128] of the archway and had Dr. Waters[129] attending me. It was reported that I was dead.

My father came to Birr every day during the week I was in it and so did the lame fellow for he knew that if I died my father would kill him for not taking care of me. I remember that after a week I came home in a covered car and was very sick after coming home. People thought I was dead for I fainted away.

Upon the doctor pronouncing me past danger Wallace got off lighter than he deserved. He was only fined a small sum or imprisoned for a few days - I forget which. The car struck me over the left eye and the mark is there yet. It will be there till it rots away in the grave[130].

Davistown, Sunday, February 13th 1859.

Morning light fog, day generally fine. I was at Eglish, Healy preached. In the evening I was out at Mr W's to read the paper. Lever is returned for Galway. Mr W said it was Father Daly[131] got him in and that Daly was a clever fellow.

Davistown, Sunday, February 20th 1859.

I was not at Eglish today on account of the sty that was on my eye. I went out to Mr W's in the forenoon to read the paper. He remarked to me that I had given myself a 'Holy Day'. By and by says he to me 'I used to hear the old people saying what would cure that' (meaning the sty WD), 'prod it with a gooseberry thorn. But I think it would be better to leave it alone, it will go of its own accord. It all comes from a cold. A cold affects one in fifty different ways. When I get a cold one of my ears gets sore.' I told him that I had a short dry cough in the mornings. 'I'll tell you what will cure that. Pound a dandelion and drink a glassful every morning, it's the best

---

128   Michael Molloy's Hotel, Connaught St. *SD*, 1856.

129   John Waters M.D. 16 Oxmantown Place. Medical officer at the District Dispensary and Fever Hospital, Connaught St., Birr. Also medical officer to the poor law union. *SD, 1856.*

130   See Appendix 2 for a contemporary newspaper account of this incident.

131   Father Peter Daly, Chairman of Galway Corporation, the Gas Company, President of the Mechanics Institute and the Commercial Society; also owner of the Lough Corrib Steam Company, chief supporter of Lever. Source: 'Politics in mid-19th Century Ireland' by K. Theodore Hoppen from *Studies in Irish history* edited by Art Cosgrove and Donal McCarthy. Published by University College Dublin, 1979.

thing could be.'

Biddulph's hounds were out hunting this side last Monday. When James came home from leaving Margaret and Charlotte in Birr he went off after them. The way he could run better he took off his boots and hid them in a furze. But when he went to look for them they were taken away and the report soon spread through the country. Today Mr W said to me that he didn't think James would get his boots back.

Davistown, Sunday, February 27th 1859.

Today was fine. The sty was gone on my eye. I was at Eglish, Healy preached. In the evening I was going out to read the paper when I saw Wm. Rigney in the orchard and stayed talking to him. He had the supplement[132] in his pocket which I read there and walked no further.

> Sale
> n.
> —
>
> **WILLIAM RIDLER,**
> WATCH AND CLOCK-MAKER
> *Cumberland-Square, Parsonstown,*
>
> **TAILORING ISTABLISHMENT**
> *38 Connaught-street, Parsonstown.*
> J. BYRNE
> BEGS to return his sincere thanks to the public and to the gentlemen of the various mercantile establishments in Parsonstown for their liberal patronage during the last 15 years.
> He would direct attention to his new pattern (military style) of Trowsers, which have given the greatest satisfaction.
> CLOTHS, TWEEDS, ALPACAS, &c. of every description, (at the lowest possible prices) can be supplied, if wished.
> The London and Paris Fashions regularly received.
> J.B. trusts by punctuality and moderate charges, to merit a further share of public business. A trial from those who have not yet favoured him with their orders is respectfully requested.
> Parsonstown, March 23, 1858.
>
> **MICHAEL CASTELLI,**
> WATCH AND CLOCK MAKER,
> *Duke-street, Parsonstown*
> BEGS to inform the Public that he has on Sale a well selected stock of Watches, Clocks, Jewellery, Fishing-tackle, Spectacles, Eye-glasses, &c. He respectfully solicits inspection.
> M. C. feels bound to express his gratitude for the patronage bestowed on him, and to assure the public that he only expects a continuance of their support by strict perseverance in the same unremitting attention and assiduity.

(d)   *Advertisements from the King's County Chronicle of 6 June 1858*

---

132   Supplement to the *Warder*. A single A3 sheet closely printed on both sides without illustrations or advertisements. Contained articles on world affairs, science and technology and news snippets taken from other papers. Overall tone of contents was educational and conservative. Copies held in Trinity College Library Dublin.

CHAPTER 5

March 1859

Eglish churchyard, the repair of a watch, bad shoes make painful feet, Charlotte's ringworm, Wesley's visit to Offaly in the eighteenth century

Davistown, Tuesday, March 8th 1859.

When I got up this morning in Birr there was snow on the ground. Lizzy came in to eat pancakes with Margaret and Charlotte. This evening Richard and I walked home.

Birr, Thursday, March 10th 1859

Fine. This morning Lizzy went home and Richard and I walked to Birr. (I forgot to mention in the original whether I was at school or not but very likely I was or I would have mentioned otherwise).

Davistown, Saturday, March 12th 1859.

Generally wet. Richard left Birr this evening a little before me and was carried from near Birr to the old road at Billy Hanlon's in the Clontyglass car, a little the Birr side of my grandfather's. I had a carrying from Jenny Heffran of Killadrown who overtook me coming from market.

Davistown, Sunday, March 13th 1859.

Morning mostly wet. This morning Richard and I went as far as Mr W's lodge to meet Dick Whitfield or Tom[133] but neither of them came and when it began to rain we turned home and didn't go to Eglish. When I went out to Mr W's he bid me get a chair. I did so and sat down.

William Smallman has a whole lot of Wesley's[134] works which belonged to his father who was a great Methodist. Among them are some of Wesley's

---

133   Children of William's uncle, Francis Whitfield of Harvest Lodge.

134   John Wesley 1703-1791, the famous Methodist preacher and co-founder of the Methodist religious movement.

journals and I do be looking over them. I saw where he says he was in Ballyboy[135] and he had a better congregation than he expected in a new place. I told Mr W about seeing the journals and remarked to him that Wesley was always travelling about.

'I have a book of his sermons' (says Mr W). 'He preached a sermon on the death of my great progenitor the Reverend George Whitefield[136]; it would be worth your while to read it.' Mr W brought out a volume of Wesley's sermons from the parlour and found out for me the sermon on Mr Whitefield's death. I looked over the most of it and put it up. Charles Coughlan then came from Frankford with the paper. Wm. Rigney was in Frankford but he was not to be home till two o'clock and he sent the paper by Charles. Mr W asked him to sit down but he said he was wet with the rain and would be going home. This evening I went out again to return the *Warder* to Mr W but he wasn't saying anything important.

Birr, Monday, March 14th 1859.

Day almost constant rain. Richard and I went to Birr this morning. Margaret and Charlotte did not come home on Saturday because the ass has to go to Tullamore tomorrow with turkeys to market and she would be too tired to go if she had to come to Birr today with the girls.

Birr, Thursday, March 17th 1859.

I was at school till after 12 o'clock. Richard went home last night as this day was Patrick's Day and there was no school at Brady's and so much he hated Birr that he went home out of it.

Davistown, Friday, March 18th 1859.

Was showery and blowing. Richard came to Birr this morning. I was at school. In the evening I left Birr to end my seventeenth birthday and begin my eighteenth year in my native home. I called at my grandfather's as I went for some American papers.[137]

---

135   John Wesley visited Ireland on many occasions between 1747 and 1789. He recorded these travels in his journals. For his visits to Offaly see the following: Wesley's tours at www.offalyhistory.com, T.W. Freeman, 'John Wesley in Ireland' in *Irish Geography*, viii (1975), pp 86-96; Dudley Levistone Cooney, *So civil a people: the story of Methodists in the Irish midlands* (Tullamore, 2004).

136   Reverend George Whitefield 1714-1770. Contemporary of John Wesley. He did much to establish Calvinistic Methodism in England, *NE*, vol. 14, p. 417. It is unlikely that he was related to Mr Whitfield of Davistown House.

137   William's uncle, William Watkins, sent these newspapers regularly from America.

Davistown, Saturday, March 19th 1859.

This day I enter my eighteenth year and seventeen years are past and gone forever. I am now in the prime of my youth. Grant o Lord that I may remember thee my creator before the evil days come in which I shall say I have no pleasure in them. The tender moments of youth will not last forever. Ah no, already it is youth vanishing away. Grant o Father that amidst the pleasure and vanity of this life I may consider my latter end, the eternal life to come, the everlasting pains of eternity and the eternal joy of heaven.

Davistown, Sunday, March 20th 1859.

Morning blowy, day rainy. I was at church. Healy preached. (Hence forward every Sunday that I am at church [in Eglish] Healy is understood to preach unless I mention otherwise.) I saw my grandfather in the churchyard before prayers. He asked me would my mother be at prayers but I told him she would not. He told us that a woman of the name of Mrs Robinson was the first that was buried in that side of the churchyard (we were standing in the new side of it) and his poor father was the second. He was buried on the 25th of May 1828. Richard, Margaret and James were with me in church. The lame fellow carried us home. He let down James and Richard at the piers and took Margaret and I to Curraghmore where we dined and took some punch. We remained there till after nightfall and then came home.

Birr, Monday, March 21st 1859.

I saw no wet. I was at school. In the evening I sent Margaret to Gunn's[138] for Wesley's *Primitive Physick* .[139] From the small portion of his works that I have read I conclude that Wesley was a man of great wisdom, a tender honest hearted man and a servant of his God. Posterity cannot judge him otherwise.

Birr, Wednesday, March 23rd 1859.

One of the new fairs was held in Birr. The first one was held on 30th June 1857. I was at school till about noon.

---

138   Mary Agnes Gunn Main St. Listed under Booksellers and Stationers in *SD*, 1856.

139   Wesley realized that medicine in England was available just to the wealthy. His aim in *Primitive physick* was to bring practical medical advice to workers and others who could not afford private doctors. Wesley first published his book anonymously in 1747. Source: m-umc.org/umhistory/wesley/primitive-physick/

Davistown, Saturday, March 26th 1859.

Day fine. I was at school. I waited in Birr listening to the trials of soldiers for assaults upon civilians but I came off before they were over. Richard was gone home and I walked home by myself.

Davistown, Sunday, March 27th 1859.

I was at Eglish. In the evening I went out to Mr W's. I was showing him a very painful corn which I had on my toe (my left little one). 'I had one of them once' (says Mr W). 'The way I cured it was I put it in hot water and I used to pick around it with my nail. I never had one since. O, a corn's a terrible thing, you can't walk with it.' I said wouldn't it do to cut it. He said a corn isn't fit to put a knife or any sharp instrument to at all. He told me to have the water middling warm and to pick around it with my nail and after two or three times it would fall out.

Rebecca had a watch which was out of repair and Castelli[140] in Birr once told her that he'd repair it for £0-12-6. She gave it to me today with the £0-12-6 to get it done.

At about nightfall a messenger came from Curraghmore to say that I was wanted there. I had a bad fitting shoe which occasioned my corn so, shoe in hand, I went near Curraghmore and then put it on and limped in. (I several times softened and picked out the corn as Mr W directed but it always came again. Now it is no way troublesome if left alone.) I stayed a while with the lame fellow in Curraghmore and supped. Then both of us hopped over to Lelaghmore across wet and miry fields. I had the shoe in my hand till I came to Lelaghmore yard but the night was dark and the lame fellow didn't see it. In Lelaghmore he told me that he wanted me to lodge money in the bank and gave me instructions. I wanted to come home, pleading that I had a sore toe and would get up early the next morning. But he said I could get up early where I was so I slept with him that night and was up before anyone else in Lelaghmore. I came home carrying my shoe in my hand as before. It rained with little intermission from the time I left Lelaghmore until the time I left home for Birr with Richard at about nine or ten o'clock.

---

140   Michael Castelli, Melsop St. in *GV* 1854, p. 88. Location given as Duke St. in *SD* 1870.

Birr, Monday, March 28th 1859.

Before we set out I cut a piece out of my shoe to make room for my corn for unless I did I couldn't walk a step and even then my shoe fitted very uneasy and I was badly able to walk. However after having our share of some wet we reached Birr a few minutes after twelve. Margaret, Charlotte and James were there a few minutes after us. None of us were at school. I left Castelli the watch. He promised to have it done against Saturday or Saturday week at the farthest and told me his charge would be 10 shillings.

Birr, Tuesday, March 29th 1859.

There was some rain and hailstones. I don't know whether I was at school, I forgot to mention. I almost say I was else I would have stated the cause of not being. In future understand that I am at school every day unless I mention otherwise. In the evening my grandmother[141] who was in Birr called to see us.

Birr, Thursday, March 31st 1859.

Day fine. Yesterday Charlotte's teacher saw ringworm on her neck and told her to stay away till she'd be well. While the rest of us were at school she took a fancy to go home and we could hardly believe it when we were told it after school.

---

141   Grandmother Watkins.

28.   *William, third earl of Rosse, died 1867*

CHAPTER 6

April 1859

Bathing for the first time this year, an anonymous letter, the death of the Marquess of Waterford, Bernard of Kinnitty and the general election of 1859.

Davistown, Saturday, April 2nd 1859.

Day wet, evening fine. When we came home we found that Charlotte had walked from Birr the seven miles, such was her strength at nine years. I went to Rebecca and told her that Castelli would have the watch repaired next week costing only ten shillings so she is now 2/6 richer than she had imagined. This morning none were in Birr on account of the wetness and Dyass of Frankford gave Margaret a carrying on his car. Richard and I walked home.

Davistown, Sunday, April 3rd 1859.

Was a little windy but I saw no rain. In the morning I bathed for the first time that year in the four drains bordering on Mr W's field of rape which is by and by now in full blossom. I was speaking to my grandfather at Eglish. We were talking of a new farm which James W[142] lately got at Killymore[143] near Tullamore. Grandfather spoke in praise of their industry saying that James had very industrious children and that he often saw them weeding potatoes at eight o'clock at night. Before parting he asked did I smoke. I told him I did not. 'Never put a pipe in your mouth by any chance, it's a hateful practise', said he.

After dinner I went out to Mr W's. 'Dear me', (says Mr W) 'how easy an accident will happen.' He then told me of the death of the Marquess of Waterford. They were out hunting a third fox after having killed two when he fell off his horse as it was going over a leap and was killed on the spot. He said he was a great loss, that he employed three hundred people.

---

142 Probably James Whitfield, husband of Eliza, (nee Davis) and brother of Francis Whitfield.

143 It is probably meant to be Kileenmore near Killeigh, Tullamore.

Birr, Tuesday, April, 5th 1859.

Morning soft misty rain tho not so much as yesterday. The day was fine. These two days were very fine and the heat of summer is at hand. So passes the year while time continues, summer and winter, day and night, seedtime and harvest time shall not cease. Time has not an end but there is an end to man's life. When once he leaves this world he leaves it for forever to return no more.

Davistown, Wednesday night, April 6th 1859.

Fine. After school I called for the watch and walked home with it. I gave it to her but I did not see Mr W.

Davistown, Sunday, April 10th 1859.

I wasn't at church for I had a sty on my eye. When I went out to Mr W in the forenoon he told me there was going to be an election and it is rumoured that Bernard will sit up for it. 'If Bernard be opposed', (says Mr W) 'there won't be a busier man in the county than your uncle James. He'll be going day and night, he'll hardly get to bed at all.'

Davistown, Sunday, April 17th 1859.

The morning was frosty and the day fine. I was at Eglish, Marcus McCausland[144] the rector of Birr preached. Mr W told me today that the election would begin on the 2nd of May.

Davistown, Thursday, April 21st 1859.

Morning was frosty and during the day there was rain and hailstones. Both Brady and Weir gave leave for Easter. Margaret and Charlotte got leave yesterday and walked home. James drove in the ass with bread and milk for our breakfast this morning. After school we three left Birr for home. Is not our life a day? With me 'tis now near noon, the morning is fast gone and the evening of life will be clouded by age and care and engrossed with the troubles of this life.

James, Richard and I spent the evening going about groves in Capalohy &c looking for wood.

Davistown, Good Friday, April 22nd 1859.

Richard, James and I were rambling about the fields nearly all day. We were

---

144   Listed as rector of Birr in *SD*, 1856 and 1870.

down in Seary's[145] in our bare feet looking for nests and when we returned we bathed in the four drains. We were just released from the unwholesome air of Birr and thus enjoyed ourselves.

Davistown, Easter Saturday, April 23rd 1859.

Morning frosty, day fine. I was at home all day. My mother went to market in Frankford. Margaret went to Birr with the lame fellow in the forenoon to get boots. I cut my name in shorthand on a little ash tree in the bottom of Mr W's lawn. Perhaps I may see it again when many now alive shall have ceased to breathe.

Davistown, Monday, April 25th 1859.

Morning and evening misty, day fine. In the morning I went to Mr W's to read the *Warder*. Mr W said I ought to go up to uncle John[146] for powder and a gun to shoot the rabbits, that I could get a nice shot at them in the morning. But I told him that I thought I should go to Birr in the morning. He said if any of us were going in the car he had a message to send by us.

I mentioned that we had a magpies nest in Maxwell's Grove and that James robbed it and now she was building another near Jack Brien's. 'Tell him to rob it again' (says Mr W). 'They're very mischievous birds that destroy every egg about the place.' But there was no occasion, this magpie only laid one egg in that nest and never hatched it. In the course of chat Mr W asked me did James ever get his boots back, I told him no.

Davistown, Tuesday, April 26th 1859.

Morning some wet, day fine. This morning Lizzy had a letter written to send to M.A. Whitfield at her new residence in Killymore but there was no ink to direct it and I brought it out to Mr W. He himself handed me a pen and ink (he was alone in the kitchen). It was a steel pen and he said 'I'd rather have a quill pen than fifty of them steel pens, I don't like them at all.'

When I went out to Mr W's in the evening Margaret was there. She had a collecting card (issued by Healy,) of 'The Society For Promoting Christianity Amongst The Jews'. She sent Frances in to Mr W with it (he was in the parlour). He gave six pence on it for which I afterwards wrote down his name. A short time after Mr W came out and gave me a shilling saying to send him a pound of cheese from Meara's[147] tomorrow and he'd be obliged to me. He said Margaret was growing very tall, that she was as tall as Lizzy.

145   Possibly the land held by William Seery at Ballindown at the time of the Griffith's valuation, *GV*, p. 14 .

146   John Davis of Curraghmore.

147   William Meara had a grocer's shop at Main St. There was another grocer's shop under the name William Meara in Market Square. *SD*, 1856.

Birr, Wednesday, April 27th 1859.

In the morning I walked to Birr by myself for Richard's leave is not yet expired. Margaret and Charlotte were driven in the ass's car by James and Lizzy. I bought the cheese in Meara's and sent it home by Lizzy and James.

Birr, Friday, April 29th 1859.

I sent a letter to Maxwell, see last leaf of this book. [On the last page of the journal William wrote -

'Let me apologise for a sarcastic letter and anonymous which I wrongfully sent to Maxwell, from Birr on Friday 29th April 1859. I have not inserted it here nor would it be any use. It was a cutting one, censuring his proceedings and his domestic arrangements which I had no right to do.']

There was some wet in the evening. Richard walked to Birr his leave being out.

Davistown, Saturday, April 30th 1859.

Morning wet, day fine. In the evening I walked home with Richard in better spirits than I came in for Weir informed us of his sorrow that his school was broken up and that Garvey (Lord Rosse's agent) took the house from him. I brought home my books.

29. *Sir John Pope Hennessy, MP for King's County, 1859-65 (courtesy of the Offaly Historical and Archaeological Society)*

CHAPTER 7

May 1859

Feelings run high about land, sowing potatoes, scandalous rumours concerning Mr Whitfield's household, running errands for uncle James. Violence, intimidation and tension accompany the election.

Davistown, Tuesday, May 3rd 1859.

Wm. Rigney was putting manure for potatoes in the field next the orchard facing the high road. I was with him part of the day. The field where the potatoes will be was formerly meadow and I never saw it broken. Later I was out at Mr W's but he was in the parlour and I had not the pleasure of his conversation.

He has lately set some ground for Burney to several people about the neighbourhood for sowing but it is reported that for this he is noticed to quit by his landlord. The land which he set for Burney is an old piece on that side of his own hill which lies next the mill. There was for a long time pasture on it. The Curraghmores are very indignant at his proceedings and rattled about it. Wm. Rigney told me once that the miserable wretch, John Davis, went through the country warning those people to whom Mr W set ground not to sow their potatoes on it for he said Aby [Mr W] would be put out of it and the potatoes seized for the rent. The covetous wretch perhaps believed that Mr W was unable to stay in it and that he'd get it. But he may slander and circulate his lies just as long as he pleases. Mr W is able to withstand him and all his character sort - perhaps when he's tired he'll stop to rest.

Davistown, Wednesday, May 4th 1859.

There was frost but the day was fine. My grandfather was at our house to bring off a little heifer which was for some time at grass with us. He is to have her in the fair of Birr tomorrow.

Davistown, Friday, May 6th 1859.

They were down from Curraghmore sowing potatoes in Cash's lower field next the old road. I was putting manure there with the ass's cart from the yard all day. John was the steward as is his custom when there is heavy work to be done. My grandfather did not sell the heifer in Birr and brought her back again.

Davistown, Saturday, May 7th 1859.

Richard walked home before the car. He told me that Weir held school all week and sent to our lodgings enquiring the cause of my absence. This shows that Weir had but little regard for the truth. I can't understand why a teacher of youth should set his school an example of lying unless perhaps that he wanted to create sympathy and get the house again. Even then he should resort to other means.

Davistown, Sunday, May 8th 1859.

Was fine. I was at Eglish. After dinner I went to Mr W's. He gave me the paper (which remains in my trunk WD) and pointed out a place in it about the war between France and Austria. He told me the first battle - Magenta[148] - was fought.

This evening my mother told me that one morning early in April Wm. Rigney went to Birr for Dr. Wallace[149] and that he delivered Rebecca (Mr W's housekeeper WD) of a girl, stillborn. How she came by this news is she was in Birr one day recently where she met a respectable woman who had just been to see Dr Wallace. This woman asked my mother was there anyone in Mr W's sick, that Dr Wallace had asked her how was the young woman at Mr W's. (My mother refused to tell me her name but she afterward said it was Tom Whitfield's wife.) The doctor told her he was called on early one morning to attend a young woman there who was prematurely confined. Dr Wallace can be at no advantage by telling a lie and if Mrs Whitfield can be believed in her story it is proof positive of Rebecca's guilt. But be this as it may it is said that she was confined of a child. I will assume the best. She was away from Mr W's lately but malicious tongues affirm that she was then sick at Mr W's previous to her delivery and caused it to be given out that she was not there at all. But I take it all for a lie. Evil persons are forever ready to say anything, no matter how scandalous, provided it hurts a person's reputation. It seems to

---

148   Italian Wars of Independence. The Franco-Piedmontese army invaded Lombardy in opposition to the domination of Austria thereby provoking the battle at Magenta where the Austrians were defeated. 4 June 1859. Source: Bryan Perret, *The Battle book*. (1996), p. 187.

149   Alexander Wallace M.D. Cumberland St. Also medical attendant at the dispensary, Castle St., *SD*, 1856.

me that she was not at Mr W's for a few days at the time for I had not seen her. There are at present at Mr W's two children, a male child about six months old and a little girl of perhaps four or five years that she brought there a few days ago. These she says are her sister Mary Anne's (Mrs Young of England WD). Back biting wretches suggest that these are also hers. (She kept the youngest and called him George. The other was sent back. I am since convinced of her guilt. WD)

Birr, Wednesday, May 11ᵗʰ 1859.

Was fine. In the evening a mob of Bland and O'Brien's came from the Roscrea direction to Birr on cars shouting and yelling dreadfully and waving hats and boughs. They were headed by their priests and joined by the mob of Birr. They went to Mathews's[150] Hotel where their leaders addressed them. Messers Bland & O'Brien were busy elsewhere and had entrusted to the priests the raising of the mob. The next day was the day appointed for the nomination of candidates and this mob was raised to oppose supporters of the candidates Kennedy, and Hennessy.[151] These four were seeking the representation of the county. Pierce [Pierse] Creagh had but lately withdrawn from the contest.

Birr, Thursday, May 12ᵗʰ 1859.

Was fine. In the morning early the mob left Birr on cars for Tullamore. They shouted and yelled through the town and waved hats and boughs as before. In the evening coming back they committed acts of violence when passing the Fivealley[152] such as breaking windows and the like. This was because the people of Eglish were in favour of other candidates. At the chapel a man of

---

150   Stephen Mathews's Hotel, Main St. *SD*,1856.

151   Tristram Kennedy,1805-1885. Born the son of a Church of Ireland clergyman at Carndonagh, Co. Donegal. Called to the bar in 1834, opened his Dublin Law Institute in 1839.While a land agent in Monaghan during the famine he strove to relieve the distress of the poor. He was returned for Louth in 1852 and in 1865. Source: Colm Kenny, *Tristram Kennedy and the revival of Irish legal training, 1835-1885*, (Dublin 1996). For further on Pierse Creagh see Kieran Sheedy, *The Clare elections* (Dublin, 1993), pp 219-31. Creagh withdrew from the King's County contest see *KCC*, 4 May 1859.

    Sir John Pope Hennessy MP for King's County 1859-1865. Born in Cork in 1834. Called to the Bar in London 1861. Became Tory MP in 1859. He was the first Catholic Conservative member with an Irish seat. Supported the earl of Derby as prime minister, opposed mixed education and supported Tenant's Rights. Source: Meehan, *Members of parliament for Laois and Offaly, 1801-1918* p. 133.

152   Here there was a confrontation between a crowd of approximately a hundred local people and fifty or sixty men travelling on sixteen cars who were supporters of Bland and O'Brien. The locals were perceived as being in favour of Kennedy and Hennessy. A large number of windows were broken and several people were badly injured. On 1st June 1859 eighteen men appeared at Thomastown petty sessions charged with rioting and assaulting people and property. There were no convictions as none of the witnesses would identify any of the accused, *KCC*, 8 June 1859.

the name of Noons[153] went out to call in his dogs which were barking and they pelted him with stones till he was almost killed. But I believe they were previously attacked by the Fivealley people and got some bruises. They did not return in a body as they went but now and again till nearly midnight. Priest Egan[154] of Birr was one of those that returned early. He addressed his party from a window of Mathews's Hotel.

Birr, Friday, May 13th 1859.

Was fine. The lame fellow since first of the election was going about on Kennedy and Hennessy's affairs but really on his own for he of course expects their interest in return for his services. James Davis will not give his assistance for nothing.

Birr, Saturday, May 14th 1859.

Weir has a drawing master Wallace who has obtained the lame fellow's consent for me to become his pupil. This is the same fellow who in 1851 went near killing me and now here he is robbing me. For I had no use of drawing that I should learn it, better I had let it alone. He pretended to attend at Weir's on Thursdays and Saturdays but very seldom he attended so often. After school on Saturday I had to attend to drawing and Richard would walk home before me alone.

Davistown, Sunday, May 15th 1859.

I bathed at the four drains for the third time this year. I was at Eglish. In the morning I gave Wm. Rigney three pence to bring me the *Leinster Reporter* which I wanted to send to my uncle William[155]. This evening Mr W said he thought Bland and O'Brien would get in. He showed me a printed letter Kennedy & Hennessy sent him requesting his vote. The election is to be tomorrow.

---

153   In contemporary newspaper accounts of the incident this man is referred to as Noonan, see, for example, *KCC*, 18 May 1859

154   "John Egan, parish priest Birr, died on 27 October 1870 aged 63 and in the 40th year of his priesthood . He was educated in Carlow and served as curate in Cloughjordan, Bournea, Roscrea, and as parish priest in Cloughprior, Dunkerrin and Birr. From Ignatius Murphy, *The diocese of Killaloe, 1850-1904* (Dublin,1992).

155   William Watkins in America.

30.   *Emmet Square, Birr with Dooly's Hotel in the background in the 1890s (courtesy of the National Library of Ireland)*

Birr, Monday, May 16ᵗʰ 1859.

I rose early and walked to Birr against about six. None of the rest came in today so I cooked for myself this day and the next. I came in out of curiosity to see an election never having seen one before. About nine I was up at the courthouse. The doors were guarded and I and Francis W (my cousin) and Willy Bulfin (since joined the police) were standing at the door but as we were not electors[156] we had no admission. After a while John Davis asked Murray[157] the priest of Eglish to get us in so he told the policeman sentry that he'd be accountable for us and we got in. I remained in the Eglish polling room till the days polling was over. John and Davy were there but

156   By the 1860s 3,449 people were qualified to vote in the county from a population of 89,064, - 3.9% of the population. The franchise was confined to adult males who occupied property with a rateable valuation of at least £12, and to some categories of leaseholders and freeholders. Source: Gerard Moran, 'Political Developments in the King's County, 1868-1885' in *Offaly history and society, in* Nolan, W & T.P O'Neill (eds) *Offaly history and society*, (1998) p. 767.

157   1) Rev. James Murray. Born Kenny, Mullingar. Studied in Navan & Maynooth.Ord. 2 October 1833. Curate to Ratoath, Kilcloon, Moynalty and Kilskyre. Appointed to Eglish 2 October 1850. Died 2 October 1889. Father Murray was interred in Eglish church. Sources: Revd A. Cogan, *The diocese of Meath*, vol.ii. (1867). Reprint by Four Courts Press 1992, p. 513 and Olive Curran (ed), *The history of the diocese of Meath 1860-1993*, vol.ii, (1995).

the lame fellow was at the polling in Tullamore. Priest Murray gave me *Saunder's Newsletter* and pointed out the place in it about the riots at the Fivealley.

Birr, Tuesday, May 17th 1859.

Today till the election was over I was back and forward from one polling booth to another. Today both sides were bringing in their reserve forces from all directions. Hennessy and O'Brien I believe were in Birr and K & B [Kennedy and Bland] in Tullamore. In the forenoon Mr W came into the Eglish booth. He was sworn by B & O'B's [Bland & O'Brien's] side and when asked for whom did he vote he said 'for Messieurs Kennedy and Hennessy.' When he came down from giving his vote Wm. Harding who acted as Deputy Assistant Sheriff for districts which were polled at the bar of the court asked him to take a seat on the bench. He refused saying he'd be going off upon which John Davis sneaked up to Mr W and prompted by his ignorance said he might as well, as if he was bound to obey his wish. Mr W afterwards said that Wm. Harding told him that H & O'B [Hennessy & O'Brien] would get in and so it has turned out. Mr W's jaunting car is out of repair and I afterwards heard that only Father Murray sent Davy with a car for him this morning Mr W would stay at home and give himself no trouble about it. Davy also showed his enthusiasm by setting the teeth of the mob on edge to strangle him. As soon as the polling was over Hennessy went to Dooly's[158] and addressed some words out of a window but his voice was drowned by the groans of the mob on the other side.

What is strange is that I heard one party groaning[159] another party's priests for still stranger the papists and their priests are divided. The Eglish priest Murray was one of Kennedy and Hennessy's maddest supporters and in consequence he was groaned terribly all down to Dooly's and both before the election at the canvassing and nomination and after it at the declaration. He had much dangers to encounter from the opposition mob. He was groaned and shouted in Frankford and on the night of the declaration the mob of Frankford were waiting his return from Tullamore till late at night to take his life but he returned another way. The lame fellow was in great danger of having his zeal appeased too by the loss of his limbs or perhaps his life and would certainly be killed if he was not guarded by the police on his return from Tullamore. Today Davy saw me in the court and what Johnny wouldn't think of he gave me a shilling and said I ought to be getting home. I think of them all he is the most honest but very little honesty is in their nature as their actions show.

---

158   Dooly's Royal Arms Hotel (family, posting and commercial). George Dooly, Cumberland Sq. *SD*, 1856.

159   A deep sound uttered in derision. Source: Virginia S. Thatcher (ed), *Webster encyclopaedic dictionary of the English language.* (1980).

I saw Maxwell vote for Kennedy. My grandfather was obliged to vote for Bland and O'Brien by his landlord Cassidy.[160] I believe Cassidy called for him at his house and brought him with him on his own car.

Birr, Roscrea and Kinnitty and their priests were for Bland & O'Brien as were Tullamore and Frankford. Kennedy and Hennessy had Eglish, Banagher, Shannonbridge, Rahan, Lord Rosse and most of the landlords and Protestants. It was more to promote strife amongst the papists and their priests that the Protestants were so warm for Kennedy & Hennessy more than regard for them for none of the candidates were worthy of their notice. For on the one side was Bland who is what is called a liberal Protestant and O'Brien a papist and on the other side Kennedy a liberal Protestant and Hennessy another papist. At the outset Bland & O'Brien who were the former Members seemed very easy and safe. But then came Pierce Creagh from Clare into the field and then both sides set to work most actively. But after a short career Pierse Creagh retired from the contest and was succeeded by Kennedy & Hennessy to whom he gave his interest. Then came mobs and speeches but all the priests who were orators and mob leaders were on Bland & O'Brien's side. Messers Bland & O'Brien called on the public in placards and by their priest orators not to elect Hennessy or Kennedy, that Hennessy was a clerk in a government office and that Kennedy was an orangeman.

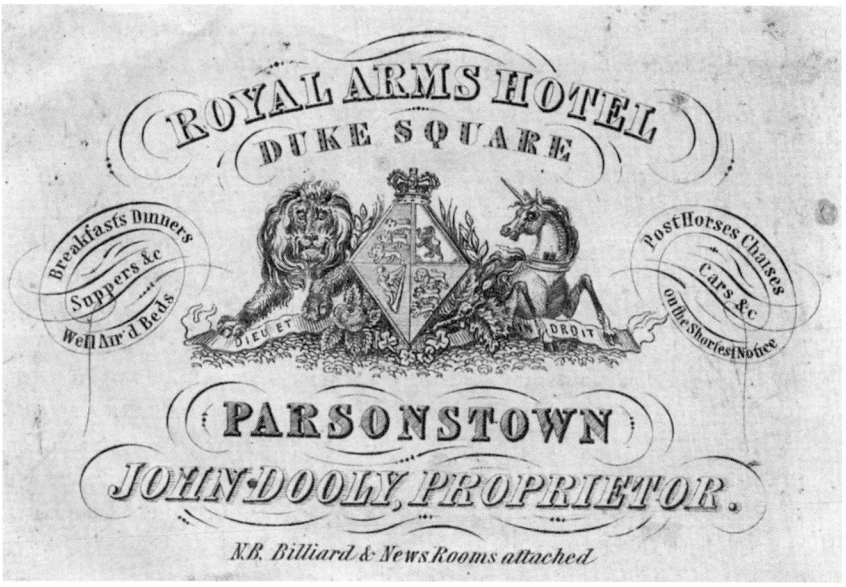

31.   *A label describing Dooly's Royal Arms Hotel, Birr in the mid-1800s (courtesy of Mr Michael Byrne)*

---

160   Probably Cassidy of Killyon. For more on this Cassidy family see Pey, *Eglish and Drumcullen.*

Birr, Wednesday, May 18th 1859.

School was continued. In the evening I sent my uncle William some papers including the Tullamore paper of Saturday. After this my uncle Wm. ceased sending me papers, I don't know for what reason. Richard &c came in to Birr in the car the election being over.

Birr, Thursday, May 19th 1859.

The day was fine. I sent my uncle Wm. the day before's *Chronicle* which contained a full account of the election majority &c and 'Savage and wanton outrages committed at the Fivealley.' I got it the evening before with 6 pence of the shilling Davy gave me.

The poll was

Hennessy-1302.

O'Brien-1290.

Kennedy-868.[161]

Davistown, Sunday, May 22nd 1859.

I was in the four drains for the day was warm. I was at Eglish and in the evening I went to Mr W's to read the paper.

Birr, Tuesday, May 24th 1859.

Margaret walked home in the evening for the dancing slippers which she forgot to bring with her yesterday.

Davistown, Sunday, May 29th 1859.

Forenoon fine, afternoon and evening some thunder and rain. The thunder was distant and I saw no lightning. I could not go to church for my shoes were bad. In the forenoon I went to Mr W's. He pointed out to me in the *Warder* an account of the battle of Mount Bello [sic] [162] which was the first time I heard of it. I saw with sorrow Mr W was reading the paper with spectacles. Before I came in Mr W said it was likely that there'd be thunder it was so calm and heavy and so there was after I coming in.

Lizzy and Margaret were the only ones of us at Eglish. When they came home they said the lame fellow wanted me. I went up to Curraghmore and

---

161   Bland secured 1,216 votes. See Brian M. Walker, *Parliamentary election results in Ireland, 1801-1922* (Dublin, 1978), p. 96

162   Italian Wars of Independence: The battle of Montebello, in the north of Italy, was fought on 20 May 1859. The Sardinian and French troops defeated a larger Austrian force.

he told me to be there again at five o'clock in the morning, that he wanted to send a message to Birr by me. He said I was to come home tomorrow evening and none of the rest were to go to Birr at all as the shearing would be on Tuesday and everyone would be wanted.

Davistown, Monday, May 30ᵗʰ 1859.

This morning I walked to Curraghmore where the lame fellow gave me fifty-five pounds and seven shillings in a cheque and notes to lodge in the bank. After I lodged it I went to school and walked home in the evening. Lizzy and M. A. Whitfield and James were in Birr in the ass and car and came home again.

Davistown, Tuesday, May 31ˢᵗ 1859.

Jack[163] called to us in the morning to clean ourselves and to drive up the sheep to be shorn, (James, Richard and I). So we did and were kept there all day, not as guests but as menials in stopping sheep and the like. Dick and James went home early in the evening. I was there till after one in the morning. Then James Digan yoked our filly to bring Curly the fiddler as far as Nanny Reilly's and I went as far as that with him. Another menial of his was also in the car, a clark he got from the poor house. After leaving the fiddler at Nanny Reilly's I came back with them as far as Mr W's lodge and came in home. It was then breaking day.

---

163   Jack Brien. He worked for James Davis.

32.   *Emmet Square in the 1890s with the King's County and Ormond Club (founded 1859) to the left and Dooly's Hotel to the right*

Chapter 8

June 1859

A nap in a field, more errands, in pursuit of serviceable boots, the death and funeral of Captain Drought, a haircut and an annoying visitor, an injury from lightning, a circus comes to Birr.

Davistown, Wednesday, June 1st 1859.

Fine. As Richard, Margaret, Charlotte and I were just ready to go to Birr, Onny our servant girl (a mere idiot but a bigot to papists) who was in Curraghmore brought word for Richard and I to bring some sheep up that remained at our house to be shorn. We breakfasted at Curraghmore and shortly after Richard, I and another were sent with sheep to Capagolan. But when I went as far as the turn of Freagh I turned back and left them to themselves. I was so fatigued that I took a few hours sleep in Parker's Grove opposite Mr W's lodge.

Margaret was in Curraghmore since yesterday and in the evening the lame fellow gave her seventeen pounds for me to lodge in the bank. Lizzy was in Curraghmore all day yesterday and last night and part of today.

Birr, Saturday, June 4th 1859.

Was wet all morning. Evening cloudy and threatening.

I went to drawing at two and Richard walked home alone. My shoes were bad and painful to my feet. Before I left Birr I told the lame fellow I wanted shoes but he was in too great a hurry to get me any.

Davistown, Sunday, June 5th 1859.

My shoes were too bad to go to Eglish. After twelve o'clock I went out to Mr W's. The morning was fine but showery and close. During a shower Mr W said this was like planet rain. I asked him what that was and he said rain coming straight down.

The Sunday before I heard distant thunder and I saw in this day's *Warder* where a man and woman were in bed with a child between them and the lightning killed them both leaving the child.

Mr W gave me a shilling to get him a pound of cheese tomorrow. He told me there are three sorts of English cheese - Stilton, Gloster and Cheshire. The Stilton is the best, the Gloster the next best (what I used to get for him WD, and the Cheshire is the workman's. Before I came in he brought me the *Warder* out of the parlour and showed me a review in it of the sermons of the heads of the Reformation (Latimer[164] &c WD), and said it was a good book.

Davistown, Monday, June 6th 1859.

A little mist, cloudy and threatening. Margaret and Charlotte went to Birr as usual but my old shoes kept me at home. James brought home Mr W's cheese.

Davistown, Tuesday, June 7th 1859.

Morning fine and warm. Evening some peals of distant thunder but no lightning that I saw. There was rain for about half an hour. My grandmother was at our house to see a letter Lizzy received a few days ago. It was from my aunt Ellen[165] in America. It was chiefly to enquire about my grandfather and grandmother, to know used Dick[166] treat them well - such is the affection of a child. Lizzy answered it today and posted it in Frankford. Her address is Aroa Post Office, London, Canada West.

Miss Skerrit of Ballinasloe is on a visit to our house for the few past days.

Davistown, Wednesday, June 8th 1859.

Knowing that I'd get no shoes at home and thinking I might see the lame fellow in Birr I got up early to go to Birr. The morning was dark and heavy. I had just crossed the fields and was in Mary Kenny's bawn[167] when a dreadful peal of thunder roared over my head. I was always afraid of lightning and now I was so terrified that I ran into an outhouse of Mary Kenny's. I was scarce in & I heard another clap but I saw no lightning with any of the peals. I stayed there till Mary Kenny was up and then I went into the house. So much was my dread of lightning that I came home when it cleared up a little and didn't go to Birr.

---

164   Hugh Latimer, circa 1485-1555. English champion of reformation and Protestant martyr. Burned at the stake as a heretic in Oxford in 1555. Source: *Webster's biographical dictionary* published by G & C Merriam Co. 1974.

165   Ellen Watkins: sister of William's mother.

166   Ellen's brother Richard Watkins.

167   An enclosure where cows were milked. Source *Oxford English dictionary*.

Davistown, Thursday, June 9th 1859.

I rose before day and walked to Birr in hopes of getting shoes. But I didn't see the lame fellow there nor could I go to school with such shoes as I then had.

Davistown, Friday, June 10th 1859.

Was fine. I was not at school and didn't see the cripple [his uncle James Davis].

Davistown, Saturday, June 11th 1859.

Day very cloudy and thunder like, though not very hot. Richard and the rest of them went home earlier in the evening. I waited and saw the lame fellow. He asked me to go up to Madden's[168] to help pack wool. When he came up he had not scruple to prove himself a liar for when he sent me up he said he'd get me shoes but he broke his word and did not. I wasn't home to our own house till near midnight.

Davistown, Sunday, June 12th 1859.

I was not at church on account of my old shoes. About twelve I went out to Mr W's. He said of the Austrian[169] War that it was a most cruel and desolating war.

'Isn't the superstition of the people terrible' (says Mr W). I then read in the paper that a man of the name of Burke was lately shot in the county Galway. At his funeral in Chapel Finerty the people refused to let the burial service be read in the churchyard for they said that if it was read there all the corpses in the churchyard would turn on their faces. So they had to lay the coffin on two chairs by the roadside and read the service there.

We were then talking of the death of Paddy Murphy, a poor old man who died in Eglish lately. Mr W told me he had been in the Eglish Yeomanry sixty years ago.

In the evening the lame fellow sent for me and gave me directions about wool in Birr. He gave me a whole lot of letters and I was to go in as early as I could the next day. If I couldn't get boots big enough I was to leave my measure. I eat my supper there and then came home.

----

168 This may have been Hugh Madden's of Market Square listed as a woollen manufacturer and grocer in *SD 1846* and pawnbroker in *SD 1856*.

169 Hostilities commenced between France and Austria in April 1859. Source: *History of the world*. General editor, Esmond Wright. Published by Viscount, 1984.

33.   *Whigsborough House in the early 1900s (from the Magan Collection, courtesy of the Offaly Historical and Archaeological Society)*

Birr, Monday, June 13th 1859.

I rose early and walked to Birr with shoes a little better than none at all. Tedy Digan came in after a few hours having been carried by Davy as far as the Fivealley. I got a shilling for myself and two shillings for Tedy from Madden's[170] as the lame fellow had instructed. I then got a car from Dooly's (on credit of course WD) and Tedy went on it to a Captain Willington's.

I got eight bags to the railway again twelve o'clock on Skerrit's wagon (eight of the bags we packed on Saturday). In the evening I pencilled down an account of the days work and sent it to the lame fellow by Tedy. I afterwards saw this note of mine on the table at Lelaghmore and I tore it.

170   This may have been Madden's as above or: Michael Madden's public house, The Fighting Cocks, Cumberland St., listed in SD, 1856.

Birr, Friday, June 17th 1859.

Morning a little misty wet, day fine. I was not at school. Pat Dulleny told me that Captain Drought[171] died last night at 11.

Davistown, Saturday, June 18th 1859.

Morning and day some little mist, day cloudy. I was not at school. When my mother came in she told me that Captain Drought was fifty-two years of age and died of inflammation. Richard walked home alone, mother and the rest of them going home in the ass's car afterwards. I waited in Birr till about seven in the hopes of getting carried, or if not, of walking home at nightfall when no one would see my old shoes. I saw James Davis going down [sic] street and he told me to go to Madden's, that Dyass was just going home and he'd carry me and his brother Richard. We went the new Rath road. When I got down I kept the road as far as Balavalla gate, then across Capalohy, down Bullock Hill and home.

Davistown, Sunday, June 19th 1859.

Day generally cloudy and a slight mist. I was not at church. About one I went out to Mr W's. He said Captain Drought left ten children after him and his wife had buried six. Captain Drought's grandfather is said to have had the greatest funeral that ever passed this road. Mr W remembered to hear tell of it. It was said that he was very fond of hares and on the day of his funeral a hare run across out of Capalohy through the crowd and went right down to Davistown. Charles Coughlan came in and they continued talking of this great funeral and how when the first of it was in Frankford the end of it was at Bullock Hill. 'He used to tell his servants on no account to beat the dogs' (says Mr W). 'He beggared his family. From forty to forty-five gentlemen used to go out of a morning to hunt. He kept the best pack of hounds in Ireland and he'd never forgive one if he found him out to kill a hare.'

I saw in today's *Warder* that the Derby government was out by a minority of thirteen and that Palmerstown is Prime minister. Hennessy voted for Derby and O'Brien for Palmerstown.

When I came in I heard from Margaret (for the rest were at Eglish) that the lame fellow left a pound to pay for my boots and to pay the taxes of our lodgings.

---

171   John Alexander Drought of Whigsborough, J.P. and captain in the King's County Militia.

Davistown, Monday, June 20th 1859.

Day bright and cloudy by turns. I did not go to school for I had no shoes. Richard brought them in to be mended. I waited in Parker's Grove to see Captain Drought's funeral pass. Tom and James Whitfield went on Tom's car to meet it. The funeral was to leave Whigsboro at eight o'clock and at nine I went over to Mr W's hill where Wm. Rigney was waiting and from that place I saw the sad procession. It was a good funeral consisting mostly of carriages, cars and horsemen. There was a good many of the tenants and workmen of the deceased walking in front of the hearse.[172]

When James came from Birr after leaving Margaret and Charlotte there I went over with Mr W's cheese. Albert brought it to him in the parlour and some time after Mr W came out to the kitchen. We were wondering how old Ned was. Mr W said he was a child of one or two years when he came to live here two and twenty years ago. He was reared at Curraghmore and wasn't very old when his mother died. I told Mr W that Sarah Davis was thirty years of age (my father's daughter by his first wife).

It is reported that Mrs Drought will leave Ireland but Mr W thinks it would be better if she stayed here and kept her children together.

Davistown, Tuesday, June 21st 1859.

Before I got up I heard it raining on the slates and it so continued the greater part of the morning. This change was welcomed by all for the corn and meadows are very backward.

Davistown, Wednesday, June 22nd 1859.

Cloudy and blowing with some light floating rain in the evening. Richard walked home with word that Keele[173] would not have my boots mended till tomorrow. He, James, Tom and I were down beyond Mr W's lodge chasing Tiger[174] for our amusement when we saw Dick Whitfield below the mill bridge repairing some bad spots on the road. I went down to him and shortly after he threw the shovel into Parker's Grove and we two came home to our house where I had my supper. Then Richard, Dick Whitfield and I went down to Art Molloy's to get my hair cut. Art not being at home Mary cut my hair. I gathered it up and consigned it to the ground in a field on the way home.

---

172   Captain John Alexander Drought, a justice of the peace, died at Whigsborough and was buried at Ballyboy, see *King's County Chronicle*, 22 June 1859.

173   Thomas Keele. boot and shoemaker, Connaught St, Birr. *SD*, 1856.

174   Their dog.

Davistown, Thursday, June 23rd 1859.

Was fine in the morning. Richard went back to school. My mother and James drove in too in our usual plain style in the ass and car. They brought home my boots. Frank Whitfield was at our house prating till late at night and sooner than go home he slept with me although I much rather he stayed at home. I am not sorry when one who makes a trade of gossiping and backbiting keeps at a distance.

Davistown, Saturday, June 25th 1859.

James and Lizzy came to Birr in the ass's car. Margaret and Charlotte got leave for the summer some day this week. Charlotte came home with my mother and James last Thursday and Margaret remained in Birr housekeeping. I went into school yesterday. This morning Weir was hearing us Euclid[175] when there were three or four flashes of lightning and peals of thunder and some rain. The lightning was very bright and the rain poured down in torrents. I was the only one in the school that was at all afraid of the lightning except Weir.

About two o'clock I went to Madden's and got five shillings from the lame fellow with which I bought a case of drawing instruments at Gunn's and went to drawing.

Davistown, Sunday, June 26th 1859.

Was in general wild and cloudy, the evening was stormy. I was in Eglish. In the evening I went across to Mr W's. He told me that Maxwell's man Pilkington was knocked down by lightning yesterday in Banagher. Wm. Rigney afterwards told me the particulars. Maxwell and his wife left Balincard yesterday to go on a visit to Portumna but when they came to Banagher they found no steamer was to sail. Pilkington went to a shop to buy a feed of oats for the horse and while there lightning struck him on the legs and knocked him senseless to the ground.[176]

---

175   They were reciting the rules of geometry as laid down by Euclid, a geometrician in Alexandria circa 300 BC, *NE* vol. 5, p. 350.

176   Three people were killed by light in Halifax in mid-June while towards the end of the month Banagher appears to have been badly hit. See *KCC*, 15 June 1859 and 29 June 1859.

Birr, Monday, June 27th 1859.

Was fine except for one smart shower. Richard and I walked to Birr this morning. We went to see Boon's Circus which had come from Banagher. We were watching them put up a tent when Tedy Digan came to tell us we should be packing wool all day with Davy and he at Madden's. We packed three bags of wool. Later when Richard and I were on our way to the Fair Green we met the lame fellow who gave us money to buy tickets for the pit. We saw great feats of horsemanship and the fooling of clowns, performing dogs, monkeys, and a great many uncommon things. We were in till near eleven o'clock at night.

Birr, Tuesday, June 28th 1859.

Fine but cloudy. The circus left Birr for Frankford early this morning. Margaret went home this morning to go to the circus there with Lizzy, James and mother.

34.   *A steamer on the River Shannon at Banagher in the 1890s*

Chapter 9

July 1859

Avoiding an exam, tales of old times in the locality, William is sent collecting taxes, a visit to grandparents Watkins, Mr Whitfield's confrontation with the rector. Tales of army life - the death of Cornet Campbell, cholera in England, bull baiting, a former army comrade seeks out Mr Whitfield in Davistown, death of a local man in the Crimean war, Mr Whitfield meets a 1798 Ferbane veteran in Stafford, a meeting with Indians in Halifax, Mr Whitfield's first visit to London at sixteen years of age, a courtmartial, gambling in Barbados, Copinger and the prostitute, tales of travel by coach.

Birr, Friday, July 1st 1859.

Was fine with a few drops of rain in the evening. There was what was called an examination at Weir's. I considered it better to be absent. The annual July vacation was given.

Davistown, Saturday, July 2nd 1859.

Morning fine, evening wet. I waited in Birr to see the lame fellow about the coat he said he would get me. He said he couldn't get me the coat today but on Monday. Thus disappointed I resolved not in future to depend upon his word in a greater matter than a coat. Had he said nothing of the coat, unasked as he was, I need not have waited in Birr today. But I find he scruples more at an honourable action than at a dishonourable one.

Richard went home before me and was overtaken on the road by the Frankford gauger and carried. At the church gate an old white-headed man overtook me in a common car. From this time he was sometimes a little before me and sometimes I was before him for he drove easy. The evening turned wet and at Nanny Reily's when we were pretty close to each other he asked me to a seat on his car. I was glad of the invitation and accepted it. I understood from him that his name was Lynam and that some time back he lived in the neighbourhood of Frankford, Ballyboy. I since heard from Wm. Rigney that his name and title is Sergeant Lynam and he herds for a gentleman in the Birr direction. He was coming to spend some time with his kinsman Bill Kelly of the mill and Heffran's.

On telling him my name he said he knew my grandmother Davis and remembered her to be married. He knew her grandfather Quorum Conroy of Derrymore[177] House and said that he was a man of family but an awful drunkard. On that account he was stripped of his commission of the peace. He used to go into any house where he expected to get drink and if there was none there he sent for it and remained there drinking for a week. Lynam went up to see Conroy about land early one morning, so early that he thought he wouldn't be up but he was. He not only gave him the land but detained him for breakfast. They had for their morning meal, ham, fowl and as a substitute for tea (which was not he said in general use at the time) they had spirits. At breakfast the discourse turned upon his son-in-law, my grandmother's father, Thomas Wilder Drought. Quorum said that he remembered Drought's estate to be worth only £200 a year and the tenants to be poor while his was worth £600 a year and his tenants rich, but now Tom Drought was worth £600 a year and his tenants rich and he was scarcely worth £200. Says he 'My tenants are all drunkards but it was myself taught them to be drunkards.'

This old man told me that Conroy had a daughter that ran off with a fellow of the name of Rafferty (a Roman Catholic, then from near Bullock Hill but now dead and gone) and that Conroy made a song about it and used to sing it. He said my grandmother was an only child and that she married not until her father's death. He remembered my father's grandfather, William Davis, whom he believed to be a trooper. Lynam spoke very much in favour of Minor Mitchell[178] and his family and said he remembered to see high banks of peat at Ballincard gate and at our gate. He said when he was young there was no distinction made between rich and poor, that they'd kill fowl and have feasts one with another. He had a lease of Quorum Conroy's yet.

On leaving him at the gate I thanked him and he said I was doubly welcome when he knew my name. Peace be to the memory of your good old people that are past and gone. Even all remembrance of ye is dying too. But time is coming when the present will be the past and all remembrance of us and our day will fade. Let us then prepare for a world that fadeth not away.

177   Probably Derrymore House, near Blueball, Tullamore. Residence of Conroy, Esq. in 1778. Source: Taylor & Skinner, *Maps of the roads of Ireland* (1778), reprinted Shannon 1969, p. 86.

178   The Christian name is unclear in the original text but it appears to be Minor. It may have been a nickname for Thomas Mitchell who planted 10,000 trees at Ballincard in 1837, Source: 'A Register of trees, King's County 1793-1913', p. 317, Offaly County Library and see Eileen McCracken, 'A register of trees, King's County, 1793-1913'in *Kildare Arch. Soc. Jn.*, xv, no. 3 (1971-76), pp 301-18.

35.   *Ballyboy former Church of Ireland church in ruins in the 1980s*

Davistown, Sunday, July 3rd 1859.

I was at Eglish. In the evening I went out to Mr W's. He told me the French had nothing to boast of, - that they were not owning to their losses at all and the Austrians were giving them enough of it. He said the Queen would be in Ireland in August.

James Gill was there and they were saying how oats were very dear. I observed that if every oats was as short as Maxwell's there would hardly be any straw in the country. 'O that's a show' (says Mr W). 'I suppose Robert put eight barrels of seed in that field and he would not have eight stone out of it at all.' (This is the general outcry. On account of the great drought of the season vegetation is very backward WD).

Afterwards I saw in the *Warder* that several people were knocked senseless in Banagher by the lightning. A great quantity of fish killed in the Shannon by lightning were taken out when the storm was over. In the same town a dog was killed lying on the hearth while a woman sitting near was permitted to escape.[179]

---

179   The storm was reported in the *King's County Chronicle* for 29 June 1859 and was particularly difficult in the Banagher area. The dog was killed at the house of a Mr John Hynes.

Davistown, Monday, July 4th 1859.

Yesterday Lizzy went to Ballyboy church with the Curraghmore people and dined with them in Curraghmore. I went up to Lelaghmore this morning as she had brought me word the lame fellow wanted me. He gave me a list to collect, taxes and income tax from a few in the neighbourhood - Crazy Willy Whitfield, Lame Tom, Bill Kelly of the mill, Mr W Davistown, Charles Coughlan, Wm. Heffran of Killadrown, Joe Brock, Mary Ward, and Mick Cleary of Balincard.

From Lelaghmore I went to Willy Whitfield's but he was in Frankford. Next to Lame Tom, but he wanted change of a pound which I hadn't. I then met Willy W near the head of his own lane coming from Frankford, but James Davis he said owed him as much as his taxes £0-9-2 and his income tax £0-2-4.

I next went to Bill Kelly's for his taxes (£0-17-4). I heard he was in Frankford last evening and stayed up all night at a party at Wm. Conway's, his nephews. I suppose this party was given to old Sergeant Lynam. Bill was in bed and his housekeeper and relative Margaret Ryan paid that. When I came home for my breakfast I found that the lame fellow had sent Jack Brien to Coughlan's and Heffran's. After breakfast I went out to Mr W's. His Co[unty] tax was £1-10-0, income tax £0-9-4, in all £1-19-4. He said he would not pay it till he'd go to Birr, that the assizes[180] would not be this three months yet. We were talking about the great amount of eels that were caught on the callows yesterday, the river being so low.

I afterwards went with Jack to Joe Brock's who was not within. Mary Ward and Mick Cleary will have it on Saturday or Sunday and Frank Smith paid me. Charles Coughlan said he would send his Co. tax (£0-7-4) in the morning.

Davistown, Tuesday, July 5th 1859.

Some hard showers. I went up to Lelaghmore before they were up. After arranging what I had collected yesterday he sent me up to Wm. Meehan's (a few perches above the new road) for taxes but he had not his taxes in the house. Lame Tom gave me his Co. [county] tax and income tax. Then I scuttled home and got my breakfast. Later I called at Dunne's and Coughlan's neither of whom paid me. From there I went to Wm. Heffran's and was paid. I entered the callows at Anne Molloy's and went up by Mary Kenny's to Parkmore. There I got Mark and Peter Downey's taxes and on my return I got Billy Hanlon's.

---

180   Court sittings.

Davistown, Wednesday, July 6th 1859.

Day fine, evening wet. Today I brought the money to the lame fellow in Lelaghmore. Later he brought me to Birr to buy me a coat, but in Birr he was so busy hopping here and there throughout the town that he had no time to keep his word. After a day spent packing wool I came home in the car with Tedy Digan. The lame fellow and his clark remained in Birr after us. It rained on us nearly all the way home.

Davistown, Friday, July 8th 1859.

I was till dinner time haymaking in Burke's field with Jack Brien, Ann Brien and Paddy Flanagan. We made four cocks and two were made in it yesterday.

Davistown, Sunday, July 10th 1859.

Close and fine, I was at Eglish. In the evening I went in to Mr W in the parlour. He told me there was an armistice between the French and Austrians[181] till the 15th of August. His tax was £1-19-4 and he gave me a £2 note asking me had I eight pence change. I hadn't the eight pence nor his receipt. I showed him in the paper where it said the Queen would not be coming to Ireland this year. I asked him for the loan of the *Home Companion*[182] for August 1853 which was on the parlour table and although it was Mrs Coughlan's he told me to keep it till I had it read.

When I went to Curraghmore with Mr W's £2 the lame fellow gave me a walk to amuse myself tomorrow. I was to go for taxes to Joe Brock's and then to Whigsboro. After that I was to go to Birr to lodge cheques at the bank and to dine at Madden's coming home by the new road to call at Cloncarbin and Springfield for taxes. I was to walk that distance and as for him he would be in the fair of Tullamore. I was to go up on Tuesday morning with whatever I got and he would have Mr W's change and receipt.

I forgot to say that earlier that day when I was out at Mr W's Rebecca showed me an old bible containing the Apocrypha[183] which she got at a Roman Catholic house because the master was wishing for an Apocryphal bible.

---

181   The French and Austrians signed the Peace Treaty of Villafranco in mid-July of 1859. Source: Esmond Wright (ed). *History of the world*, (1984)

182   A weekly magazine.

183   This refers to the fourteen books included as an appendix to the Old Testament in the Septuagint and the Vulgate versions of the bible. The Church of Rome adopted them as being part of the Old Testament at the Council of Trent in 1545-63. The Established Church of England recommended them for study but not as a means to establish doctrine. As the nineteenth century wore on it became more usual for bibles to be published without the Apocrypha. *NE*, vol. i, p. 334.

Davistown, Monday, July 11th 1859.

Was hot, at least to me that was on foot all day. I started after breakfast to Joe Brock's and then for a few perches I went along the old road over through Mrs Mohan's ground to Whigsboro, but I got only a few shillings there. From James Read I got 10d and Pat Dooley of the same place gave me £0-5-10. Several others to whom I went made excuses, most of them said they would pay it on Saturday. Leaving Whigsboro I came by the Fivealley to Birr and lodged two cheques at the bank. After getting some bread and porter at Madden's I left Birr by the new road on my way to Cloncarbin and Springfield. By the time I came to Mr Molloy's lodge I was much fatigued with the heat of the day and walking, but I took a drink at the spa well there and felt refreshed. I went by the lane opposite the spa well through Cloncarbin, getting nothing, and came to my grandfather's where I took some drinks of milk and some of water.

I asked him about his mother's people and he told me that his mother's mother's name was Margaret Morrow when she was a young woman. 'She died in that room above,' said he pointing the room over where we were sitting in the parlour. She was originally a north country woman and was buried in Eglish graveyard. His mother Margaret Ranger was from Loughrea.

From there I came across the fields to Springfield. Tom Hernon paid me his taxes all but one penny which remained unpaid for want of change. Wm. Bell met me and invited me to eat in his house but I wished to be home so I refused. I came home tired and weary.

After resting a while I went out to Mr W's and in to the parlour where he was drinking his punch. I left the kitchen to be out of the way of men who were coming in from cutting Mr W's rape and I look upon this as a happy evening when I first sat and conversed with Mr W and listened to his advice. When he asked me to drink a glass of punch with him I thanked him but said I used not take any. Mr W spoke favourably about the Apocrypha which I was reading and forcibly said more than once that he believed every word of it. The discourse turned upon Healy. 'Healy prides himself on his preaching extempore - that is without notes' (says Mr W). 'But I could refute him in several things. He said in his sermon one day that when Christ said 'I come not to call the righteous but sinners to repentance' he meant by righteous the self righteous and I never thought anything about him since. I told him at his house one day 'Healy your an ignoramus. You don't know the duties of the Scriptures or of the pulpit'. He said none were righteous, but I told him not to bamboozle me. Would Christ send his disciples to preach the gospel if they were unrighteous, weren't the self righteous sinners?' (Most true WD) 'He came to call the sinners and therefore he came to call the self-righteous so that when he said 'I come not to call the righteous' he did not mean self-righteous.' (Note. This would be absurd, I came not to call self-righteous people sinners but sinners to repentance. This reading of it would be most incorrect WD.)

Mr W then told me about Aldolphus Drought[184] who is a great friend of his. He preaches great sermons but would sometimes be up all Saturday night preparing them. He is first cousin to Captain Drought and son of old Colonel Drought. Aldolphus had the parish of Aghancon but his wife Miss Nixon did not like the place and he got a living in the county Clare. Hereabouts in the conversation Mr W told me that I should go to Edinburgh and get on a man of war as assistant surgeon like another young man he knew. This man Hunt went on to be surgeon after tho' he had first studied for the church. 'O' (says Mr W) 'why doesn't James Davis give you your father's situation. He has no right to monopolise it from you, it's your right. He wants to have the whip hand and keep you a child that knows nothing. If you go to Col. Bernard he'll give you the collecting of the taxes. Go up and rap on the door and tell him you're your father's eldest son and that he monopolises the collecting of the taxes from you since your father's death. He'll take you by the hand as he did him,' (the lame fellow). 'He'd bring you before the grand jury[185] and give you the collecting. I'll give you a letter that'll do you no harm. You needn't tell your mind to anyone, but you can come out and talk to me. I'll make you an independent man if you take my advice. I would not for the world tell you anything wrong. Jas. Davis is a keenshaver and wants to keep you a child. You ought to leave no stone unturned to get the collecting of the taxes'.

During the evening I asked him would his spectacles answer all sights. He said no but for me to try them. To my sight they did not magnify much but I could read with them. I gave him the 8d change from his taxes telling him all I walked today which he said was too much.

Davistown, Tuesday, July 12th 1859.

Was warm in the morning. I went to Lelaghmore with what money I collected yesterday and got my instructions for today. As I was coming away down Curraghmore lane I lost one of the poor rate receipts. I went first to Mr W's with his income tax receipt. When I said I was on my way to Maxwell's he asked how much had Robert to pay and I told him. At Tom Dunne's Mrs Dunne told me he was at the bog but that he would bring his taxes to the lame fellow in the evening. I found Maxwell on his lawn with some workmen. When he read the bill he exclaimed in astonishment 'O my soul!' I got nothing from him but he asked what was my uncle giving for wool at present. I said he was buying it for £0-22-6 [sic] and Maxwell

---

184   Aldolphus Drought was rector of Aghancon from circa 1841 - 1851. Not to be confused with William Drought see footnote 221 below, RCB Library.

185   The principal governing body in every county was a non-elected grand jury whose main function was to finance and supervise public works. The grand juries were also entrusted with deciding which cases should be sent for trial at the assizes. Source: S. Clark, *Social origins of the Irish Land War*, p. 186.

talked of sending over a man about it in the evening.

Then I set off for Joe Mahon's. The lame fellow has decided that he need not pay his poor rate this year, but that he must do so from this out. I gave Joe his receipt but I kept the unwelcome part of the story to myself. It had been a custom of my father's to forgive Joe his taxes and poor rate for work done by him (which was only a little). The lame fellow has done so till now but I think he has been kind long enough and Joe must escape payment no longer. Big Will Bulfin said he'd have his taxes and poor rate on Saturday.

Later in Mr W's when I was reading the Apocrypha I saw that it was a very old one. It was printed in Dublin by George Grierson, Essex St. in 1741. Some time after when I was sitting in the kitchen Rebecca brought out a drawer of Mr W's writing desk from the parlour and I delighted myself very much by reading the superscriptions of the letters therein. Some of them were addressed to him as an ensign[186] and others as Lieutenant. Some of them were sent to Dublin, others to Bridgetown and more of them to Weedon, Northamptonshire, Liverpool and Gosport. By and by Mr W came out and explained all I asked him about them. He said he had a letter from William the 4th and it began 'Our trustworthy and well beloved' and that William the 4th signed his commission. I brought the drawer back to the parlour and put it in the desk. Mr W told me how to fasten it with a pin that passed through it from the inside and so holds it. It is locked then and must be opened to get out the drawer. He said that desk crossed the Atlantic four times and he had the key in his pocket for forty years.

Later he told me that one evening a fine young man, Cornet[187] Campbell asked him to his room after mess. 'When I came to his room' (says Mr W), 'I saw a blazing flash of light. He had a whole lot of candles lighting and he up on the table making a speech. The table was full of brandy and water and cigars. Well a few weeks after we landed in Barbados we heard he was dead. He killed himself drinking brandy and water. He wouldn't get up till one o'clock and then he'd drink brandy and water and smoke all day. He was seventeen years of age. You'd meet every sort of the world's queer characters in the army. William if you travelled.... all you'd see!

'A Captain in my regiment called Thene used to amuse himself by looking at churchyards, old castles and old Roman camps. One time he brought a couple of us to a place called the Spencerian chapel, a beautiful place. You'd see every King and Queen of England and their dress and every sort of arm. Bows, arrows, spears and lances sculptured in the rock. It was well worth going to see. Thene - he was half Saxon and half English - was a bad marcher. There was nothing he hated more than a march up a hill. He'd have his pockets full of bread that he'd divide amongst us as we went.

'One day while on a march Captain Lowe, Johnny Henderson and myself

---

186   The lowest rank of commissioned infantry officer in the British army.

187   The lowest rank of commissioned cavalry officer in the British army.

stopped at Woolhampton - a town about twice as big as Kinnitty - to find our billets. Henderson and I had a fine drink of ale at the hotel where we were billeted. In England they keep the barrels down in a ground cellar and pump up the liquor - like with a force pump. Well it was the most delightful liquor ever I tasted. The landlord told us it was seven year old and I thought to myself, well, that bangs Banagher!

'The cholera[188] was raging that time and the strawberries were in the hotel garden in heaps for the doctor forbid the people to eat fruit. The landlord gave us the key of the garden and we helped ourselves. When we could eat no more we went down to see how Lowe was getting on at his billet. There was Lowe and the landlady balaragging like two fisherwomen. 'She's striving', says he, 'to impose stinking mutton on me for my dinner, she's striving to impose stinking mutton on me!' We brought him off to our billet and from that out he ate with us. Poor Lowe delighted in eating fruit. He was a consumptive and was very fond of fishing for he used to get his health better near the water.'

Mr W told me that every officer used to have a name and he was called Ben after his Captain Benjamin Hatwell. I asked Mr W were any of the officers who served with him alive still. He said that Captain Galloway was commanding the 70th now in India. One day Galloway had been marching through Frankford and came out with Francis Bennett to see Mr W but he was in Banagher at the fair. Poor Galloway waited as long as he could, but when he saw that Mr W wasn't coming he put a cigar on one end of the chimneypiece, another on the far end and a pipe in the middle. He wrote two notes and put them between the two cigars so Mr W came home to find the chimneypiece 'decked out'. Francis Bennett and his brother were in the army. One of them was killed in the Russian War - his mother getting £780 from the compensation fund.[189] Mr W told me they were in Lemington once where they put up at the Regent Hotel. A powdered waiter met them and ushered them into the breakfast room. There they had pigeon pies, cold meats and all sorts. 'Captain Hatwell took up a fork,' (says Mr W) 'looked at it and gave it to me
'Whit' says he, 'is that silver?'
'I looked at it,'
(here Mr W takes the silver spoon he was stirring his punch with - for Mr W was at his punch - and looked at it). 'It's not the sort they make the shillings out of at any rate' says I. Then Hatwell gave the bell a terrible pull and the waiter run up frightened. 'How dare you' (says Hatwell) 'not leave silver

---

188   This probably refers to the cholera epidemic of 1832 which killed over 14,000 people in England. *NE*, vol. 4, p. 67

189   Ft. Lieutenant Valentine Bennett of the 33rd Foot was killed at Sebastopol in the Crimea on 18 June 1855. Lieutenant Francis Bennett, 33rd Foot, retired from the army in 1848. The Royal Patriotic Fund Corporation was set up during the Crimean War for relief of dependants of veterans. It was funded from public subscription and the War Office. Sources: 1) Pey, Brian (ed.), *Eglish and Drumcullen*, p. 82. 2) Army Record of Service card index, National Records Office, Kew, England. 3) Veterans Review website.

forks for us?' Well the waiter thought he'd be shot. He run and gathered them up and brought silver ones. They thought we would steal silver forks if they left them out - we being soldiers.

'Once when we were on detachment in Stafford I went to engage lodgings for myself and Captain Galloway. He disliked looking for lodgings and would always send me on this errand. At the house of people named Guinan I took a bedroom and parlour for Galloway and the same for myself. Guinan the landlord told me that he was born and reared near Ferbane but had to fly in '98 with his daughter.'

Mr W told me another pleasing little anecdote. It shows the kindness to be had from strangers. He said that in marching they halted for five minutes every hour to 'pump ship' or anything. One day they halted at a beautiful cottage with grapes all growing in front of it. 'I walked up and plucked some,' (says Mr W) 'and I was putting one into my mouth when a woman came to the door. 'Lady' says I, 'how much is these a dozen?'
'O sir' says she 'you're heartily welcome to them, I know you'd like a grape this hot day'.
The English are a good hearted people. The sun never sets on the British Dominions from east to west, north or south. There isn't a house in it smaller than this one, it's the garden of the world and why wouldn't it be with the wealth of the world coming into it every day in ships and steamers.'

When he was in Dublin Mr W was often on bank guard. A man would come out from the bank with a book for you to sign your name and a waiter would come over from the Shades, give you a big bow and ask if there was anything you wanted. It took a whole regiment for the different guards in the city. There's white glass eight inches thick in the roof of the bank. 'You could walk along it and see the heaps of bullion under you'.

Mr W above all things wishes me well and is deeply interested in my success. This evening while in the parlour he said affectionately to me 'It's time William to do something for yourself, you're too big to be going to school. Call your uncle James aside and talk sensibly to him, don't be afraid of him. If you could get him to lodge £450 and get your name on the Commander in Chief's list you'd get your commission. Or.... tell your uncle James to go to Colonel Bernard and he'll get you an ensigncy in the militia. They'll be called in on Friday. James Davis could give you fifty pounds and if you had a certain number of volunteers you'd get an ensigncy in the line. There's no time to lose, they muster on Friday. It's time William to do something for yourself and not be walking about the fields. What makes you so much afraid of him? Let him assist you into the army or have him give you up your father's situation. I'll be your security. If you were in the army all you'd have to do is mind yourself. The table is spread there and walk in and make no compliments or apologies. Sit down in the first empty seat you find and call to the waiter for whatever you like. The Queen would come and dine with you and what better company could there be.'

Earlier when I was in the kitchen looking through his letters I lit on one dated 1816 and Mr W said that was the year he joined the army when he was about eighteen, which leaves him now at sixty-one years of age. O Lord preserve him from his enemies and comfort and bless him in this life. At the last receive him into thine heavenly rest for Christ your son's sake amen.

Davistown, Wednesday, July 13th 1859.

Was fine in the morning. This morning at Curraghmore lane I gave Tom Dunne a receipt for his poor rates which he had that minute paid the lame fellow. The cripple [his uncle James Davis] was coming down to our place to sow turnip seed and I turned back with him. I told him the militia was being called in on Friday and that if he went to Colonel Bernard he could get me an ensigncy in the line which was worth £450. But he acted the rascal and the liar as will shortly appear. He said to come up on Friday as he would be going to Tom Manifold's and I could go with him to enquire about it. I almost forgot to say that a man found the receipt that I lost the other day and gave it to the lame fellow this morning.

As Maxwell didn't send a man about the wool the lame fellow told me to tell him he would give him £0-22-6 [sic] for hoggits wool but only £0-22-3 [sic] for ewe wool. When the lame fellow had the turnip seed sown (not a turnip of the same sowing ever came to be worth pulling and half of them never came up on account of not being sown in time) he had his breakfast at our house.

At Maxwell's house I found the little man in the big house which he built in the day that he considered himself too big for Minor Mitchell's house. He would not give the wool for less than twenty-three shillings and the lame fellow would not pay that.

Later when I went out to Mr W's we chatted in the kitchen for a while and then went into the parlour where Mr W took his punch. 'Halifax' (says Mr W), 'is a fine town. The people are nearly all Irish and nearly their whole trade is in timber and saw pits. Our ship the *Roslin Castle* had fifty carpenters repairing her. They have robins there bigger than blackbirds, I often saw them. One day about the end of April a lot of us took an Irish guide of about fourteen or fifteen years of age with us and went seven or eight miles to see the Indians in their wigwams. They're in the woods like a sugar loaf and the Indians sit round a fire that's in the middle. We raised up a blanket that hangs at the door and walked in. We gave them presents and they gave us porcupine quills and we came on great terms with them. We could not understand a word they said. We left Halifax on the fifth of May. It was still cold that time and I asked the people when would the summer come and they said 'In two days'!

'The first time I was in London I was about your age. I travelled from Liverpool to London which was about 204 miles. There was opposition coaches on the route and the fare was very cheap. We used to be going a night and a day and part of another night and we used stop the car for breakfast. When we got into Charring Cross I called for a car to take me to thirty-four Fritz Street, Soho Square. Miss Christy - an old maid of about forty - came to the door. 'I'm a friend of Doctor Hunt' says I and O.......she gave me a great welcome' (this was the Doctor Hunt who was educated in Maynooth but joined the navy). 'Miss Christy's lodgers were all pursers and Captains in the navy. One said 'Only for Dr. Hunt I'd be dead of the measles long ago'. 'O' said another officer 'he cured me of the yellow fever.' 'After breakfast the next morning a purser - that's a paymaster in the navy - showed me the way to Greenwood's offices. I pushed in the green baize[190] door and walked in. It was just like the aisle of a church and the men writing in every nine or ten pews. I walked down a good piece and asked a middle aged man who was it that wrote for the West Indian Regiment. It was himself and he was the perfect gentleman. He said there was no point in me buying regimentals for the West Indian regiments were to be disembodied.[191]

'A few days after that I was ordered to the Isle of Wight and from there I went to Hilsey barracks outside Southampton. There the Commandant was going to put me in lodgings, but as young as I was I was up to him. I don't know how it came to my mouth but I said to him I'd prefer being in barracks. The barracks sergeant, a big red headed fellow with a great big bunch of keys, brought me to my room. The furniture was a table, two chairs, a set of fire irons and a water bucket. The bed you must provide yourself. I sent out for my dinner and such little things as I wanted. Then there was a rap on the door and in walked Lieutenant Lorimar who was of my regiment. A while later in came ensign Montgomery of the 3rd West Indian. He was seventeen years old. We three had rooms next one another and would always mess together. Every night Lorimar would play the fiddle to perfection and I would play the flute while Montgomery would dance. When we'd be done playing Montgomery would go out trailing after the girls. He had plenty of money but I doubted that he was the son of the Earl of Enniskillin by some fine girl of the north and thought he assumed the name Montgomery. Lorimar was a Scotchman married to a lady in Cork.'

They stopped at Hilsey playing and dancing for six weeks. When they memorialled[192] the government they were sent home on half pay to save the expense of keeping them in barracks till the regiment was disembodied. Montgomery's regiment the 3rd West Indian was kept up. The outfit costs about fifty pounds. Mr W got his from Fisher, 37 Duke St, London. 'He'll send them to you and you needn't pay him till it's convenient. Many a five pounds and ten pounds I sent him in half notes, I never paid till it was convenient. It's a great loss to you that the Derby government is out. Hennessy

---

190   Doors were sometimes covered with green baize material to deaden sound. At times there was a layer of cotton wool underneath the baize to further aid noise reduction. Source: Cecil English.

191   Disbanded.

192   Petitioned.

[the member of parliament] would only have to seek a commission in the line for you and you'd get it. It was they put me where I am.'

I asked Mr W would an officer salute his superiors every time he met them. He said no, that you only salute them after parade and not again till the next morning. It is different for privates who must salute always unless told not to. 'I always said 'Walk on sentry', I'd never put them to the trouble.'

Davistown, Thursday, July 14th 1859.

Was warm. I was at home all day only that in the evening I went out to Mr W. When he was some little time at his punch I went in to the parlour. He sat facing the fire at the left side of the table as you go in leaning his left arm on the table and resting his head on his left hand. His feet were on a footstool, his hair parted over his left eye. This is his general position at punch. A pint of spirits did Mr W for about two evenings. He suffered no inconvenience from it that I could perceive and took it merely as a daily cordial after dinner but never before.

Mr W does not talk without pausing. He makes frequent thoughtful pauses before he speaks anything. Then he speaks nothing but what comes from the heart, the language of truth, good nature and sincerity. I record his stories as I do every saying of his in this journal as well as I can remember in his own words without any vain polish as he told me. I wrote his own words only for my own addition and personal reading and meditation in after days when I can no longer sit and listen to his voice. When that head is perhaps low and that noble spirit among the joys of glory would it not then be poor comfort to me if I were to by any vain addition pervert his previous words of truth and candour.

This evening Mr W told me the story of Sir Burdett, the greatest brewer in England. 'He said one night in the House of Commons', (says Mr W) 'that he would not give the old hoops in his brewery yard for £100,000'. At any rate he arranged for a beautiful young girl that worked at the brewery to be a servant in his house. He soon brought her to the church and made her his wife. They had no children when he died a short time after and left her all his property in his will. But then the other heir came and said he'd run a cart through his uncle's will. He ordered her to quit and take nothing but her wardrobe. A nephew of a friend of the widow who was a brief-less barrister, the then young counsellor Hyde, undertook to plead for her. 'But' says she, 'I have not a penny to pay you'.
'Won't you pay me if I gain your case?'
'This least I may do.'
He employed an attorney to state his case and reserved himself to address the jury. Well, he made the Four Courts of London ring. The jury never left the box till they gave the verdict in his favour and from that day his fame spread far and wide. He came to visit the young widow and she asked him did he bring his bill. 'Yes' says he 'I'll be well paid if you give me

your hand' and they were married. He afterwards became Lord Clarendon, Lord Chancellor of England. His daughter Ann Hyde was married to James 2nd.[193]

I'll tell you another story and it's true, I saw part of it myself. I was marching one day and I saw on before me a lady in a barouche[194] with grand gold liveried servants shining. 'Begad' says I to myself, 'this must be one of the Royal Family'. As it came nearer it shone more and when it came up I ordered the men to incline to the left. I was going to order present arms but I didn't. I remember it as well as if it was yesterday. She was leaning back in the barouche, sallow complexion, a round face and a little fat. A man told me it was the Duchess of St Albans.

When I was in Stafford I asked Guinan about her and he told me this story. There was a poor man and his wife that lived in Stafford of the name of Mellon. They had one child called Lucy. When the mother and father died an old aunt took her in. One day a set of strolling players came to Southampton and the old aunt and Lucy went to see the play. From that day on Lucy said she wanted to be an actress. Two years later when the players came to Stafford, Lucy went off with them to London.

Mr Coutts, a rich middle-aged gentleman, saw her and sent her a note when he took a liking to her. Not long after that they were married. He had a large banking establishment next to the Bank of England. Didn't you ever hear of Coutts and Company? At any rate he didn't live long till he died. She had no children and he willed her his whole share in the bank.

Now the Duke of St. Albans was the highest peer in England next to the king but he was also the poorest. His income was only £6,000 a year which wasn't near able to support his extravagance. He came to visit Mrs Coutts offering to marry her. She of course accepted his offer but she said to him 'Now I'll give you £1,000 for pocket money and I won't ask to touch any of your estate at all'[195]. So now William, didn't them two play well?' I said they did.

I asked Mr W was he ever on a court-martial. 'If you had five pounds for every time I was you'd be a rich man' (says Mr W). 'Many a one I wrote down and if you go in the army you'll have to write down many a one. It's the fairest trial in the world. The prisoner is brought up at the foot of the table between two sentinels and the articles of war are open there. The witnesses are called and sworn, then the Adjutant is called to give his

---

193   Mr Whitfield has intertwined fact with fantasy here. Perhaps he has rolled two separate factual stories into one. Lord Clarendon married twice. Both marriages were to daughters of titled gentlemen. His daughter did marry James 2nd.

194   A four-wheeled horse drawn carriage which seated four people plus the driver. Source: *Collins English dictionary*.

195   This story refers to Harriot Mellon c. 1777 – 1837. First appeared, 1787, at Drury Lane, 1795 -1815, playing an extensive round of characters. Married Thomas Coutts , the banker 1815. After his death she married William Aubrey De Vere, 9th Duke of St. Albans, 1827. From: George Smith, *The concise dictionary of national biography* (1930).

character. If it be a good one it stands for him, if it be a bad one it tells against him. Then they begin by asking the junior member,. ..say you're the junior member,... 'Mr Davis, is he guilty?' Of course you answer in justice to your conscience. 'He is'. Then it goes on till it comes to the President. Then if the prisoner be guilty he's asked what has he to say in his defence. The different penalties are read and they begin again by asking the junior member 'What punishment do you give him?' 'Fourteen days solitary confinement' or 'two-hundred lashes' and so on.'

I asked Mr W if the sentence be death would the prisoner be hung. 'No' (says Mr W) 'he'd be shot. He'd be brought out and put behind his coffin', (here Mr W illustrated the coffin by placing the silver spoon with which he stirred his punch on the table for the coffin and his hand behind it for the prisoner), 'and the men'll be brought out. They'll put ten balls through him and if that don't kill him I don't know what will.

'I was on the court-martial of a Captain Vincent of the engineers in St. Lucia for five weeks one time. He was honourably acquitted. Colonel Moore was mad,.....Moore of the 35th. He had some disagreement with him about flagstaffs and he asked for a court of enquiry but the government wouldn't give it to him. So he made up a whole lot of charges again him, but they were all frivolous.'

I asked Mr W was there no appeal from the verdict of a court-martial. He said 'No, but you can be sent back to reconsider your verdict. In Barbados one time we were sent back to reconsider but we did not change the sentence. When they came to me I said I had come to my former resolution after mature deliberation and we sent back the former verdict. The man on trial had been drunk. It was Colonel Mallet thought the sentence not severe enough. He was a fine old soldier, but he was very severe upon the men.

'Barbados is a queer place. You put a big glass thing like a barrel over your candlestick at night the way the wind passing through your room won't blow it out. You have to leave your door open all night, you couldn't live in it if you didn't. I used to keep a goat, you'd get one there for four shillings. She could graze about the barrack yard and I could have milk for my tea. Then there's an allowance of a shilling a day for a black servant and you'll get one for half that. I had one of the name of Harriet. She'd be watching for me when parade would be over and there she'd be waiting after with a bowl of coffee'.'I'll tell you a strange story. A large draught of men came out from Ireland to Barbados. One morning I was drilling the men and I noticed one of these standing in the rear. I asked the sergeant why wasn't that man in line with the rest.
'O' says he 'that man is sick'.
I went up to him after parade and asked what ailed him, he was as healthy a man in the face as you'd see. He said he was sick in his inward parts and I sent him to the hospital. The next morning I saw him in the same place. I went to him again and spoke sharply to him. We had two excellent doctors who said nothing ailed him. When he said once more that he was sick I

went to the Colonel about it. He had him sent to the cook's room for a few days but when he came back he still stood in the rear. The Colonel told me to bring him to court-martial, but I filled in the form in as slight a manner as I could and he was sentenced to fourteen days solitary confinement with bread and water. He wasn't long in the cell when he had to be sent to the hospital where he died shortly after. In the way that nothing would ever come again Dr Cunningham or me the doctor took out his heart and preserved it in a bottle of brandy. He had as fine a heart as could be. All we ever heard about him was that he had married a girl in Cork and that she wouldn't be let come out with him. Dr Cunningham was a very nice man. He was lame. He walked like your uncle James.' Another story more dreadful he told me was of a self murder. 'Every Saturday the mess kits are inspected to see that they have the proper number of shirts, stockings, shoe brushes &c. One Saturday the Captain was sick and I inspected the kits. We were on the lower veranda which is flagged, the upper veranda is boarded. The men had all their kits open and I went along the line. When I reached the fourth man drops of blood were coming down onto his shirt in his kit from the veranda above. 'Go up sergeant' says I 'someone's killing a fowl or committing some depredation above.' When he ran back down says he 'Sergeant so and so's after cutting his throat!' I run up with my sword drawn and there he was with his throat cut to the bone and the razor grasped in his hand this way'. Mr W illustrated it by stretching his right hand down to his knee. 'He was giving his last gasp when I went up, I never saw such a terrible sight'. (Mr W shuts his eyes and opens and shuts his mouth in imitation of the man. WD)

Then there was the dirty fellow in their regiment in Jamaica of the name of Young. He used to get the heads of pirates that were hanged at Port Royal and hang them up around his room. Mr W went into his room once but never again.

He told me that when I'd report to a barracks there'd be a room for me and the first thing I must do is see if there's ere a cracked pane and if there is to run my sword through it. 'If you don't' (says Mr W) 'it'll be put down in damages again you when you're going off. Just run your sword through it and say 'Sergeant, get a pane of glass in that'. O yes, when you're in barracks your room is your castle. If you like you can smash everything in it so long as you pay for it. Suppose you want another table. The barracks sergeant won't get you one, but you can ask him for the key to such a room and he'll give it to you. Then you can take whatever you want out of that and put it back again. If you were a married man you could use it as a bedroom. There are two or three ways of killing a cat.'

Davistown, Friday July 15th 1859.

I had fresh proof of the lame fellow's villainy and falsehood. I went to Lelaghmore as he had told me for today he was to enquire about the militia. He went to Maxwell's and on coming back told me to go home. He said he could not make any enquires about the militia today as Tom Manifold told him that Colonel Bernard would not be home till tomorrow on the train. We will see about it tomorrow in Birr. I am to walk in as the lame fellow says he does not know if he will go the Thomastown or Eglish road.

[The Eglish road was nearer to William's house than the Thomastown road. SR.]

Davistown, Saturday, July 16th 1859.

Was very hot. I walked to Birr in the morning. Richard and Margaret were there too, chiefly on the business of the rogues of Curraghmore who find work for everyone and payment for none but those who compel them. I waited till evening when I saw the lame fellow. He began to mutter through his nose that he was talking to Colonel Bernard and nothing could be done. There was no vacancy in the militia. But I knew that he told me a lie. A lying scoundrel he is, one that lives by his lies and plans, a fellow with no desire above grabbing money. At one time buying wool - another time jobbing on cattle - always a cunning rogue. But as his means are so is his success, he is not much better by all his trickery. I suppose he told me yesterday to walk to Birr thinking that would discourage me and that I would stay at home. This morning I saw him passing by on the Eglish road in his car as I was about to set out and he didn't even call for me.

I walked home nearly all the way, Margaret and Dick overtaking me our side of the Fivealley. When we reached Nanny Reily's I sat up on the car. This is now our only way of travelling - an old ass and car. We had horses at the time of my father's death but they were taken away from us. Let him do what he likes while he has any liberty in Davistown. But if I can he'll pay here for his villainy. His end will not be anything the better for having robbed us.

After coming home I went into Mr W's and told him all. 'In my opinion' (says Mr W) 'he did not see Colonel Bernard at all. He's keeping you wasting your time at school to let people see what education he's giving you.' Mr W advised me very earnestly to go to Col. Bernard myself and not let it pass Monday, to go early and tell no one my business. He said if he wasn't at Kinnitty he'd be in Birr and that I should walk up to him and not be afraid. 'Don't be afraid and tell him your story. Tell him your uncle took your father's situation and that he's doing nothing for you. If he wants to know why your uncle didn't come with you tell him 'He's more intent on his own business than on mine'. Tell him your delight is to join the army and would he have the goodness to get you an ensigncy in the militia. Give my name as a reference. He drank punch at that table there', (Mr W pointing to the parlour table) 'and smoked a cigar - what he didn't do at Curraghmore. He was chatting me in the fair of Frankford and never fear he won't forget me now.'

I said if I got my commission I'd have to get an outfit and the lame fellow wouldn't get it for me. Mr W told me he would see about it. As I was coming in he enquired if I could get him a history of England. I will get the second volume of Hume's[196] the next day I go to Birr, but it has small print.

Davistown, Sunday, July 17th 1859.

Was warm with a few drops of rain. I walked to Eglish. After dinner I went out to Mr W's. He told me a treaty of peace is after being signed between France and Austria which both astonished and alarmed the English. He also said there were several people killed in England with sunstroke.

It seems the militia is only to be kept in for a month's training and I now see there is no use in me going to see Colonel Bernard.

I afterwards went down to the river of Broughal where Richard and James were gone to bathe. I did not bathe myself for there was too great a rabble. There was only a few in it whose company I could at all like - a few of James Whitfield's children and Tom and Davy and those for whom I always had a greater liking - a few of the Harvest Lodge children, William, Tom and Dick. As we were going home a big headed scoundrel from Freagh of the name of Shameen Conrahy thought to take a pipe from James. James refused to give it but called him (Conrahy) names. Shameen caught him, but as soon as James got out he called him names again. Shameen caught him again and was just going to beat him when I interfered. I gave him some good boxes, but as I was not used to boxing he held me down by the hair and hit me twice or thrice in the face with my head kept down. I could do nothing and he refused to let go his grip so I caught him by the leg and brought him to the ground. Here I could have repaid the rascal if I wished but I let him up and it was all over. I was not pained at all only that I had a pair of black eyes. He had none, but I dare say he felt it as much as I did. He was about my age, but thicker and stronger and not so tall. He was, if anything, more than my match and I wouldn't have anything to do with the fellow but that I was called on by a sense of honour.

---

196   David Hume, philosopher, historian and political economist, 1711 - 1776. There were numerous editions of Hume's *History* which continued to be published up to the end of the nineteenth century, *NE vol.*7, p. 245.

36.   *Castle Bernard, Kinnitty in the early 1900s*

Davistown, Monday, July 18ᵗʰ 1859.

Day some distant thunder and heavy rain. Margaret and Charlotte returned
to school, James driving them in the ass and car. We lodged at 30 Cumberland
Street [Birr] with William Smallman my grandmother's brother in a little
cottage. He is an unmarried man and supports himself on the rent of some
houses in Dublin, the remains of a considerable property. He lost the rest
partly by being unable to repair houses and partly by the dishonesty of
tenants. A quiet and friendly man he is and strictly honest in his dealings
with everyone. I told Margaret to get from him the second volume of Hume's
England and send it home by James. Later I brought it out to Mr W but he
did not say anything about my black eyes. He told Frances to go out and
turn our cattle lest they should break out into his fields. I went after them
to drive them off and then came home. Shortly after there was some distant
thunder but I saw no lightning.

Davistown, Tuesday, July 19ᵗʰ 1859.

Morning wet, day some wet and a little distant thunder. This morning Tedy
Digan brought me a paper to go to Derrinlough for taxes. Having no desire
to exhibit my black eyes and not being very careful to oblige the lame fellow
who had so often disobliged me, I did not go today. About dinner time I was
walking along the pond with Wm. Rigney when we espied an eel lying at its
ease in the sunshine near a stick that was placed across to prevent the cattle
going across to Mr W's. The water was almost all dried up and I stepped
across to catch him but as soon as I put my hand near him he made off. He
was lying nearer to the bank than to the middle of the pond. We made dams

and got dishes to drain it and then Wm. Rigney stuck a fork in him and pitched him up on the bank. Beck wanted me to bring him in to our house but I wouldn't. I told her to keep it for the master's dinner.

In the evening I went out to Mr W in the parlour where he was at his punch. He got a summons a few days ago to attend on the petty jury[197] at the assizes and I read it as it lay on the table. I said during the course of chat that one of the Hobbs was a Colonel and says Mr W 'I'll tell you how old Captain Hobbs got in the army. The 92nd - a Scotch regiment - came to Frankford and they encamped at Inchymore, between Frankford and Barnaboy. Hobbs lived in Barnaboy then and the Colonel of the regiment, Colonel Lamont, took a liking to Hobbs's sister and married her. He afterwards got an ensigncy for her brother in his regiment. Captain Hobbs was married to a daughter of Simpson Hackett's who's alive in Barnaboy yet.'

37.   *Hunt meet at Syngefield House in the early 1900s (courtesy of the Offaly Historical and Archaeological Society)*

---

197   Serious criminal cases were tried at the assizes by public juries presided over by justices of the higher courts and is to be distinguished from the county grand jury. Source: S. Clark, *Social Origins of the Irish Land War*. p. 186.

'We were going on detachment to Downpatrick one time' (says Mr W), 'and I told the Adjutant to only give me soldiers with good characters. 'I can only confine them to barracks if they commit any crimes' says I, 'or give them so many hours drill. If their crimes exceed my punishment I'll send them back here at the expense of the government to be punished.' 'O very well' says he 'I'll give you none but good characters.' When I came to Downpatrick I made a speech to the men in the barrack yard. 'Now', says I 'I'll give you every indulgence in my power if you deserve it, but if you misbehave I'll send you back to Newry to be punished.' They took good care to know that what I said was the truth. We were there in June and the General in Armagh sent me word to watch the July procession and be in communication with two or more magistrates. He feared there might be trouble on the 12th - the great day. At any rate there were no processions, just dinners in hotels. We should have been relieved in three months but they left us there for five. The Colonel was disagreeable about it and sent a Major to inspect us hoping to catch us unawares. But the Major sent word that he was coming and it all went well in the end.

'There was a ball alley in the barrack yard there and one day the barracks sergeant - a veteran sergeant, he lost a leg - came hopping up to me with a letter. It was a petition from the townspeople asking to be allowed to play ball with the men. I said 'To be sure!' and they came every day playing for drinks of ale. One townsman used to spend too much of his time and money there making his wife jealous. A letter came to me with no name on it which said as sure as my name was Whitfield they'd report me to the government if I let the townspeople play anymore in the ball alley. I gave the letter to the sergeant and told him to tell the people. He did so and they put on their coats and walked off quietly saying that if they knew who wrote the letter they'd tear her to pieces. I never made any enquiries for I knew the person could injure me but I suspected this woman.'

I asked Mr W was he lonesome there but he said no. He sent for Johny McBride who was only a little fellow then and he came to him. He had a horse and gig which he used to drive out into the country every day and free entrance into the newsroom any time he liked. He also had a seat in the Marquess of Downshire's pew in the Cathedral every Sunday.

Shortly after this Mr W continued 'One time when I was in Northwiche [sic] I heard there was to be a bull beat[198] a piece from the town. I was never at one before so off I went dressed in plain clothes. The bull was in the middle of a ring and the owners of the dogs outside with their dogs between their legs. The dogs all came there in slips[199] and every one was numbered. As soon as one dog was tired another would be called. There was a butcher from Northwiche [sic] there with a milk white bitch. She used to take the

---

198   The correct term was bull-bait. A bull was tethered to a post in the centre of a ring and set upon by dogs, NE vol. 3, p. 239.

199   A type of dog-lead which allows for the quick release of the dog.

bull by the underlip and he would toss her up in the air. The butcher would catch her coming down to break the fall and then she'd be after the bull again. He was so elated that he clapped me on the shoulder and said 'Look at my bitch officer!' I didn't think anyone would know me in plain clothes. It was a dirty and brutal amusement. I never was at one before and never will again.' He told me he had a bitch once by the name of Fury and she would take any cow or bull by the nose but she would not go near a weasel.

Later we were talking of marching and Mr W said 'The hardest march ever I had was from Fort Augusta to Spanishtown in Jamaica. It was only nine miles, but the day was burning hot with no sea breeze and the dust was lying. We left Fort Augusta at four o'clock in the evening with seventy men. After two and a half miles I allowed the men to stop for a drink of ginger beer. When we had gone on another piece the men run off with a big basketful of oranges belonging to a black man, they were so thirsty. When I heard the terrible cries I run up to see what was happening and tried to reason cases with the black man. I gave him £0-1-6, a quarter dollar and a half quarter dollar. The finest oranges in the world grew in Spanishtown.'

Mr W told me that one of his duties in Bridgetown was inspecting the powder magazine guard. 'The lightning would be flashing in my face' (says Mr W), 'and I'd think the powder would be blown up every minute and me with it. There was as much powder in it as would blow up the whole world. There does be great lightning in the West Indies. We had conducting wires but that wouldn't save me.'

Davistown, Wednesday, July 20th 1859.

In the morning and the early part of the day there was some wet. My black eyes were a good deal better today and I went on Jas. Davis's affairs to Derrinlough. I went across by Mary Kenny's and the first I called on was Joe Brock of Ballincard. He said he'd bring his taxes against Friday. I then crossed over the hills to the Mohons of Derryadd and then came to a bog which brought me out on the road leading to Cloghan from Derrinlough.

The first I went to there was William Coughlan, a son-in-law to Billy Hanlon of Glebe. He lives a good piece below 'Mobby' Berry on the same road. An old woman in the house (not his wife) told me he was at the bog and promised to let him know that his taxes were called for. John Donnelly who lives a few perches at the rear of Coughlan's was likewise on the bog. Mrs Donnelly said she would tell him I called. Next was William Harding. His home is down a good piece from any of the rest by the roadside just at the lower boundary of Derrinlough. He told me he had paid his taxes to Jas. Davis in Birr a fortnight ago so I came home none the better for my walk.

After eating my dinner I went out to Mr W's. This evening for the first time I saw Mr W mixing porter with his punch. Two bottles were on the table, one with spirits and the other porter. He used to pour a little of the porter into the tumbler while making the punch. I was looking at some books that were on a side table between the two parlour windows. He advised me to read a book of the name of *Roderick Random*[200] for there is a great deal of instruction in it. He said it is older than *The Vicar of Wakefield*.

'We had a beautiful library in Bridgetown.' (I think it was Bridgetown Mr W said WD.) 'You could get any book you wanted in it. There was a book in it called *Notes From The Diary Of A Physician*, that is, what his patients told him. There was an account of the Martyred Philosopher - a man that used to lie down and call on his servant to walk on his back to try to get the pain out. Another thing in it was '*Man About Town*', an account of a man that died of venereal disease and it was awful.' I asked Mr W would it be good to keep a journal of where you'd be every day. He said 'It would, and write down everything you'd see and hear.'

Hume's *History* was opened at an advanced page and I remarked to Mr W that he had got through a good deal of it. He said he would have read more but he had to be out today. (He had to be minding our cattle from breaking out on his ground for William Rigney was gone to Birr to enquire the price of rape which Mr W is going to thrash. Wallace told him he would give him the highest price. The Dublin price isn't struck yet. As for Jack Brien he is minding his own business and not our cattle WD.)

About now in the discourse Mr W said that the first time he was going out to the West Indies there was a Captain Stuart with him. 'He was as perfect a gentleman as ever stood on two feet' (says Mr W), 'and as good a soldier as ever wore a red coat. He served fourteen years in the East Indies. He married a Church of England clergyman's daughter and had his wife and family in Scotland. When the weather was fine he and I used to walk the deck - that is when we could walk it in safety. One day when we were walking up and down he found a small lead spoon in his pocket. Well, he took out his handkerchief and started to cry. One of his children had put the spoon in his pocket when he had been at home. When we came into the warm latitudes he gave me his cabin on account of me being a married man and his wife was in Scotland (he had his own on account of being a Captain). At night he'd come down to the cabin, 'Well Whit' he'd say, 'are you asleep?'
'No.'
'Well, what do you want?'
'A song.' Well he'd sit down and sing me a song, and two songs and three songs until I'd be asleep. When we landed in Barbados he used to come into my room every night and drink coffee and brandy and water till it'd be time to go to bed. But he had the one fault only ever I could see and that was he was given to gambling. There was a whist club in Bridgetown where they used to meet every second night and they would stay there till morning drinking wine and playing cards. I would advise Stuart to go off

---

200   *The adventures of Roderick Random* published 1748. Tobias Smollett's first novel which follows the hero through his adventures at sea and in the army. Source: Margaret Drabble, *Oxford companion to English literature* (1985), p. 838.

on detachment so that he'd get away from the whist and save all his pay. On detachment you'd be invited to one planter's house one night and a different one the next, they'd make a king of you. This was before emancipation. They were afraid of their slaves rebelling and would make a fuss of you.

'One morning I was out on the veranda buckling on my sword before parade when Stuart came up to me with a bag of money. 'Look at what I won last night, £75!'
'That'll do, stick to that, says I.
I took the bag and threw it into my room and off we went. The next morning he came home without any bag.
'Well Captain Stuart, where's the bag today?' He never made me any answer only 'Eme, eme' (groaned with the mouth shut WD). He doted on his wife and children. He used to say 'I love my wife and children but I love gambling better.' I used to advise him as best I could but I took my orders from him. O, he was a Scotchman to the marrow. He used to sing Scottish songs for me till I'd be tired. I'd have to say 'Captain Stuart I'm asleep!'
I was telling Mr W about being out collecting taxes. He said he thought Wm. Harding was Pat Cash's father in law and that Harding was an industrious man (Pat Cash who went to America a long time ago from Clontyglass WD). 'Wm. Harding would go to his neck in the river for me' (says Mr W). 'I'm £300 security for him for receiving the rents of the Fivealley and Moate for Berry's.' (Mr W mentioned some other places but I forget them WD.) I asked him did any of this generation see Garrycastle old castle inhabited. Mr W said no, that that wasn't inhabited this 400 years. I said I stayed up there all night at Kennedy's (who live in a house close to the ruins of the castle) all night one night a long time ago before the sheep fair of Banagher. Tedy Digan and Ned Molloy (since gone to Australia) and I walked to Kennedy's with sheep the fair eve. 'The country is covered with the ruins of them castles (says Mr W). There's one here below at Killadrown and an old one near John Manifold's and one there outside Killyon.' (John Manifold came to live to the mill of Eglish lately and since poor Mr W died he made away to Australia on account of debts which he was unable to pay. Saturday March 10, 1860.)

I asked Mr W which was the oldest Ballyboy or Eglish church. He said he thought Eglish was the oldest and that James Gill's great grandfather was the first sexton of Ballyboy after the reformation. Eglish was founded by a party of Whitefriars. Mr W saw the old church there. It was on the left as you go into the present one. There was an old manuscript found at the old church at Drumcullen and it says the church of Drumcullen was there 1400 years ago.

GARRY CASTLE.
KING'S COUNTY

38. *The ruins of Garrycastle at Banagher from a drawing by George Petrie from Excursions through Ireland, vol. i, Leinster (Dublin, 1821)*

The discourse turned to the reformation. 'The reformation' (says Mr W), 'came from heaven. There was a sum of money needed for the building of St Peter's Church in Rome and Luther was sent to Germany to sell indulgences to gather the money for it. He was a sensible man and after a few days he knew he was on a wrong mission and he began the reformation. Give me so much money' (says Mr W) 'and I will forgive your sins for five years ... sure how could he forgive sins?' Mr W told me that it is written in a book of Jane Gill's (a small book belonging to James Gill's wife, I was reading it a few days ago at Mr W's, WD) that one of the popes said to one of his cardinals 'Why don't you stop that fellow's mouth' (Luther WD) 'with silver or gold?' 'O,' says the cardinal 'He doesn't care for it'. I said to Mr W wasn't it a wonder some of them of the present day didn't see their mistake. Mr W in all charity replied 'Time'll tell all things.'

I asked him what did he think of the revival (a movement then going on in the north of Ireland, accounts of which used to appear weekly for some time in the *Warder*.[201] Persons are said to be publicly struck down with a conviction of their sins WD). 'I can't give you any opinion about it' says Mr W. 'But one thing is certain that can't be contradicted, our Saviour tells us not to make a show of our religion nor pray in the streets nor say a multitude of words like the heathens, but to go into our closets and pray there.' Here I noticed the custom of people putting their hats to their faces to pray when they go to church (I never do it WD). 'They do it' (says Mr W), 'because they see others do it. Can't you crave a blessing of God Almighty in your heart without putting up your hat to your eyes?'

Towards the latter end of our discourse poor Mr W told me to speak to Jas. Davis and tell him to lodge £450 in Birr. 'Penchin'[202] (a clerk at the bank WD) 'will give you a receipt and if Colonel Bernard recommends you maybe you'll get your commission. Tell James Davis you can get your outfit on credit from Fisher, he was my tailor and I used to get my outfit on credit.' I said he would not lodge that much money, that he was too fond of it. 'Does he want to keep you till you're an old man with grey hairs? Can't you speak to him, sure he won't beat you! If you wait much longer they'll ask you 'Why didn't you come sooner?' I said I had but small chance of getting into the army now that the militia wasn't being kept up.

About here I said I'd heard that old Colonel Drought would sleep on no bed save that made of beech leaves (my grandfather was telling me last Sunday in the churchyard). 'You heard what was true'(says Mr W). 'I had a general invitation to the house, what very few had. One morning I was there on business and was asked to breakfast. About the middle of the meal he came in and laid his hands on my chair. "Well Mr Whitfield" says he, "I see you have tea for your breakfast."
'Yes Colonel, tea's my favourite breakfast, I see a great many old ladies in the country drink it'.
"It's not salutary to old age'"
'I see a good many old ladies drink it'.
"There'd be more if they drank spring water" says he.'
I don't know how he drew it down but in the course of conversation Mr W said that Montreal should be pronounced Montrayaul and not Montreal.

201 This evangelical movement began in Antrim in late 1858 following news of a religious revival sweeping the eastern United States. A hundred thousand people, mostly Protestants, were said to have been converted around this time. Source: Sean Connolly, *Religion and society in 19th Century Ireland*. (1985) p. 45. Part of a series *Studies in Irish Economic and Social History*.

202 This may be John Penchin who had a house and eleven acres of land at Townparks, Birr, GV p. 84-86.

39.   *The fair at Banagher in the 1890s*

Davistown, Thursday, July 21st 1859.

Morning was foggy till about noon, then there was some thunder but no lightning. This morning I went to Curraghmore to say I got no taxes in Derrinlough. James Davis was displeased that I didn't tell him sooner but I cared nothing for his displeasure. Dan Neal and Rigney were thrashing Mr W's rape today but didn't finish it.

This evening I went out to Mr W when he was having his punch in the parlour. Beck came in to ask Mr W to tell about the man that was travelling by coach and stopped at a hotel for breakfast. This man wasn't finished eating when the coach was going off, so he hid the silver spoons in the teapot and gave the alarm that they were stolen. By the time the coach was searched he had enough eaten and was in time for it. The spoons were found in the teapot after. Mr W said he never heard of it.

He began out of this to tell me there was a man of the name of Dempsey that used to drive the coach from Dublin to Mountmellick, his family lived near Monasterevin. 'Everyone would be trying to sit with him on the coach. He used never stop telling stories and telling about everyone along the road and what they were. The coach would start from Dawson Street and I would make sure and be there early so as to get a seat beside him. When the coach would be full that was the time when he'd really be in the humour for telling stories, he'd tell you anything. He told me about the time he saw a car on before him and was determined to overtake it. He was a good coachman and prided himself out of his whip hand. At any rate the two cars got entangled and down came Dempsey and the coach was broke. He had to hire cars to take the passengers on to Mountmellick.

'There was a fine lot of coachmen in England before steam was got up. One time I was travelling from Stafford to Liverpool, ninety miles, and was sitting with the coachman. Fifteen miles from Liverpool there is a town called Warrington and all along outside the town is a beautiful copse. "Did you ever hear the nightingale sing?" says he to me. 'No, I haven't had the pleasure to hear her sing' says I. "Well you'll hear her now", and he drew up the horses till he brought them to a dead stop. And there she was singing in the woods at twelve o'clock.

'I'll tell you another story but it's a long one. It happened about fifty years ago. It shows what it is to rear children and instil pride into them. There was a family in Westmeath of the name of Leigh' (pronounced Lay WD). 'Their daughter married a London merchant whom she met at a ball in Dublin. They moved to London where in less than a year she presented him with a handsome daughter whom they called Roasmond. Some time after', (I think it was a year Mr W said WD) 'from causes not well explained, he became insolvent and died. He left behind his wife, Roasmond and an old female servant named Molly with nothing but thirty pounds a year to live on while the mother lived. Some years after this they moved to a small cottage outside London. No back doors as the saying is, fasting in Lent on a meal a day and a collation[203] to stretch the thirty pounds.'Not far from their house was a castle belonging to the Wilsons who were at that time on a visit to Paris. Roasmond's mother had known them in better days. When they returned they sent out many invitations for a big ball and one came for Roasmond and her mother. They had great difficulty getting dresses, but they went at any rate. At the ball Roasmond met a man of the name of Sentillon who proposed to her. The marriage was set for a few weeks hence and in the meantime he had some business to attend to in Wales. Then came a letter from his banker saying that his presence was required in Jamaica. There was a rebellion amongst his slaves and nothing but his presence would put it down. He had a plantation there - I know the place - and his slaves rebelled saying the overseer was an impostor and there was no such person as Sentillon in the world at all. So off went Sentillon to Jamaica.

'Roasmond's mother died shortly after of a broken down constitution. When Roasmond was going through her father's papers after the funeral she found a paper giving instructions that if ever Roasmond was left unprovided for an enclosed letter should be sent to the vicar of Merrioneth, an old friend of his in Wales. This she did and in due time she was accepted into the vicar's family and the cottage &c was sold off. Roasmond grew very intimate with Ruth Williams who also lived at the vicar's house and they used always

203   A light meal permitted on fast days. Source: *Collins English dictionary*.

be together. Roasmond would be telling Ruth about Sentillon and what a fine young man he was. But she did not know that Sentillon had promised to marry Ruth Williams and his journey to Wales had been to get released from the engagement.

'Sentillon returned from Jamaica and wrote to Roasmond saying everything was settled in a prosperous way and in a few days time he'd come and marry her. When Ruth heard of him coming she made preparations to go away. She gave Roasmond a casket of jewels which had belonged to her grandmother. Miss Williams was the heiress to a fine old castle but she had come to live with the vicar till she'd be married, not wanting to be a maid alone at home.

'After Roasmond and Sentillon were married they set out for Paris and to make a tour through Europe. Before they were a year away Roasmond presented her husband with a daughter whom they called Little Sentillon. In Paris the Sentillons took to gambling and they were sure to lose every night. Roasmond had been gambling with a French Count and was greatly in debt. This man used to flatter her and she was so infatuated in playing with him that he insinuated in to her head that when she hadn't the money to pay him she could pay him in another way. And that was to elope with him to Italy, which she did. By this time Sentillon had received word that his banker had failed and he was now penniless. The Wilsons who happened to be in Paris at the time persuaded Sentillon and Little Sentillon to come home with them. Mr Wilson obtained a situation for Sentillon in Calcutta and Little Sentillon was sent to live with Ruth Williams in Wales.

40. *Dermody's shop at Fivealley in the 1980s*

'Time passed by for six years and one day Ruth was sitting beside the fire and Little Sentillon was by the door when a harper came by and started to play. I believe it is the custom in Wales for harpers to play before the doors of castles in the evenings. When he was finished he asked to see 'the lady' and she went out to him. 'My Lady' says he 'as I was coming here I saw a woman at such a cross in clothes not to be described and by what she said I think she wished to see you'. Something struck Ruth that minute and she put on her shawl and bonnet, called some servants and together they went to the cross. These crosses are quite common in England - large stone crosses with benches round them to sit on. They found a woman sitting there with her face in her hands dressed in an old bonnet, an old mantle with twenty patches and a sort of old flounced coat. Ruth raised up her head and saw that it was Roasmond. "Roasmond!"

"Don't call me by that name, I am not worthy of it."

"How is the child?"

"Get up and come home, you will see soon enough."

"No, I won't pollute your peaceful hall."

Ruth called the servants and the men made a chair of their arms for Roasmond while the women walked one behind and one in front. She was put to bed when they got her home and given a posset[204] which Ruth had made for her. When she wakened she asked to see the child and was brought to where the child was sleeping. She would not kiss the child saying "No, I won't touch that angel with my polluted lips."

She knelt down to say some prayers and asked them to send for the curate. They sent for him and she died' (or more beautifully expressed by Mr W but I forget it WD). 'The moral of that story is that it shows the weakness of some females and the staminus of others.' (In staminus Mr W pronounced a and i long WD). 'When Sentillon came home from India with an immense fortune he asked Ruth to marry him.

"Are you in earnest?" says she.

"I am."

"Well I suppose you want an answer."

"I do."

"Well you are welcome to my house every day and hour and moment that you wish, but never ask me that question again."

"Hadn't that girl a staminus William!" I said she had. I asked him had he ever been in Wales. He said no.

---

204   Drink of hot milk curdled with ale, beer etc, flavoured with spices, formerly used as a remedy for colds. Source: *Collins English dictionary*.

Davistown, Sunday, July 24th 1859.

The day was very warm, I was at Eglish. In the evening I went out to Mr W. Poor Mr W spoke very earnestly and affectionately to me about my prospects in life. 'Why doesn't that fellow buy you a commission in the army? Tell him to buy you a commission or give up your father's situation to you. Tell him if he does not you'll go to Colonel Bernard. It was I got him to be where he is. He wouldn't have the collecting of the taxes only for all the letters I wrote for him. I'm afraid you're too much afraid of him do his worst. What can he do, only what your father left you and we'll say that's nothing. I'm afraid you have your hand in the lion's mouth and take it out as easy as you can. It's only a humbug to have you at school. You're a young man and speak to him as such. He'll keep you at school for another year and then get you some trifling situation and say to all, Look what I done for that fellow!'

Poor Mr W showed as great an interest in my welfare as if I were his own son. In justice to the dead I say he loved me more than my father. This evening as I was going off I thanked him for his advice to which he replied 'That's my way of living, fair, honest and agreeable with everyone.'

Davistown, Monday July 25th 1859.

Was cloudy but fine. Richard drove Margaret and Charlotte to Birr and came back in the afternoon. Mr W did not go to the assizes to serve on the petty jury.

In the evening I went into him in the parlour. The following is the substance of the evening's discourse. I shall always regret that I was not able to write Mr W's words as they fell from his lips. However there is sufficient likeness to his own words in what I have recorded that I will often think of the happy evenings which I have spent in his company.

He was telling me this evening that when he was going to Barbados he was seasick for ten days. There was a box of raisins stowed under his berth and for them ten days he lived on nothing only raisins and water (I think it was water but raisins at any rate WD).

There was a young chap going out with them of the name of Copinger, (they always called him Cop WD), an ensign from Dublin. 'He was' (says Mr W), 'very fond of girls and reading. One day in Liverpool I met him coming up Dale St. with a book in his hand, he had got it at the library. To my surprise a few minutes later I saw him coming back with the book. What happened to you? says I.

"O wait till I tell you" says he. "I'm after seeing one of the nicest girls there above. I gave my last guinea in pledge for this book and I'm going to get it back."

41.   The meeting rooms on the first floor of the *King's County Chronicle* printing
      offices at Emmet Street (formerly Cumberland Street), Birr erected in the 1850s
      and damaged by fire in 1903 (courtesy of Mr Michael Byrne)

'He was senior ensign when he went out to Barbados and he was gazetted[205]
to be a Lieutenant', (or it might have been Adjutant, I put Adjutant in the
original from which this is transcribed, but I didn't know much of the army
then and I might have mistook Lieutenant for Adjutant WD). 'Whether that
affected him or not I don't know but he went out of his mind shortly after
and there had to be two men minding him in his room. He went home and
recovered and joined the 16th.'

Mr W asked me did he ever tell me about Lieutenant Grant. I said no.
'The way he used to amuse himself was turning with the lathe. The
greatest present you could give him was the hardest piece of wood on the
whole island and he'd turn egg cups and chessmen out of that. He kept
a pot full of chisels and hammers and hatchets in his room. His room
was on a corner and was a great meeting place. One day that I was there
the wheel was too light. "If I had some lead" says he, "it'd turn right."
'Says I, do you think will it rain soon?'
He went to the window, "It'll rain in ten minutes" says he. Well, I took up
a hatchet and waited, and in about ten minutes there was a terrible fall of
rain. When I was sure no one would see me I went out into it and chopped
off a piece of a lead spout and brought it in to Grant. We got two black

---

205   To have one's name announced in the Gazette as being appointed to some post or
      promoted to some rank. Source, Virginia S. Thatcher, (ed) *The new Webster encyclopedic
      dictionary of the English language.* (1980)

fellows to make a fire in the cellar - you're allowed a black servant on foreign service but not a white one - and we melted it in a big greassit and you would think we were two vulcans coming up we were so black. Grant bored holes all around on the wheel with an auger about an inch asunder and you'd think it'd cut iron it went so well.'

Mr W told me that when he went to Barbados first he thought it was wonderful to see the houses without any chimneys or glass windows and to see the cabbage trees[206] with the leaves all on top. That time he used to wear a big hat with a big leaf called a Panama hat. One morning he would have arrived at parade with it on only quartermaster Williamson stopped him.

Davistown, Tuesday July 26th 1859.

Was warm although a little cloudy. The evening was a little blowing and towards dusk there was some wet. Mr W said he would like me to get him the other part of Hume's *History*. I said I thought Hume to be an infidel but he said it did not appear so from his writings.

I gave it as my opinion that the Quakers were an honest upright people. Mr W agreed with me saying 'You'll always find them in business minding their business.'

Note. Since that time the Quakers have built a new meeting house at the end of the haymarket[207] close to Lord Rosse's wall. 'They have a burying ground up graveyard.[208] I was at it with Joe Robinson's funeral. He lived here at the mill. They call it a sleeping place, a very good name'(says Mr W). Mr W was telling me of a man he knew when he (Mr W) was a little fellow. 'His name was John Walker, father to John of the Fivealley. He said - and I think there is some foundation for it - from the creation to the flood was 2000 years and from the flood to the birth of Christ was 2000 years and he said there'd be some great change in the world 2000 years from that. They used to call him Walker the Anabaptist.[209] He used to come to my father's when I was a little fellow and give me three pence to put in a purse.'

---

206   Areca Oleracea. Grows to a height of between one hundred and two hundred feet with a trunk of not more than seven inches in diameter. The leaves which grow at the top were considered to be a great delicacy either raw or boiled, *NE* vol.1, p. 401.

207   Now called the Green. The Society of Friends meeting house is now the Masonic Hall.

208   A nick name for High Street because of the Society of Friends graveyard there. Source: Mr Tadgh Pey, Birr.

209   A group of Protestant Christians. One of their articles of belief was that baptism ought only be administered to adults and by immersion. They accordingly rebaptised those who joined them. They disliked this title which had previously referred to the ultra radicals of the reformation. They preferred to be called Baptists, *NE* vol.1, p. 251 and vol. 2, p. 242.

I was telling Mr W that I would like to have the whole of *Humphrey Clinker*[210] - a book in two volumes. He had it there and told me to take it with me to read, but through neglect the second part has ever since remained at our house. It was written by Dr Tobias Smollet[211] of Dunbarton who lived in or about the year 1770. He is also the author of Mr W's favourite book *Roderick Random*. He says there is a great deal of information in it for one that would be going to travel.

Later in the course of chat I told Mr W that I had been confirmed by the Bishop of Meath. 'How long since is that?' I said it was a couple of years. 'And when will you see him again?' It was my opinion that I would never see him again, they only go round their diocese about once every three years to confirm children. 'Poor fellow,' (says Mr W) 'isn't he to be pitied, that has to go round his diocese in three or four years. They could make themselves very useful if they liked - inspecting schools and contributing to their support and the like.'

Davistown, Wednesday, July 27th 1859.

Was fine. Richard went to Birr with provisions for Margaret and Charlotte. I sent him to William Smallman's for Wesley's *Life*. William Smallman is a brother of my grandmother's. He stops in the same house as us, 30 Cumberland Street, a little thatched house. We pay half the rent - two pounds - and he the other half.

JOHN WESLEY.   *Methodist Publishing*

42. *John Wesley, the founder of Methodism and a frequent visitor to Ireland over the period of the 1740s to the 1780s*

---

210 *The expedition of Humphrey Clinker* published 1771, the story of a journey through Wales, England and Scotland. A study of how the same events affect different people in different ways. Source: Margaret Drabble, *Oxford companion to English literature* (1985), p. 483.

211 Scottish author. 1721-1771. Used his time as a surgeon's mate in the British navy as background material for some of his writings, *NE* vol.12, p. 407.

Davistown, Thursday, July 28th 1859.

I went out to Mr W's with Wesley's *Life*. He was walking up and down outside the hall door as was his custom when the weather was fine. He was waiting for Beck's sister Frances to come from Frankford with the spirits and porter for his punch. Later I joined him in the parlour to have the pleasure of his conversation.

'One time' (says Mr W), 'my old comrade Thene was commanding men at Chester and he had a refractory soldier. He wrote to the Colonel to have a court-martial on him. We were in Liverpool that time and the Major and four or five of us went down to Chester for it. When the court-martial was over Thene brought me round the ruins of the old walls of Chester. He would never tire of looking at old ruins. Well, we stayed looking at this castle and that castle, and this old house and that old house and when we were finished the others had gone without us. 'Come' says Thene 'and we'll try to get a coach to Birkenhead'. It's twelve miles from Chester to Birkenhead and four miles from Birkenhead to Liverpool by boat across the river. I just got the coach to Birkenhead but when I got to Birkenhead I was told I'd have to wait an hour and a half for the steamer. So I sat down by the fire and lit a cigar and was very comfortable. By and by I came out and there was the Major and the others coming marching along full of puddle and wet and dirt for it was a wet day in October. Hadn't they taken a coach to the wrong boat office and then had to march six miles to Birkenhead at a great rate so as to be on time for the steamer. I put my hand this way', (here Mr W put his hand to his eyes as if to look against the sun WD), 'What happened ye or where were ye, says I. They wouldn't speak to me. O, they were full of puddle and wet.'

Davistown, Friday July 29th 1859.

Fine. This evening I went out to Mr W before he went to his dinner. He asked me would any of us be going to Birr tomorrow, that he wanted to send for a pound of cheese. I said someone would go. (I have seen Mr W sit but little before his dinner. He used generally to be pacing across the kitchen, or sometimes outside the hall door and some years before he died he used almost every day take to the hill and down again). He was always very fond of gathering little twigs and branches for burning, the turf he used to get in the moor below the house being black and heavy and not easily kindled without sticks.

Beck was there with her son Albert, son of Tom Murray with whom she went to America about the time of my father's death. She disliked working for her bread and soon after returned when the child was born about 1855.[212] Her husband was a son of old John Murray of Clontyglass. He enlisted

---

212   Albert Murray, born January 25, 1855 son of Thomas and Rebecca Murray of Eglish.
       Baptised 25 February, 1855. Source: Birr Church of Ireland baptism records.

after coming from America, but deserted before he was long in the army and went to America. Then Beck took with Jas. Kenny (her villainy all this time was either unknown to Mr W or else he pardoned it and forgot it for he was of a most merciful and humane nature WD). About Christmas '58 it was reported that she was delivered of a son and in about the beginning of April of this year '59 Rigney went early one morning for Dr Wallace of Birr and she was delivered of a child dead or prematurely born. This story is not without foundation for about this time I did not see her for some days and on Sunday February 27th Rigney met me in the orchard with the supplement and made some excuse that the paper was borrowed the way I wouldn't ask to go out. It is further affirmed that the child lived and was privately conveyed by night to Dublin, Rigney acting as accessory and that some woman of the name of Davis kept it there. At any rate at the beginning of May she brought two children there, a girl of about three and a boy about six months which she kept and called George and sent back the other. She pretended that they were her sister's, but it is a falsehood.

'I had an uncle' (says Mr W), 'of the name of Tom Freer. He was in Italy during the Spanish War[213] and when he came home he went to live in Ballinasloe. There was an old man of the name of Billy Pierce beyond in Ballinnacarrig, an honest simple man, a high Protestant. My uncle had a great liking for him. One day Billy was in Ballinasloe at my uncle's and he told him he could prove from a verse in the bible how long anyone would live.
'And did you try how long yourself had to live?' says my uncle Tom.
'I did', says Billy, 'I'll live for fifteen years yet'. Well six months after when I was down with him in Ballinasloe Tom asked me 'Abey, do you know Billy Pierce?'
'I did know him' says I.
'Why don't you know him now?'
'Because he's dead these six months.' Well, he leaned back in his chair and laughed for half an hour. He had been here looking for a place to live. There was so many people in Frankford that he knew. There was a barracks where Crommer lives now and the house was to be set. He went and agreed for the house, but there was a large heap of dung and whoever bought the house should buy the dung. It was to be sold for fifty pounds and he wouldn't give that so it was all knocked on the head. I went back with him to Ballinasloe to stay a while, I was about like Richard[214] that time. He was an asthmatic and used to keep seven or eight horses (or one or two but I forget how many horses Mr W told me he kept WD). He was the best judge of horses I ever saw, he used to buy horses for the regiment. You might as well hit himself with a stick as hit a horse. He wouldn't let you hit a horse at all. In the morning he wouldn't be able to ride so he would put a horse under a

---

213   The Peninsular War, 1807-1814. The Spanish, assisted by Wellington's British army, eventually defeated the French army of invasion, *NE*, vol. 12, p. 470.

214   Thirteen years of age.

car and drive out. Then about two o'clock he'd get strong and ride out. The horses got oats and bran every day and their hooves would be stuffed with cow dung every night to keep them cool. After dinner he'd drink wine and I'd drink punch. Then he'd be very strong and never stop talking.

One evening when I got him in good humour I said to him Uncle when you're dividing your land you ought to leave me _____ ' (Mr W mentioning the name of an estate which I forget WD). 'That was what I said - When you're dividing it' - I didn't say, when you're dying. But I wasn't of his name and he wouldn't leave it outside his name. He was asking me about all the people here. He was always talking of Crommer's house and how it needed repairs. I told him if he wrote down all that needed to be done I would oversee the work. "Well" says he, "let you ride to Birr in the morning to Simpson Hackett to lodge the money." Simpson Hackett and Bernard kept a bank there that time.[215] I knew that if he got Crommer's he'd leave it to me. But my aunt had her ear to the keyhole and she did not want to go live in Frankford. When I went to bed that night she brought a lot of the Mahers in - one of them was married to my cousin Abraham Freer - and they put upon my uncle not to leave. At any rate around midnight she sent up word that I need not go to Birr and that was the end of it. Uncle dropped down dead off his horse in ___ months after.' (Mr W told me the number of months but I forget, I suppose it was six or nine months WD.)

'Abraham Freer was off in Italy guarding the pope, and his wife - the Miss Maher - would come up to my uncle's and condole with me on the poor lot of a soldier's wife. She was good to me but my aunt did not care for me.'

I asked Mr W who lived in Davistown all this time. 'Tom Davis lived in it. I was at his funeral. He was a big fat man with a hooked nose and weighed ____ .' (Mr W mentioning some great weight, I think it was eighteen stone WD). I don't think he was related to your family, I think he was related to the Davises of the Leap and Drumoyle and your family was the Garryheather. I think they're distant relations.

'Tom Davis was bound to a shoemaker, but he'd rather have farming and at that time he wasn't worth fourteen pounds by what I heard. He went and married a Miss Evans from Dungar near Roscrea', (Mr W pronounced it Eve-ans WD) 'and he got one hundred pounds with her, that was considered a good fortune that time. Davy Barber lived in Davistown this time and he had a great many friends in America who used to be writing to him to come out. When Tom Davis - who cared nothing for shoemaking - heard of this he went and gave him the hundred pounds for his goodwill of Davistown. He asked his wife's friends to make up another hundred pounds saying he would repay them before two years were out. He set up a dairy here making

---

215   Cooke refers to this old bank in his 1826 history as a ruined building near Emmet
        Square, see [T.L. Cooke], *The picture of Parsonstown in the King's County
        containing the history of that town from the earliest period to the year* 1798,
        together with its description at the present day (Dublin 1826, reprinted in part, Birr,
        1929), p. 222.

butter and cheese. Capalohy was to be set that time and he got that. He burned it flat there to the right as you go up to Curraghmore and sowed rape in it. He had a good crop and got three hundred pounds for it. His wife used to eat a cold roast duck for her breakfast with one foot on the grate there' says Mr W, pointing to the kitchen grate. I asked him was the proper name for this place Davidstown or Davistown. He said David Barber called it Davidstown and when Tom Davis came he called it Davistown.[216]

'I'll tell you the first history of this place. The first name of this place was Cornawinchin.[217] There was an old Protestant woman living in Clontyglass this time that was dying and she sent for Mr Carr the curate of Eglish and Drumcullen who lodged in Ballincard house with two old maiden sisters. She told Mr Carr a secret about the nursing of a child and he sent for a magistrate who took down what she said and made her swear to it. Everyone knew that time that Awly Magawly had a lawsuit in the Four Courts, about a child and if it went again him it would break him. Carr met Magawly at the Four Courts with the old woman's deposition and when he gave it to his counsel the lawsuit went in his favour that minute.
'Well', says Magawly 'I must give you something to repay you for what you've done for me'. Carr was fond of shooting and at that time the bog came up to the bottom of the lawn. It was full of wild fowl. The Lisduff people used to come by a road called 'The Black Avenue' to get turf out of it. 'Well', says Carr 'Give me Cornawinchin.'
'I'll give you that for nothing.'
'No, you must name a rent and give me a long lease.'
So he gave him a lease of it forever - Magawly would give an ever lease to anyone that'd ask him. He made my grandfather take out a lease forever of Ballincloghan. At any rate Carr got it[218] for fourteen pounds and when the currency changed[219] it was eleven pounds.' (I think Mr W said eleven pounds and some shillings and some pence but I forget WD.) 'I pay that every year to Sanderson's agent in county Cavan, I send it in half notes.'

---

216 See Brian Pey, *Eglish and Drumcullen*, p. 333.

217 Also spelled as Coranawynchin and Cornawynchin. Would seem to be an Anglicisation of Corr na bhFuinseann 'the (rounded) hill of the ash trees'. Source: Letter from Conchubhar O Crualaoich of the Placenames Branch, Department of Arts, Heritage, Gaeltacht and the Islands.

218 1737 McAwley of Kilcormac leased lands of Coranawynchin als Davidstown part of Bullock Hill containing 154 acres to Rev. David Roberts, Ballincard for 300 years, renewable after each 100 years. Deed witnessed by Thomas Kennedy Ballincloghan, Joseph Calcutt Mountrath and Richard Calcutt, Ballincard. Source: paper of David Maxwell's, Ballincard, given to him by Mr Brian Pey. I have been unable to verify Mr W's story. See also Pey, *Eglish and Drumcullen*, pp 333-4.

219 This refers to the amalgamation of the Irish and English exchequers. The Irish currency was abolished from 6 January 1826. Source: G.L. Barrow, *The emergence of The Irish banking system*. (1975) pp 28-29.

Mr W told me this was the head rent and said Tom Manifold asked him to pay it for him and then it was subtracted from Mr W's rent every year along with the poor rates and income tax.

'When Carr came here he built a lodge, part of this house. When he died or was leaving it he set it to people of the name of Nugents and they built the rest of the house and planted these trees and built walls and planted the garden. The Nugents left it to Davy Barber and Tom Davis bought it from Barber. Then Wm. Woods came in for Davistown by being married to a daughter of Tom Davis's and now it's an undivided property between Wm. Woods's four daughters. If I owed them rent or you owed them rent they wouldn't know whose cow to take, they couldn't tell who to distrain[220] for it. If one of them came to you and said 'I want my rent' and you didn't have it you could play the mischief with her if she took your cow. It being undivided who is to say whose cow is on whose part of it.' (When Maxwell came to Ballincard it was his fancy to build a big house on a hill and he made use of this venerable house as a laundry WD.)

Hereabouts in the discourse Mr W said 'When I came here first there was a nice curate in Eglish of the name of Drought.[221] He stopped in Whigsboro. He would come here to me two or three times a week and we would have breakfast together and then drive round the parish. When the new church was going to be built in Eglish he was gathering subscriptions and we used to be saying how it should be built on glebe land.[222] The Eglish glebe lands are at that farmer's house next Tommy Neals, the one next to Hanlons - Dooly's. But the commissioners said no, that at the dissolution of the union of Funchawn every parish would have its church. Coote[223] pays curates for all the parishes of Funchawn and at his death every one of them parishes will have a church and rector. He pays eighty pounds a year to every one of them. It's likely that Healy has one hundred pounds on account of having Drumcullen, but Ballyboy has only eighty pounds.'

As I was coming away Mr W gave me a shilling for the cheese and said he was troublesome. I assured him he was not, that it was no trouble.

220   To seize from. Source: *Collins English dictionary*.

221   A William Drought was curate of Eglish in 1840 when he published "A funeral address", in *New Irish pulpit*. Source: RCB Library. A William Drought is also listed as clergyman in Parish of Gallen in 1874. Source: John Healy, *History of the diocese of Meath*, vol. ii. (1908)

222   Eglish Church of Ireland church was built in 1839 by the Ecclesiastical Commissioners. Source: Pey, *Eglish and Drumcullen*, p.33.

223   Rev. Ralph Coote, vicar of Fercall 1827 – 68, married Harriet or Henrietta Close, daughter of Rev. Samuel Close of Elm Park on 4 May 1828. She died 20 September 1866. He died 24 November, 1868. RCB.

43. *Kinnitty village in the early 1900s*

Davistown, Saturday, July 30th 1859.

Blowing, in the evening there was a mist which gradually turned to a heavy shower. My mother and Richard went to Birr. When they returned I went across to Mr W with the cheese. It was pouring rain and he said it was badly needed. He remarked 'John Wesley must have had a strong constitution and a strong mind to bear all the hardships he went through. He was a very learned man in Latin and Greek and Hebrew. The first verse in the Bible is 'In six days God created Heaven and Earth', but Wesley showed that's not the right translation. It should be 'The Gods created Heaven and Earth'. In the same way where it says 'God placed Cherubim and a flaming sword to keep the way of the tree of life', it should be 'the Majesties of Heaven'. Wesley and Whitefield disagreed on some points, but I think Whitefield was the most popular. There's a great many of Dean Swift's[224] works out. Now he was a most curious man. One morning he called his servant for his boots and says he, 'Are they clean John?'
'O sir, what use in cleaning them, they'll be spattery as ever tonight?'
'O very well, get the horses.'
'I wonder why sir you don't stop for breakfast?'

224   Jonathan Swift, 1667-1745. Author of *Gulliver's travels* and many other works. Became Dean of St. Patrick's in Dublin in 1713. He founded St Patrick's Hospital for imbeciles which opened in 1757. In later life he suffered from what is now thought to have been Ménière's Disease and not insanity as had been previously suspected. Source: Margaret Drabble, *Oxford companion to English literature*. (1985), p. 952.

'O what use? You'll want another breakfast in the morning.' That was a good answer. He founded an hospital and endowed it, it's there yet, Swift's hospital. Himself was the first lunatic in it and he died there.'

Here after pausing a while Mr W said, 'Well I'll give you my opinion of our rectors and curates. There's Shaw the rector in Kinnitty. He's paid so much a year for visiting the parishioners and attending to the church. He'll go and preach a sermon and then that'll do till next Sunday. Now Travers, who was minister of Kinnitty', (I believe he was Healy's uncle and is now dead WD), 'he was worthy of being called a minister. Then there's Healy, the curate in Eglish. He'll go and preach a sermon and the rest of the week he'll be at his farm. I often saw him and I going to Birr and he looking at a few poor labourers instead of going round his parishes and minding the church.' I told Mr W that grandmother Davis was sick not long before and Healy did not come to see her for a long time. When he did come she reproved him for not coming sooner instead of attending to his farm. Some Sundays after he said in his sermon that self examination was necessary for the parishioners, that people should mind themselves instead of telling him that he was more attentive to his farming pursuits than his calling. 'When Coote put him there' (says Mr W), 'he did not intend him to be a farmer. He's allowed a liberal salary and he should go through his parishioners at least once a week instead of standing there minding a few poor labourers tilling his farm. How often is he at your house?' I told Mr W that he wasn't at it these six months and that he often stays a year and a half without coming. Mr W was astonished.

'I won't say he's wrong', (says Mr W). 'God forbid that I should judge anyone, it's not my province.' (And how Healy dared to judge Mr W as he lay on his deathbed, upbraiding him with impenitence to my mother, but God is the judge of all WD.) 'I never saw such a coward as Healy. He bawled at me one Sunday, you might often hear of it - I walked out.' I said I barely remembered it but I was at church that Sunday. (I heard my mother say that before this Mr W went regularly to church.) 'Next morning was Monday and I went up to his house and rapped on the door. A girl came and said Mr Healy was in the yard. I walked round and there he was hedged in in a little cow house. 'What are you afraid of?' says I, 'Come out you idiot until I talk to you!'
'I was afraid you were come to assault me' says he.
But I had no other intention than to speak plain and reason cases with him. Says I 'You're a disgrace to the gown; it's a pity that ever you got ordination, you mistook your profession.'
'You know nothing about it' says he.
'I do know more than you and if I go back to your father he sold gloves on Essex bridge in Dublin. He sent you to college and put you into the church and it was the greatest mistake ever happened. And now you idiot, I leave you in your ignorance.' I never put a foot in his church since nor never will. What call had he to meddle in my private affairs. What is it to him what

servant I keep in my house? I think he repented of what he said to me.' (Mr W has since told me this story again and instead of the cow house he said hen house WD.)

'I saw him since once. Tom Healy was killed in the Russian War and a paper came home from the War Office to be signed by the curate.' (Tom was Beck's brother who went in the land transport corps at the time of the Russian War[225] WD.) 'A girl came to the door and let me in. I saluted him and he saluted me. I handed him the papers and says I, 'Put your name to these when you look over them in order that Rebecca Murray may have the amount.' He looked at them and put his name to them that minute. I saluted him and he saluted me and I came off. Before he came he was curate to Jack Travers in Kinnitty, he may be his nephew. Before the break up he used to come here looking for subscriptions and I would always give him something.

'Did you ever hear the story about the little Protestant boy? One day someone asked a Protestant boy where was his religion before the time of Elizabeth and he couldn't answer him and was told to ask his minister. 'Tell him' says the minister, it was like his face, it was in the dirt and wanted to be washed'.

'O, that was a very passionate woman, that Queen Elizabeth. One day she saw either Essex or Leicester joking with one of the maids of honour and she gave her a slap on the jaw. Another time she gave Essex a box in the face and all he said was 'I wouldn't take that from your father!' Her father Henry[226] was a terrible passionate man. The lower orders of the Roman Catholics would tell you he was the cause of the reformation but he had no more religion in him than that fender. He was but one degree removed from the beast - a beast in human form. He only wanted hooves and horns to make a beast of him.' Mr Whitfield asked me if I could get the other part of the *History of England*, but alas, in the small circle of my acquaintance in Birr I never could get it for him.

Davistown, Sunday, July 31st 1859.

Morning showery, day generally cool and blowing. I was not at church. Before dinner time I went out to Mr W's but Wm. Rigney was not home with the paper. When it came I went back to look over it till Richard came to call me to my Colcannon[227] for it was Garland Sunday.[228] Later I read

---

225   Crimean War, 1854-1855.

226   Henry VIII.

227   From the Irish, cál ceannann - a white headed cabbage. First meal from the new potato crop. Milk, salt, onions and butter were added to mashed potatoes. In some places vegetables and spices were also included. Source: T.P. O'Neill, *Life and tradition in rural Ireland* (1977) p. 65.

228   Garland Sunday. 'Last Sunday in July also known as Bilberry, Height, Fraughan, or Lammas Sunday'. Source: Bernard Share, *Naming names* (2001) pp 138, 141.

that Hennessy speaks betimes in parliament and is in favour of abolishing the Queen's Colleges[229] in Ireland for it is his opinion they are a failure.

Frank Smith was at Mr W's. Mr W said to him that John Camon - of Frankford who has potatoes on the hill - deserved to be put in the pillory for disgracing the hill with his late potatoes. It is the news all over Ireland this time - the small potatoes. Frank Smith had some turnips on the hill and Albert began to tell him how young Mary Brien (Jack Brien's daughter WD) used to pull his turnips. Beck told him the same. Smith said he should watch them, that Jack Brien has two big pigs there and nothing to feed them.

When Mr W went to his punch I told him that they were striving to revise the prayer book, (accounts of it used to appear in the parliamentary reports of the *Warder* WD). Mr W observed that they could shorten the service by reading a lesson from the New Testament one Sunday and one from the Old Testament the next. 'People object to repeating the Lord's Prayer so often in the service but I find no fault in it at all. The prayer book was settled the way it is now at the time of James the 1st and there were sensible men out that time.'

I asked him were the four forms of prayer for the Restoration, gunpowder, treason &c[230] used now and he said 'No, and I don't fault them for that at all. I'm afraid our curates and rectors think that when they read the service and preach a sermon they can have the rest of the week to themselves looking after their farms or hunting. Couldn't you or I read the service as well and couldn't we preach a sermon if it was written for us? It's not your or my duty to say they're wrong - only our own private opinion. If they'd imitate Wesley they'd profit by it'.

I said the priests weren't careless of seeing to their flock and I gave it as my opinion that if our clergy minded their parishes and left controversy alone it would better become them.

Later that evening one came into the parlour to say that Frank Smith was after getting an eel in the pond. This was the third eel caught there this year. James caught the first one. I wondered how they came to be in the pond when it had no communication with the river. Mr W said he didn't know if cranes - fishing cranes - didn't drop them in it.

I asked him which season of the year would he sooner have. He said from this to November when it's neither too hot nor too cold and one can be more abroad. He asked me did I ever see Shakespeare's *Seven Ages of Man*, at the same time handing me down an engraving of Shakespeare from the chimney

---

229   Established in Ireland in 1849 to give a high class education to students of all religious denominations. Colleges at Cork, Galway Dublin and Belfast formed the Queen's University in Ireland, *NE*, vol. 7, p. 499.

230   This refers to prayers giving thanks for the restoration of the monarchy, the failure of the gunpowder plot and the martyrdom of Charles the First contained in the Book of Common Prayer.

piece - the front piece of some book which Beck put in a little frame. I said I did not and he repeated to me words like these. 'At first the infant mewling and pewking in the nurse's arms, then the schoolboy creeping like a snail to school, then the soldier, I thrust them here, I dart them there, then the lover singing songs to his mistress's apron strings'.[231] He said he had Hume's *England* and Wesley's *Life* read and I brought them in to our house.

44. *Birr Castle about 1900 (courtesy of the National Library of Ireland)*

---

231   From Shakespeare's play *As You Like It*, Act 2, scene VII.

CHAPTER 10

August 1859

An encounter on the way to Athlone fair, the distress of Mrs Burriss, the funeral of George Stoney, Mr Whitfield and uncle James Davis strike a bargain, Jack Carroll the piper, sailing to Barbados, the strangeness of the natives, Mr Whitfield challenges Major Harty, fever in Jamaica, Mr Whitfield meets the Duke of Cumberland.

Birr, Monday, August 1st 1859.

Morning showery, cool and blowing. Richard, Margaret and Charlotte returned to Birr to attend school. I left home for the same purpose about one and was in Birr before three. I heard that Weir was not at home nor wouldn't be till next Monday. He was in Killarney and his wife's illness was the cause of his delay. I brought back Hume's *England* and Wesley's *Life* to William Smallman.

Davistown, Tuesday, August 2nd 1859.

Morning and evening some showers, day fine. I remained in Birr till eight this evening to see if Weir would be home. It was night a long time before I arrived at our house.

Davistown, Wednesday, August 3rd 1859.

Morning and forenoon some weighty showers, rest of the day fine. This evening when Mr W was at his punch I asked him was he going to the races. (This was a horse race got up by Bernard and Bennett &c which took place at Raheenglass near Thomastown on the Friday after WD.) Mr W didn't think he would go. He was asking me about Weir's school and I told him that Weir has about thirty scholars and one boarder. When I went there first it was a good school but he took to gambling and drinking and the school declined. I told him how he used to spend nights at Mick Madden's[232] till two o'clock.

---

232   The Fighting Cocks public house, Cumberland St., Birr, *SD*, 1856.

45.   *Eglish Castle in the 1970s (courtesy of Mr Michael Byrne)*

After a pause Mr W said 'I never won at cards but once. One night I was going to the fair of Athlone and I put up at a house about a mile from the town. It was January this time and there was a good many there. We had bacon and cabbage and roast goose for dinner. There was a man there of the name of Finegan, he had a custodiam of Lettybrook. He would have plenty of money at any rate - Drought owes him £1200.' (It might be that Mr W said more or less or it might not be Colonel Drought although I think it was, yet it was some of the Droughts WD.) 'He lived in Westmeath, a cute old fellow - you'd think he was Solomon. At any rate the two of us played cards again two more. We played for six pence a piece and a drink of punch. We two won thirty shillings and what punch we drank! That was the first and last time I won at cards.

'I was telling you about Stuart, he used to go play cards every night. Creagh was another one, a cunning fellow, as wary as fox. We were standing on the veranda in Bridgetown one day and I saw a ship coming in. The time passed so heavy that we'd be out to see what news by the ships. Creagh took up the glass and looked at her and I did the same. I had good sight and saw the Blue Peter. 'There's troops on board' says I. Creagh said there was none. 'I bet you eight dollars' says I.
'Done.'
When she came a little nearer he took up the glass again to look. He never said a word but put his hand in his pocket and gave me eight dollars. O, there's no port in the world a ship would sooner go into than Barbados. Captain Cannon, the first sea captain ever I sailed with told me you can drop

anchor any time of the night without taking on a pilot. We sailed in the *Brig Robert*. The *Irlam* which was the finest ship in Liverpool sailed out with us. Stuart often cursed the agent Brown for not putting us in her, the villain took a bribe. At any rate we sailed out together. But when we came to Waterford there was a great wind and we separated. We went into the Bay of Biscay and they went up by North America. When we got to Bridgetown I asked the pilot when had the *Irlam* come in. "No *Irlam* massa, no *Irlam* massa.'" [233]

I understood from what Mr W said that the pilot was a black. I asked him do they speak English. He told me yes, that they import no slaves - they're born on the island. Mr W told me that in Bridgetown there are Mulattoes[234], Samboes[235] and Scramboes and what not. They are very fond of bottled porter and have a dance called a Joe and John.

'One day the Colonel allowed them to have a Joe and John in the barrack yard. They all brought in bottled porter and gingerbread. The blacks rushed in amongst the 500 soldiers that were in barracks and.... such confusion to see them all.... blacks and redcoats together, you'd think it was the end of the world. The Colonel would not let them have another Joe and John there if he got half Barbados. They're a queer people. The women carry the children on their backs. They don't call them child at all but pickaninny. I'd go over and give the pickaninny a punch and he'd give a great jump, wouldn't cry at all only give a great jump. She'd turn round, 'Massa pinched pickaninny!'

'O, he's leaping with the heat.'

'No, pickaninny no leap with the heat, massa pinched pickaninny!'

'In Barbados there was a merchant of the name of Maguffy, a Scotchman, an excellent worthy fellow. He kept a horse and gig and gave great dinners to his fellow merchants. He wasn't married but had a large family by a Mulatto woman. He sent some of them home to England to be educated. I had no enemies in the army, I was always free and agreeable. Some made enemies for themselves with their bad temper. I remember we were on detachment in Stafford one time. We had about three companies and we had squad drill every day - agreeable I suppose to headquarters. At any rate one morning I was looking at the sergeant drilling the men and the Major, an imperious haughty coxcomb of a fellow, made use of 'dog or devil' or some dirty expression as he was passing my company. Lowe's company was near mine and as soon as drill was over Lowe spoke to me about what the Major had said. He told me that I should get an explanation for it and he would stand by me. I went up to the

---

233   The *Irlam* remained in service till at least August 1829 when on a journey from Liverpool to St.Vincent the ship was attacked by drunken pirates 500 miles SW of Madeira. A large quantity of provisions were stolen and three of *Irlam's* crew were murdered. Source: An extract from *The Times*, 11 Sept 1829 obtained from *Digest of piracy reports from the London Times 1826-1831* in the Pirate Document Library, Dept. of History, University of Melbourne. Information supplied by the Royal Ulster Rifles Museum Research, 5 Waring St. Belfast BT1 2EW

234   'Person having one negro and one white parent', source: *Collins English dictionary*.

235   'The offspring of a negro and a member of another race or a mulatto', source: *Collins English dictionary*.

Major and says I 'Major Harty, you made use of an expression passing my company today which I don't like. Did you allude that to me?'

'O no, O no!'

'That'll do ...will that do Captain Lowe?'

'O that'll do.'

We had a nice little fellow of the name of Plunkett from Dublin with us and he burst out into an immoderate roar of laughter. 'Begad Whit' says he 'I thought every minute you'd have the Major trembling on a daisy.'

'So I would' says I 'only it was his own fault, it was him showed the white feather.'

I would pistol him that minute' (says Mr W to me) 'if he didn't apologise.'

This evening Mr W said to me again that Jas. Davis should buy me a commission, that the government were in want of money now and not to let the opportunity pass by. 'Tell him that you will buy your own outfit and that you will not make any claim on him or Davistown after that. You can turn it in your mind but if I was you I wouldn't let it pass the morning.'

Ah, it was little Mr W knew James Davis.

Davistown, Friday, August 5th 1859.

After breakfast my brother James and I went across Glebe bog to the races of Raheenglass. There were some heavy showers while we were crossing the bog. They had a high pole peeled and soaped but no one could climb it. I met James Davis there. When I told him that Weir was not in Birr and I had no school he said that was what I liked, such is the unkindness of the man. He said I would have some other excuse when there would be school - I said I had schooling enough.

46.   *Eglish Lodge, 2009 (courtesy of Mr Ger Murphy)*

Davistown, Sunday, August 7th 1859.

It rained constantly all day and cleared up in the evening. No one out of our house was at church today. James Gill was at Mr W's. When I was out with him Mr W asked me to write on two pieces of paper "Meadowing to be set at Davistown on Monday the fifteenth instant." I was to put one up at the Fivealley and another at the chapel.

Mr W said he saw in the paper where there are only one or two commissions being given out without purchase. He impressed upon me that the government needed money badly and that this was the time to buy a commission. 'You'll have to buy an iron bedstead and a mattress and your mother'll have to make curtains for you. You'll have three months on full pay before you join your regiment. The way you won't go in a greenhorn or a ninnyhammer go to Birr and get a sergeant to teach you your drill for a few shillings. I joined the 86th at Newry. You may have to go to Templemore or some place in England.'

But I am afraid that Jas. Davis will not deal honestly with me. I never knew him to be fair and honest. When Mr Burriss died (husband to my grandfather Watkins's sister Catherine) he plundered all of his substance that he could lay hands on. Mrs Burriss came to live at grandfather's in Eglish till she died. I remember to hear her crying in agony of spirit and praying that her substance might melt away like the snow from those who plundered her. Will the aged and helpless widow's curse fall unavenged to the ground? Vengeance is mine sayeth the Lord. I will avenge.

Mr W called James Davis an old screwpocket and said he had his hand open to grab all the world. 'The old hop and go constant. William you don't know what it is to sit down to a mess table. You walk in with your hands behind your back and sit down in any chair you like, call for whatever you like and walk off to your room whenever you like. Your mess bill and wine bill will come in to you every month and you be punctual in paying them. There's a president and vice president there to see how long you sit at mess. You needn't sit to drink wine till you get over your difficulties. You need only drink a glass of wine and walk off to your room. If I were you I'd go up to Lelaghmore in the morning. Be up there before he is up. What can he do only refuse you - you're only a fool if you don't do something for yourself.'

Birr, Monday, August 8th 1859.

Fine. I returned to Birr. James drove the car with Margaret, Charlotte and Richard and I walked along by the side. At the Fivealley I nailed up one of Mr W's notices at the big tree at the head of the Whigsboro road. When we came near the chapel I saw I had made a mistake and had put Monday the twenty-fifth instant instead of the fifteenth. I turned back and at Jude Mulrooney's public house I got papers and pen and wrote two proper advertisements and put them up.

I was at school that day for the first time since June although I was heartily tired of Weir and his school.

47.   *The Birr telescope in the 1880s*

Birr, Wednesday, August 10ᵗʰ 1859.

Fine. This morning George Stoney's funeral left Birr for Ballyboy. Some years ago he left Frankford and went to Australia. He came home again, got married, came to live in Birr, went mad and died.

Davistown, Friday, August 12ᵗʰ 1859.

Richard and I walked home after school for we came short of provisions. We left Birr at four and got home at six. At Ballynaguilsha big hill we saw my grandfather off a piece in his own field. He said I had schooling enough and it was time to do something for me. I said I liked the army. Before we parted he said 'I wish I may live to see you in some good situation, nothing in the world would give me greater pleasure. It's time to do something for you now.'

After eating my dinner I went out to Mr W's. Beck told me that he was near going to bed so I didn't go in. I got the *Warder* and was sitting on the window stool just at the door leading from the kitchen to the hall door when a large red flash of lightning passed and a little time after it a peal of thunder. I was very much frightened. What if I was cut off that instant, sudden and unprepared to stand before my judge? I stayed there for a while till the rain was over and came off in.

Davistown, Saturday, August 13ᵗʰ 1859.

Before I got up this morning I heard rain on the slates. Day fine. James went to Birr this morning with provisions. Richard and I were carried with him.

After school Margaret told me she got Mrs Marshall's school money from James Davis. It was generally very hard for Margaret to get the price of her schooling from him. He told her that we were not doing much good at school and asked was I there today. She said I had had enough of school and would go in to the army. He supposed he could get me to be a gauger. She told him I would not be a gauger but an officer in the army.

Saturday was one of Wallace's days to attend to teach drawing - Thursday the other. While we were waiting for him today a schoolfellow of mine Phil Robinson showed me a letter from the War Office nominating him to a commission when he would be prepared to pass an examination (this was in right of his brother who died in the service WD). The subjects of the examination will be Greek, Latin, French &c. After drawing I walked home by myself.

When I was out in Mr W's this evening he told me about the time he joined the regiment in Jamaica (the 33ʳᵈ after his promotion from the 86ᵗʰ WD). 'I was left with two companies in Port Royal and didn't I take a complaint in my bowels. Captain Westmore sent me to the doctor and it was intermittent fever I had. I had to lay down my head on the table with the pain in it, then that pain would go and the pain would come in my bowels and so on. But I recovered after some time.

'After about three months at Port Royal we were sent to Up Park Camp.[236] It's nine miles by water and then four and a half miles by land. We went in boats rowed by blacks. There was a spring near where we landed and we couldn't stop the men from drinking the water. Thirst is a terrible thing. Out of the one hundred and eighty men we only had seventy or eighty when we got to camp. All the others took sick from drinking the water, we had to leave them by the way in twos and threes under the _____ trees', (Mr W mentioning the name of the trees but I forget WD). 'So isn't thirst a terrible thing. The only way to avoid fever in the West Indies is to live temperate and not expose yourself to the sun. The men there drink all the rum they can lay their hands on & it sets them mad. They stay out with their regiments on foreign service for ten years. Then return for five before being sent out again. Drafts are sent out from the depot to replace the men that die.'

Mr W told me that he often had to attend two funerals a day. He recommended to me a book called *Six Months in the West Indies* by a young man of the name of Colderidge [sic].[237]

---

236   Up Park Camp, Kingston, Jamaica.

237   Nelson Coleridge, *Six months in the West Indies in 1825* (1826).

Before I came in Mr W earnestly advised me to go up and see the lame fellow about the commission. I said I'd go up Monday morning with the excuse I wanted stationary.

Davistown, Sunday, August 14th 1859.

Fine. I was at Eglish. Mr W was out with people about the meadowing for some time. I was with him in the parlour when James came for me and I returned to our house. Mother said she had met the lame fellow up near Jack Brien's and that he was looking for me. When I heard this I went back to Mr W's, determined that if James Davis wanted me he might look for me. Mr W remarked to me about all the horses out in our field. We had at this time - as always when we have good grass - a whole lot of James Davis's horses. I said that for want of a horse to carry us we might walk to church. 'It's not right to have all them horses there and the cattle and sheep left to starve all year round. Your poor father should have left you more power. Your mama ought to have more authority.'

One came in and said James Davis was abroad in the lawn with Rigney. Says Mr W to me 'Don't you stir till he comes in. I think that fellow does be thinking while he's asleep on the bargains he will make the next day. He goes to church and stays there as long as Healy but what does he be thinking of ? It's not his prayers at any rate!'

By and by Rigney came in to say that Jas. Davis wanted to see Mr W so he went out to the hall door while I remained in the parlour. After saluting Mr W he addressed him as Sir, (here is the lame fellow's hypocrisy, in Mr W's absence he only calls him Abey WD). He wanted three acres of meadowing saying that he wanted it 'for these people here abroad' meaning us. I suppose he told Mr W this to show how careful he was of our affairs but Mr W knew he was a dissembler.

Mr W said five pounds, the lame fellow said four pounds. He went to walk through it and came in to the parlour when he was done. When he saw me there he seemed astonished. Beck came in to give him some whiskey. He would not give more that four pounds for the meadow saying that it would perhaps make pasture but not meadow for it would run through the rake. Mr W said there would be plenty here tomorrow who would take it and James Davis was so afraid of losing it offered him four pounds and ten shillings. Mr W said 'I'll never be a Quaker' and told him he might have it for that. Although Mr W intended speaking to him to buy me a commission he could not for the lame fellow stayed only a few minutes.

MAIN STREET, BANAGHER.

48.   *The town of Banagher in the early 1900s*

Birr, Monday, August 15th 1859.

Was fine. James Davis with his clark overtook me on the high road this morning in a gig, I suppose going to the fair of Cloghan. I got no chance to speak with him he was in such haste. Today I gave James the Goldsmith's[238] *History of England* to bring home to Mr W.

Davistown, Saturday, August 20th 1859.

Was fine and part of the day warm. James, who was in with the ass and car told Richard and I to go to Madden's where the lame fellow was waiting for us. There he gave us a tumbler of porter each. Then we were to spend the day haymaking in Fortle. I walked out the Mile Tree and Kingsboro road till I came to Syngefield corner where Richard and he overtook me in the gig and I got up. We left the pony in Kingsboro yard and went down to the moor near the old castle of Fortle. This is a place the lame fellow got not long before about two miles from Birr. About seven Richard went home with the lame fellow. Jack Brien, Tom Rourke - a chap of Jas. Davis's, and I, went across the fields in a common car, out beyond the Killyon road and home by Killyon and Rath and Curraghmore lane. We got home before the lame fellow.

---

238   Oliver Goldsmith c 1730-1774. Graduated from Trinity College, Dublin, 1750, author of *The Vicar of Wakefield* and other works including a number of histories. Source: Margaret Drabble, *Oxford companion to English literature* (1985) p. 401.

Davistown, Sunday, August 21ˢᵗ 1859.

Was fine approaching to warm. Margaret and Richard walked to Eglish, I did not go. Lizzy went to Curraghmore and was carried with the churchgoers of that house. As soon as these left home James and I thought to bathing. We went accordingly to a part of the river of Broughal at the back of Clontyglass called Sandy Banks, stripped off our clothes and got in. I could make but little attempt to swim, I could give only one stroke and no more without sinking. But as the place was of no great depth we were safe.

After coming from bathing I went out to Mr W's. I read the *Warder* and an American paper called the *Weekly Reville* sent to Mr W by the McBrides from the town of St Charles in the United States. In this paper there was an advertisement stating that one of them (I think William, there are three of them WD) had opened his new store with $20,000 worth of goods (£4,000 WD). Mr W frequently got papers from his McBride nephews. I have seen four of the McBrides - Henry who remains at home, Margaret who went some years ago to Australia, John and George. John followed the business of butcher for some time in Birr although it was more from whimsical fancy than from necessity. He afterwards went to St. Charles to his brother William. George also went to St. Charles a year before this. This was also a whim for he could live comfortably at home. He went by Galway since the time that Lever established his packets there. I never saw William who was the first to settle in St. Charles.

Today Peter Molloy was at Mr W's and agreed with him for a half acre of meadow for I think twenty five shillings. Mr W said if it was to be done again he wouldn't give John Camon an inch of ground. He gave him good ground for potatoes and he wouldn't sow them early.

Later he said to me 'I saw the Duke of Cumberland once and had a couple of bows from him. I was after coming home from the West Indies and had a nice fellow of the name of Bligh with me in London. We stopped at the Salopian Hotel near Charing Cross. Bligh wished to go on a walking tour through Scotland - I wanted to return to Ireland. We both went to the Horse Guards[239] to ask for leave. It's called the Horse Guards because there are two Dragoons on horseback with swords drawn guarding the gate - one on each side.

'We wrote our names in a book there to see the Adjutant General and went back the next day. The waiting room was full of books and you can read or sit down while you wait but when your name is called you must run. When I went in Sir Herbert was sitting at a table covered with letters. I walked in bold and he shook hands with me.
"Mr Whitfield, are you anything to Captain Whitfield of the 18ᵗʰ?"
'I am a relation of his, Sir Herbert' says I.

---

239   The building in Whitehall which was the headquarters of the commander in chief of the British army. Source: *NE*, vol. 7, p. 222.

"I had the pleasure of seeing him here once. Well, Mr Whitfield, what do you wish me to do for you?"

'Sir Herbert, I have been out in the West Indies these two years and I'm burned and I'd wish for a few months leave of absence'.

(This was probably when Mr W was after coming from Barbados after getting promotion into the 33rd for I think that when he told me last Sunday that he was in the West Indies four years it was Jamaica not Barbados he meant. He was abroad with the 86th first in the windward isles and in Jamaica with the 33rd. He joined the 33rd in Burnley, Lancashire WD).

"If you go to the depot you'll get leave of absence there."

'I'm aware of that but I'm passing through town and it would inconvenience me to go to the depot.'

'Then a servant came to the door and announced the Duke of Cumberland so I retired for a few minutes. I met the Duke coming in and he bowed to me and I to him. He had a little blue frock coat and black silk buttons on it. The Adjutant General gave me four months leave of absence after. I think the Captain Whitfield of the 18th was a first cousin of my father. 'Sir Herbert was a son of one of the unmarried daughters of George the 3rd. Taylor was his surname. Another son of one of these unmarried daughters was Sir Willoughby who came out to Jamaica a Major General, he inspected us at Up Park Camp.

'You'd get your dinner cheaper in London than you would in Frankford. Walk up without ceremony and the waiter would be there and tell you what was for dinner. There'd be a speaking trumpet down to the cook and he'd order up a plate of mutton or beef and you'd get three potatoes, two peeled and one not and a cut of bread for one and six and three pence more if you got plum pudding. Give the waiter a penny and he'll thank you for it.' I asked Mr W why was one of the potatoes not peeled but he didn't know.

About this time word came from the kitchen that Rody Mahon wanted to see Mr W about the meadowing. (Rody is brother to Joe the smith WD.) But Mr W and he could not make an agreement about it.

From our discourse this evening I computed the following. That Mr W remained at home till 1816 when he was about eighteen. He was on half pay to the 8th West Indian till 1827 when he was about twenty nine. He then spent two years in the 86th and six years in the 33rd retiring at about the age of thirty seven. I think Mr W married in Kinnitty while he was on half pay and lived there for a time. He also spent some time there after leaving the army before coming to Davistown where he lived for twenty three years. He died at about sixty years.[240]

Mr W said he would try and get the lame fellow in while he was at the hay and talk to him about me. 'I'll tell him that you will pay him twenty pounds a year out of your pay as an officer until the £450 is paid. And if he shuts his eyes and says "I have no money"' (Mr W stuttering in imitation of him

---

240   See Appendix 3 for details of Mr Whitfield's' army service.

WD) 'I'll say if you haven't the money you can get it. All he cares about is selling cattle and wool & keeping poor men to their work.'

Birr, Thursday, August 25th 1859.

Fair of Birr. Morning foggy, day fine. This morning Richard and I left Birr before five and met Jack Brien and another with sheep near Syngefield's gate as the lame fellow had told us to do yesterday. The other man turned back and we three drove the sheep into Birr by about seven. The lame fellow sold some of them to Davis of Kilnaparsons and I and Jack Brien drove them to Madden's yard. Here James Davis gave me a shilling as I went to school. Richard who had no school remained with the sheep that were unsold and did not come to the lodgings till after eight at night.

I saw Anne Flanagan (the potter's daughter) in Birr and she told me that my uncle Richard who is about one year married had a young son yesterday.

49.	*The town of Ferbane about 1930*

50.   *The town of Kilcormac about 1900*

Davistown, Saturday, August 27th 1859.

There was a few drops of rain. Fearful that there would be lightning I did not leave Birr with the others but was home as soon as them at any rate.

Mr W had not spoken to the lame fellow about me. He said James Davis was in Ballinnacarrig today mowing oats (a place he lately got beyond Ballyboy). Mr W asked me to give a message to John Abraham in Eglish tomorrow. Abrahams are a family of respectable farmers from the Queen's County who hold land in Eglish. 'Tell him' (says Mr W), 'that I have seven or eight cocks of hay and they are tormenting me for them in twos and threes all week. Tell him I'll keep them for him altogether. I'll give them to him for less than the value.'

On this day as I was coming from Birr I met my grandfather and I remarked to him that there was a young son to be a papist if he lived. He said he never saw it and didn't wish to see it. I told him there was a photographer in Birr that would take his likeness for a shilling and he could send it to Ellen as she had asked. He said he would come in on Monday and call for me.[241]

---

241   A Mr Ilvie was advertising photographic portraits at 5s and upwards in Birr in June 1858 – see *King's County Chronicle*, 16 June 1858

Davistown, Sunday August 28th 1859

Was fine. I was in Eglish. I told John Abraham that Mr W wished to sell him his hay, but he was a clown and very improperly gave me no answer. He only said it would be hard to get hay this year and that Henry McBride told him that Mr W had all his hay sold. John Abraham is in my opinion an ignorant boor.

When I told Mr W about it he said no more of it. For some time past accounts appeared in the *Warder* of the imprisonment and trial of Dr. Smethurst in London for the murder of Miss Banks so as to come by her money. He has been found guilty and sentenced to death. Mr W had an aversion to anyone being hanged and hoped that he would be transported. In the *Warder* today we saw where the day of his execution had been put back and this is thought to be a sign that he will be transported.

Beck's sister Frances (who I believe came from the union[242] many years ago to Mr W's, she was then about eighteen and exceedingly immoral in words and deeds for her years) came in and said that a lot of little brats were at the apples in the garden and wouldn't go out of it for her. Mr W went out and they went away.

Later several of Beck's acquaintances were in the kitchen together with William Barber who was playing the flute (a fellow of two faces and two ways). In the parlour Mr W asked me was it Johnny Tooher playing. He began out of this to talk about Jack Carroll who he said was the best piper ever. 'He used to live in Frankford. I remember seeing him when I was a little fellow. He was blind. If you met him on the road and asked him what o'clock was it he'd put his hand on the dial plate and tell you to the minute.

'One time the Queen's County Militia' (I think it was the Queen's County Militia Mr W told me) 'was in Frankford and Colonel La Touche sent for Carroll. John Gill told me this story.' (A plain man many years dead, father to James Gill WD.)'Says La Touche "Well, are you Carole?"' (Mr W pronouncing it Carole in imitation of La Touche WD.)
"I am your honour."
"You can play on that bagpipes?"
"I can play a little."
"What tune can you play?"
"I can play the Fox Hunter's Jig."
"Well, wait till you hear my pipes play the Fox Hunter's Jig." When he was done – "Well, how do you like that?" says La Touche.
"O", says Carroll "I'd put the chanter under my legs and play it as well."
And when Carroll played it La Touche was so pleased with him that he paid his own piper the next day and sent him home. Carroll was a very haughty fellow. There was only a few houses he'd play at, he was independent. He

242   The workhouse

played for the Bernard family [of Castle Bernard]. The grandfather of the present Bernard had Carroll to play at a ball one night and insisted on getting a man to help him. Carroll got them to send for Jack Daly from Frankford but he didn't want anyone at all. He tied the neck of the chanter the way no wind would get in and put Daly to squeeze it. After a time a fine lady came up and said she never heard two men playing better!'

Mr W told me something about how Carroll used to teach someone to play the pipes and he'd never begin to teach him till all the family be in bed but I regret that I do not remember the particulars.

Later he talked of the army and the disgust he had for drilling - in his opinion a useless pastime. 'The only drill ever I liked was the manual and platoon exercise.' I asked him of what did the manual and platoon exercise consist. He told me it was firing in a field. 'William if they can't fire in a field how can they fire when they're before the enemy. You say ready, present, fire. The last word was dropped when I was there. When you'd say fire maybe some of them wouldn't have their aim taken and the shot would go up in the air or down in the ground. When you only say ready and present they fire when they are ready.'

This evening before I came in Beck came in to the parlour and said that James Davis was there abroad and wouldn't come in. By and by Mr W asked me where he was now. I said he was hopping off near the blue gate. He bid me go and tell him to come in, but I foolishly said that I was afraid that he wouldn't come back (for I did not like to speak to the lame fellow at all). Mr W told Frances Healy to bring him in but she would not. 'O,' says Mr W 'I'll catch him next week.'

Birr, Monday, August 29th 1859.

Was wet in the morning, the day generally showery and cool. Richard and I walked to Birr taking our time so that we did not reach Birr till after eleven half an hour. Even the car with the others did not get in till after ten. Charlotte, Richard and Margaret went to school while I remained absent. I saw my grandmother in the town and James carried her home in the car.

Parsonstown Classical and English School

Mr. Brady T.C.D. Principal

Mr. Brady begs to inform the inhabitants of Parsonstown, and its vicinity, that he has taken the extensive premises in Cumberland-street (opposite the Church), lately occupied by Mr. Weir where business shall be resumed (D.V.) on Monday the 16th day of January 1860, when the punctual return of pupils is requested.

Mr. Brady has secured the services of well qualified assistants and assures his many kind friends that the utmost exertions shall be used to merit a continuance of their approval.
Parsonston January 11th 1860.

(E)   Notice for the Brady school from the King's County Chronicle, 11 January 1860

CHAPTER 11

September 1859

William despairs of school, a photographer in Birr, sad tales of illness and death, haggling over the hay, a rare glimpse of Mrs Whitfield, a scathing summary of some relatives, a nutting foray, William and little brother James succumb to temptation, Captain Young offers advice, uncle Francis has a terrible injury, aunt Sally loses her mind and the court-martial of Sergeant Tremble of Kinnitty.

Birr, Thursday, September 1st 1859.

Was fine but not warm. In the middle of the day my grandfather called for me at Weir's. Weir followed me down to see was it the lame fellow for on this day and many days before I had not learned a word of a lesson for I knew that I had learning enough for as much as I wanted. At my age every day spent at school was so much time thrown away. I asked my grandfather would he get two likenesses taken as I wanted one but he said no for he had to borrow the three shillings to get the one done and he was only doing it to gratify Ellen. Later he brought the likeness to our lodgings and it was a very correct one only his eyes weren't taken clear and the hair was whiter than his own. We prevailed upon him to stay for a dinner of fried bacon and potatoes.

He told me he had five brothers, Humphrey, Tom, Sam, George and Frederick. Humphrey the eldest had planned with Robin Hackett (Micky Hackett's brother and a libertine who lived in the mill of Eglish WD) to go off and enlist in the militia where he got to be sergeant in the Life Company. When he left them he went to Liverpool where he took a situation on board a ship bound for Jamaica. The night before they landed he took a pain in his head and died a short time after. A man in Liverpool wrote to grandfather about his death.

Tom was a clerk in Dublin. He took sick there, came home and died in the parlour.

Sam built the house that George Perry lives in (George Perry is a shopkeeper at the corner of Church Lane in Birr WD). He went to America forty years ago on the 21st of April 1819. He was alive and well when William wrote a year ago. He was eighty five yesterday having been born on the last day of August 1774.

George had a shop in Tullamore and was a hatter. Grandfather served his time there. He died in London. Frederick died when he was nine. There were three sisters. Catherine was Mrs Burriss. Ellen was married to Tom Alexander. (NB An inferior with whom she run away. The Alexanders live above Birr. I have a faint remembrance of seeing Mrs Alexander at our house - Davistown. She is now buried with her husband's family. I have heard my mother say that Mrs Burriss disliked her for making a bad match.)

Charlotte was the other sister whom my sister is called after. She died when she was eleven years of age. She took a swelling in her thigh and old Dr Kelly attended her (the father of Charley Kelly who lives a few doors from our lodgings WD). He put some poison to it that made a hole and all the substance of her body came out of it.

I wanted to go up on Saturday to have a look at the book where all their ages are written down, but grandfather said no that there was an o Caun in it (a child WD). Sally Kinsella told me that they would call it William. Better for them to call it Peter or Martin. (It was afterwards called William WD.)

Davistown, Saturday, September 3rd 1859.

Day fine. I waited in Birr after Richard went home hoping to see the lame fellow and be released from the frightful waste of my time at school. Margaret waited also as she wanted books but did not like to ask Miss Gunn for them because she wasn't paid for books we got long before. When we saw the lame fellow she went out after him, telling him about the books and showing him the bill. He said he would pay her after the fair of Banagher and gave her two shillings to buy turf &c for next week. I did not speak to him. My mother was in Birr and she, Margaret, Charlotte and James went home in the ass's car. I walked home calling at my grandfather's on the way. He showed me an old *Scripture Concordance*[243] bearing the name of my great grandfather Samuel Watkins 1762. On the front flyleaves of it was recorded in a fine old hand the date of my great grandfather's marriage to his wife Margaret, also the successive birthdates of their nine children. Grandfather had in his turn written the time of his marriage and the days on which his six children were born. While I was writing Frederick's age into a book he told me that 'He died in a bed that was there', pointing to the corner. 'He died of some disorder that was going through the country. It was well for him that he died so soon while he was young and innocent.'

Some time before my uncle William wrote from Brantford C.W. saying that my granduncle Sam had built his tomb and inscribed it all but the date and

---

243   A dictionary or index of all the important words in the Bible alphabetically arranged for the purpose of finding passages and of comparing the meanings of words. Source, *NE*, vol. 4, p. 223.

wished to know his age. William said that his uncle Sam had all his family settled round him in trade, that he lived on the banks of Lake Huron (I think WD) and spent his time fishing on the lake.

On my way home near Jude Mulrooney's public house at the Fivealley I found two little parcels tied together. The larger one was in brown paper and the other was in white paper. I suppose half a pound of sugar and a half-ounce of tea. I gave the parcels to Mrs Gill who was in a car outside Jude's. Near Joe Mahon's the car belonging to James Gill overtook me and also a cart belonging to old Bill Kelly of the mill. Cashin, Bill Kelly's boy asked me up but if I'd known what was afterwards to happen I would not on any account have consented to sit on that cart. It was to the owner of that cart's mill that Mr W's oats was sent and concealed the day he died. From what I have seen of the lower orders of the Irish they are one and all of them a band of unfaithful thieves and robbers ready at all times to rob and plunder and as an act of piety, to cut the throat of a Protestant. Bigotedly ignorant, most of them are ungrateful thieves, liars and slanderers. I write this from sad experience.

Davistown, Sunday, September 4th 1859.

Was fine. I was not at Eglish. I went out to Mr W's before twelve but the paper was not brought from Frankford. After a while Mary Dulleny called on her way from mass with it. In the supplement I saw that Smethurst[244] the murderer had been given a respite and that Pearse [sic] Creagh would contest the county at the election next year.

After dinner I strolled down to Cash's boteen where James was enjoying his childhood - leaping one of the asses (for we had mother and foal WD) over a stick that was laid across the two ditches of the lane.

That evening while I was at Mr W's a brother of Johnny Dooly's of Glebe called to look at the hay. He asked for some spring water and Mr W gave him some with some whiskey in it. Dooley would not give the twenty four shillings a cock that Mr W asked saying that two of the cocks were heated. Mr W said that was no harm, it was only the freshness of the grass. He told us that in England they put fresh grass in hay to make it heat and offered to make up two other cocks for Dooley. But Dooley, as if he paid Mr W a compliment by coming, said that as he came he'd buy them all as they were but they were too dear. Shortly after Rigney came in and after him Beck with an escort of her companions (to say no worse), Pat Rogers, young Will Troy and James Gill. Dooley was still peddling about the hay. He wanted Mr W to give him the seven cocks for seven pounds and for him to give back seven shillings out of that.

244   This English trial created controversy at the time. Dr Smethurst received a pardon of the conviction for murder. He was later found guilty of a bigamous marriage to Miss Banks and was sentenced to one year's imprisonment. Source: Minnesota Law Library bibliography.

'O, I won't be peddling with you, I'll give it to you for that!' says Mr W and the deal was made. Dooley went off and Mr W retired to the parlour. Young Troy began to play the flute.

Mr W may have been censured for letting his house be resorted by people such as these but he is perfectly blameless. They were not brought there by his wish but by Beck. He participated not in their sports but withdrew to his parlour where it was his custom to be holy in all his conversation, and if any degree of criminality be attached to these meetings in his house I protest that he was entirely innocent. But why did he permit them to assemble in his house? He did so because he wished to live peacefully and agreeably with all. He did not wish to shut his door against them and although they sinned in Sabbath breaking he did not dare to judge them but left it to God and their own conscience. He knew not their villainy. He did not think that they should plunder his effects when he would be gone. Of any wrong which was committed under his roof I protest that he was entirely innocent. His character has been blackened for putting away his wife, but he never put her away. It was he who once told me that she was a great trouble to him. Slanderous lies were circulated of him. His wife would upbraid him with unfaithfulness, but I believe in my heart that he was innocent. My mother told me that Mrs W would go to Frankford and coming home a miserable old woman since dead (the mother of Art Molloy, an illegitimate son) used to follow her from where she lived in Freagh to Mr W's lodge telling her lies of Mr W's inconstancy. Then when she'd come home she'd upbraid him with what she heard. He would never say a word but stand up from the table and walk out. Then he disdained of speaking to his wife. For years he never spoke to her. At last of her own consent she went to live in Kinnitty where Mr W supported her with a yearly sum until his death. She left shortly after Beck came to the house. Previous to this there was a servant at Mr W's house who had an illegitimate child by a manservant of Mr W's. He sent away the servants and the child was sent to Pat Cash's of Clontyglass, since gone to America. Because it was born under his roof Mr W would not let it starve and paid for its support till it died a short time after. The world while it lasts will be given to lying and slandering, thus they slandered the upright of every age even the Lord of Glory. That devouring wolf Healy, that greedy dog, the mercenary pastor, the hireling of the Gospel slandered my friend.

When Mr W was done eating his white bread and eggs I asked him did he think the lame fellow would ever marry. 'I don't think he will' (says Mr W). 'He was full sure he would be married to one of his cousin's daughters one time and she wouldn't have him. That was the time he had Ballincard, that's what made your papa give him the house part. No, nor I think John will never marry.' (From the time Minor Mitchell left Ballincard till Maxwell came James Davis and my father possessed it jointly WD.) I gave it as my opinion that John would never marry and that the three of them were housed up in an unnatural way.

I believe my grandmother had a family of twelve. My father was the eldest.

Then there is Elizia married to James Whitfield, she is a backbiter. Sarah another sister married his brother Francis Whitfield.

Richard is a rogue. He was going to Curraghmore early one morning and a yew belonging to people of the name of Mahon was after yeaning twins in a field he passed through. He was accused of taking one of the lambs and hiding it under a furze in James Davis's field till he'd be coming back. But Richard Davis was seen passing the field and the lamb was found and he was prosecuted at Birr quarter sessions[245] on charge of stealing it. My mother told me his friends got a packed[246] jury and he was thus acquitted. Once, a long time ago, Beck asked Mr Whitfield in the kitchen in my presence did he think Richard Davis stole the lamb? Mr W said he was afraid he did.

Drought Davis died. I heard he was a fine young man but I don't remember him.
Chusen also died when she was young.
Ellen died in my memory in Ballincard. I was in Aghancon at her funeral.
Tom went to America with his family from Lelaghmore in the spring of 1849. He was given to drinking, but my father looked upon him as the most honest of the family. He used to write from America, but none of his letters were answered.
Mary Anne is a backbiter.
John is a liar and a boaster. He lives at Curraghmore with my grandmother.
James is a rogue and unprincipled.
Davy also lives at Curraghmore, but he talks of going to Kingsboro. It would be long to enumerate half their acts of meanness and dishonesty to us since my father's death.
The discourse with Mr W turned upon Wesley. Athlone was Wesley's favourite place, Mountmellick and Birr the worst. In his journal of Tuesday 3rd of May 1748 I find the following – 'I rode to Birr twenty miles from Athlone. The key to session house not to be found I declared the grace of our Lord Jesus Christ in the street to a dull rude senseless multitude. Many laughed the greater part of the time - some went away just in the middle of a sentence. And yet when one cried out (a Carmelite friar, clerk of the priest) 'You lie, you lie!' the zealous Protestants cried out 'Knock him down!' and it was no sooner said than done. I saw some bustle but knew not what was the matter till the whole was over. In the evening we rode to Ballyboy. There being no house that could contain the congregation I preached here also in the street. I was afraid in a new place there would be but few in the morning but there was a considerable number, such a blessing as I had scarce found since landing in Ireland.' The journal for Easter day April 10th 1748 says

---

245   Local court held once every quarter.

246   A rigged jury.

'Never was such a congregation seen before at the sacrament in Athlone. I preached at three, an abundance of papists flocked to hear. The priest seeing that his command did not avail came in person at six and drove them away before him like a flock of sheep.'

I told Mr W that my grandfather had five brothers and three sisters and of all of them there was none alive but his brother Sam that went to America in 1819 and now lives near New London. Mr W said his brother John lived not far from there at a place called Farnham. He liked to sit in his garden watching the men working. One of his sons who is called after Mr W[247] came to see Mr W some time ago. He had been in England, Barbados (where his brother had died) and Ireland and out of the three he liked Ireland the best. He wished to remain here but had to return to America.

'When I was in Barbados' says Mr W, 'Major Richardson and I would go bathing nearly every morning to a place called the shark's hole. We would take a calabash with us to wash the sand from our feet after we getting up. The calabash is made of a big nut cut in half and they make cups of them. The black women would walk along with a calabash on their heads full of eggs or anything and they would never put a hand to it. We would tease them that we would knock them off.

'One time when we got a rout to Antigua, Montserrat and St. Kitts Major Richardson said I could go with Captain Stuart to St. Kitts. Major Richardson was a nice fellow, you'd live with him forever. He would come into my room to drink punch. He'd say "I can't stand the noise and talk of them fellows there below, they give me a pain in the head." At any rate when I was being sent to St. Kitts my brother George who was a merchant in Barbados said that pistareens[248] were all in vogue in St. Kitts and he kept all that came in for me. Just before we went the packet came in with stores and newspapers and the like. A nice fellow of the name of Holt saw in one of the papers that I had got promotion to the 33rd and he run all the way down to tell me. I had to get a fatigue party to get all of my things out of the ship. Major Richardson gave me gold for my pistareens and Johnson from Cork offered me £100 to go to the depot in my place but I wouldn't take it and scuttled home. I might as well have taken the £100 for I wasn't home five months before I was sent out again. A bloody villain of the name of Rolers wouldn't go out, he went on half pay sooner than go out. I had to go in his place.' (Mr W went to Barbados in Captain Cannon's ship *Brig Robert* and came home in the *William Harris*. The *William Harris* was an old rotten ship that had been going about the islands gathering old military stores to bring home. He went to Jamaica in *Stephen's Ship* and came home in the *Robin Castle* WD.)

I asked Mr W who got in his place when he retired. 'A nice young fellow

247   Abraham.

248   A Spanish coin used in the U.S. and the West Indies. By this time it was no longer in common usage. Source: *Collins English dictionary*.

of the name of Ironside from England. He died of consumption five months later, about your age. He liked nothing better than to keep a horse. He had a little fellow he called his tiger to look after his horse.'

Before I came in Mr W said he would speak to the lame fellow if he saw him about getting me a commission. He asked me to get him a pound of cheese tomorrow in Birr.

Birr, Monday, September 5th 1859.

Was fine, evening wet. We all left the house at the same time. Richard and I kept up with the ass's car till we came to Ballynaguilsha big hill when we began to lose sight of it. Old Dan Molloy from Ballindown (a Protestant) overtook us and asked us up on his car. He said he remembered when that road was made and long enough before. I understood from him that the road from Birr to Dublin that time was by the lane at Tom Connor's on by Fagan's, out at Sally Kinsella's, across the present road, by Ann Connor's cabin, out by my grandfather's door, and crossed out on the present road at the bridge of Eglish. From that it was as it is now. He told me that people used to go to Dublin that time with four stone of oats in a sack. He remembered my grandfather's brother Sam to be a good horseman in old Captain Drought's company of Horse Volunteers in the rebellion of '98. Sam also kept a tan-yard in Birr where Perry lives now.

In Birr I heard that Weir was gone to Limerick since Saturday so I did not go to school today. Wat Keating the assistant taught a few children that attended. Keating, (about twenty years) was a son to Hackett's miller at Whiteford. He used to teach the junior classes English. Richard got Mr W's cheese from Meara's which we packed in some hay and sent home with James when the ass was rested.

I saw five fellows going out towards Eglish to pick nuts - two Lloyds, sons of an army officer (deceased)[249] and three of the scholars. There was Meara,[250] a Roman Catholic country fellow and Shep Smith a little scamp of a fellow generally on the streets. He went to Trinity when Weir left Birr. The fifth was Phil Robinson[251] the only one of them I had any regard for; he was a nice little fellow. I found everyone else in the school to be deceitful to me. I went out the road with them sooner than be confined in Birr. We were

---

249 Possibly Lieutenant Colonel H. Lloyd D.L., Gloster, Shinrone, *SD 1846*. In Patrick Meehan's book (see footnote 86), Lieut. Col. Lloyd is said to have died in 1860 so this is possibly not him as William refers to him as deceased. But perhaps H. Lloyd was alive in 1859 when William wrote the original notes and was dead by the time he transcribed them into this journal, just like his comments on the death of Mr Whitfield. However Lloyd's age at this time (born 1782) suggests that the Lloyd referred to by William may not have been this man.

250 This boy may have been related to one of the Meara families who owned businesses in the town at this time.

251 Possibly son of Thomas Robinson Esq, Cumberland Street, Birr, *SD1856*.

leaping over drains and ditches till we came to Dan Molloy's when a little fellow overtook us driving a mule's car. All but Meara and I leaped up and every time we would go to get up they would push us down. They got down at Tom Connor's house and we went up the old road where an old woman directed us to Clughill scrub. This was where the nuts grew, but she said she thought they were nearly all pulled. We only got a few handfuls and sat down on the grass to eat them. A little distance from us there was a great big hill. When I was going to Eglish school I used to hear my aunt Ellen (my school fellow) talking of it, Scernaboragh.[252] It is about a mile at the back of Ryalls's house. It is the highest hill I saw yet.

They all craved me to go to the Fivealley and get them a glass of spirits each promising to pay me tomorrow. When we came to Jude's [Mulrooney's] I called for five glasses of spirits and a glass of cordial for Meara - a teetotaller. I told her I'd pay her in a few days, as to the others I told them I would bear the expense. We drank it in a room next to Carten's of the Post Office. They all said it was the worst of the sort ever they tasted. Jude is notorious for keeping her spirits bad. After this they made up two pence to buy a loaf of bread. When it was eaten Smith said his father (NB. An attorney in Birr. WD)[253] had given him a shilling to buy a book and that he would buy some ale with it. He got half a gallon of ale which like the spirits was the vilest compound ever invented. (I was always fond of ale or porter but never liked spirits WD.) Meara who had spent some time standing outside looking at us through the window went off. The bill was one shilling and five and a half pence.

Later we went into the graveyard and from there up to the top of Ballynaguilsha big hill. On the way to Birr we were overtaken by five car loads of hay coming from Duggan's of Eglish Castle. Robinson and Smith and one of the Lloyds (they used to call him Prince Lloyd) got on top of one of the loads. Fred Lloyd and I had to walk, but it was raining by this time and we were as well off walking as we would have been on the car. Lloyd was very angry at not being let up but I took it in good parts. When they got down in Birr they were twice as stiff and sore as we were, both from the bad drink we got and the rain which fell.

252   Peak 273 ft

253   Probably attorney John Smith, John's Mall, Birr, *SD 1856*.

The departure of Mr Weir from Birr in November 1859

I beg to inform the public that in consequence of the delicate state of my wife's health, I shall be obliged to close my school in this town on Thursday next.

I take this opportunity of recommending to the support of the public, Mr. Brady, a gentleman who, for many years, has satisfactorily conducted a public school in this town. He is a man of high acquirements as a scholar, long experience as a teacher, unobtrusive in his manners and utterly devoid of that vulgar pedantry, which always characterises the presuming impostor who, mentally conscious of his own inferiority tries to force himself into public notice, by heralding his own praises and laying claims to knowledge which he does not possess, where he can do it with safety.

The few pupils that came to me from Mr. Brady's school, were far better grounded both in Classics and English then those who came from any other establishment in this or the neighbouring counties.

In making these remarks I wish it to be distinctly understood that I have no interested motive, but merely wish to serve a brother teacher and one whom I consider to be a man of merit.

The public are, I believe, aware that I have for sometime past, decided on leaving this town for Limerick. It is not from want of support that I take this step, but from want of sufficient accommodation to conduct my business in a satisfactory and respectable manner, I have lately refused to take several pupils, both boarders and day scholars, and for several months past, I have had all my spare hours occupied in reading with private pupils.

During my residence here I have tried to do my duty, both to my pupils and to the public, as conscientiously as I could, and if I have failed in giving satisfaction to all parties it is not from want of good intentions on my part. I have been instrumental in preparing a good number of young men for the Universities and other examinations, and I leave after me several promising pupils who I have trained up to this time and who, if their education continues to be properly conducted will I hope hereafter distinguish themselves in whatever career of life it may please the Lord to place them.

N. B. As I have some pressing demands to meet both in this town and elsewhere which I am anxious to liquidate at once, I request that those who are indebted to me will settle with me before Friday next and I cannot help remarking that some parties who have repeatedly promised me payment against a certain day and as frequently disappointed me are treating me very badly knowing as they do the circumstances in which I am placed. The labourer is worthy of his hire and the labour of a teacher who discharges his duty conscientiously ought to be remunerated without grudge or delay.

James W. Weir, A.B., ex-Sch., T.C.D.

(F)   Notice of the departure of James Weir from Birr, from the *King's County Chronicle* of 2 November 1859

Birr, Tuesday, September 6th 1859.

Was generally showery. Weir did not come home. Keating taught some of the junior classes. About twelve o'clock a little fellow of the name of Hill (the sub-inspector's son in Birr WD) came to our lodgings and said that Weir sent him to tell me to come say my French lessons. I went and waited for him to come downstairs but I at last found out that Weir had not come back at all, that they had only played a trick on me and I came off. We rightly supposed that Weir was all this time looking for a school in Limerick.

Birr, Wednesday, September 7th 1859.

Some showers through the day. Weir returned by one of the evening trains. James brought provisions to us with the ass and car. He told me he was to bring home a hive of honey from Madden's for the Curraghmore people and we planned to deprive them of some of it. When he was going home I went outside the town with him and between us we devoured a sidecomb of it.

This morning Margaret left Birr for Eglish to collect money there for the Society For Promoting Christianity Amongst The Jews. She went to Mrs Molloy's of Clonbeal, widow of the late Daniel who died April 25th 1856. (I remember I was at his funeral in Ballyboy barefooted. I met it near Clonbeal and walked to Ballyboy. I was going to school in Frankford that time to a fellow of the name of Cahill. He went mad after and his family left Frankford WD.) At Clonbeal Margaret saw one of the Misses Molloy who was watering the geraniums. She brought the card to her mama who subscribed a shilling. Margaret then went to Thomastown where Frederick Bennett gave a shilling with the remark that the Jews were the worst people in the world. The total amount collected on this card was eighteen shillings.

Birr, Friday, September 9th 1859.

Morning some wet. The weather begins to grow cool and wintery. Yesterday Weir told us he had a school in Limerick and that he would be going there in two months. Today Wallace gave me his account for a quarter's tuition in drawing - fifteen shillings and nine pence. I had not attended his lessons for some time past.

Davistown, Saturday, September 10th 1859.

Some wet. Richard was out of school before me and got a carry with Healy. I showed James Davis Wallace's bill but he said he would not pay it till Monday. Lizzy and James came to collect Margaret and Charlotte. I walked home.

After dinner I went out to Mr W's. Beck &c were out stacking oats in the orchard and I went in by the front door, the kitchen door being bolted.

'Great fellow, great fellow' (says Mr W). 'I attacked the lame fellow since, I gave him a severe attack. He said he was afraid you wouldn't pass the examination but I told him I'd make you pass. 'It was never easier to get in' says I. 'All you have to do is lodge £450 in Birr and send the receipt to Greenwood and Cox and get Colonel Bernard's letter.'
'O' says he 'I'll get Colonel Drought's letter.'
'You won't want that' says I, 'get Colonel Bernard's letter. William will pay you back twenty pounds a year and buy his own outfit. That won't be more than forty-five pounds.'
'Well I'll see about it' says he 'I'm thankful to you for speaking to me about it.'

'So now William when you go to Birr find out the Adjutant of the militia, he used to lodge at Lynn's of the square and ask him what examinations you have to pass. Or salute one of them young fellows out of the barracks and ask him. Then sit down and study for one month or ready. Leave him no hole to two or for however long need be. Then go tell him you're creep into. I laid the foundation and now you build on it, let nothing cool. If you're gazetted to the 19th you have a cousin and namesake there - John Davis's son. If you went into the 70th I'd give you a letter for Galloway that'd do you good. If you got an army list it would be worth your while. Shields's[254] would send for one for you. I got one some time ago to see where Galloway was, an old traveller of mine. He was with the 70th in India.'

---

254   John Shields, booksellers and stationers, Cumberland Sq. *SD*, 1856.

During the discourse Mr W talked of Fisher, his military tailor. 'He'll see your name in the gazette and he'll write to you telling you of his ready money prices and his credit prices. He came seventy or eighty miles to me in Gosport one time to take my measure. Get your outfit on credit and pay him when you have the money. I used to send him the money in half notes when I'd have it.'

Before I came in Mr W repeatedly warned me to leave James Davis no hole to creep into.

Davistown, Sunday, September 11th 1859.

Early this morning when very few were up I was out in Mr W's orchard looking through the trees for apples, but they were shook and I only got one or two. Mr W came out and asked me was the dew cold for I was in my bare feet. It was only a little. He shortly after went in remarking that he had a sore foot.

I was not at church today as I preferred Mr W's company to Healy's. After dinner I took a walk down Cash's field and returned to Mr W's to find him walking up and down outside the hall door. When he came into the parlour he unlocked the door opposite me on the right as I go in and brought out some apples. 'If I don't lock that door', (says Mr W) 'Albert would eat every one of them apples in a day.' I took my old seat at the corner of the table opposite Mr W. The table was opposite the parlour fire and I sat at the corner next the window and to the door of Mr W's room. Mr W sat opposite next the door to the apple room. This was where he always ate and drank his punch.

The discourse turned to the escape from drowning of Mr Alexander Carson and Mr R.W. Guinness at Castlerock as recorded in last Sunday's *Warder*. They were pulled out by the tide and narrowly escaped death when people on shore sent out a boat to rescue them. I since got the *Warder* that contains the article and see that one of the men is a brother to Rev. H.G. Guinness. I heard H.G. Guinness preach in the Presbyterian chapel, Castle Street Birr the time I was going to school to Weir while we stopped at Muirison's in '58. His sermon was very pathetic - the whole of the first psalm - the tears fell from his eyes as he spoke. He appeared to be one and twenty years old. He commented on the different progressive degrees of hardness into which the sinner enters. First walking in the counsel of the ungodly. Next standing in the way of sinners and then the perilous position of sitting in the seat of the scornful.

Mr W continued 'I think it was last March there was a vessel wrecked near Drogheda and there was a sailor on the mast' (Mr W might have told me there was more than one but I forget WD). 'They sent out two boats to try and rescue him but each time they were driven back. Then a fisherman who was in the crowd called his two sons and together they went out in their own open boat and brought the man to safety. The very minute the Lord

Lieutenant heard of it he sent the fisherman thirty pounds. He had a right to send him £1,000 - I never heard of such a brave turn.'

I said to Mr W that it was great bravery of a soldier to throw a burning shell ready to burst. 'It was often done. They put their hand to the fuse, throw it off as far as they can and lie down flat on their faces. That way it'll fly over them when it bursts. They do it at the peril of their lives.' I told Mr W I heard that in France they have a whole lot of furnaces melting metal every day and casting cannon. They are then taken out and after being filed and smoothed are put in a pit that's out of the way. Here they are filled with bricks and powder and any cannon that does not burst is proof.

'If you want to try a gun', (says Mr W) 'I'll tell you a good way. Put in a good charge then put the gun up in a tree, settle the match to the touch hole and light it. If it doesn't burst it'll do.' I suggested it would be safer to tie a long cord to the trigger and go off a good distance before pulling it.

'I was firing one day' (says Mr W) 'with the men on a hill near Newry. One of the men who was loading his rifle gave it three rams and it went off. I don't know how he escaped but he wasn't hurted. The ramrod went off and I didn't see it for a week. One of the country people found it and brought it in.' I said Art Molloy would tell you a great many stories of army deserters. 'O, Art would bother you! He'd tell you the same story forty times. He was in the 75th but he had bad eyesight. A fellow who had great eyesight was one of our sergeants when we were at Weedon one time. He was down in the village one day when the coach came in and who did he see on it only a fellow that had deserted four or five years earlier. He arrested him and he got four or five days imprisonment. We were content to have him back for he was an excellent tailor. All the men's clothes had just come down from London and we didn't know what to do with them so we put him to work on the lot.

'I'll tell you how the Fogaballaghs[255] got that name. They were fighting in Spain and their ammunition ran out and the enemy was pressing them. "Fogaballagh" says they - give them the butt end of the gun. So they did and ran them and have been called Fogaballaghs ever since.

'My brother William was out in Spain. He got an ensigncy in a black regiment - The West Indian Rangers. Through his acquaintances he got a Lieutenancy in a Spanish regiment and when he went out there he met General James Weldon Carroll from Tipperary and became his secretary. A Connaught Ranger that was in the regiment became his servant. He was a terrible rogue that never stopped thieving but my brother never said much about it as a lot of it was to his advantage.

---

255   "Faugh-a-Ballagh", the regimental motto of the Royal Irish Fusiliers. It means "Clear
         the way". Originates from an incident during the battle of Barossa on 5 March 1811 in
         Spain involving the 87th regiment (a forerunner of the Royal Irish regiment) when the
         French standard was captured. Source: Letter from The Royal Irish Fusiliers Regimental
         Museum, 29 January 2002.

'Now William if you go out to the West Indies there's nothing you'll be more fond of than bottled porter. It's very dear there, a shilling a bottle. We used to get it out ourselves and bottle it. After freight and everything we could have it at eight pence a bottle. Half an hour before you go to mess the porter bottles are laid on a stand outside the mess with an iron shade full of holes put over them. They throw water on it and let it drip down to cool them.

'I'll tell you a queer thing about St. Lucia. There's two hills just like a bottle or a sugar loaf called the Pitons[256] all covered in brushwood. One on the right and one on the left as you go into the town. When we got the island first we built the barracks on the hill on the right. The men couldn't live on it with the fever. They died in their dozens. Then we built it on the left hill and they usedn't die at all. My first cousin Freer who had a commission in a West Indian regiment went one day to see the Pitons - he took fever and died.'

About here I asked Mr W had the pensioners ensigns and Lieutenants over them. He said no that they had only one officer who paid them. 'Stoney in Birr used to pay them. I knew all his family. They're not related to the Stoneys of Frankford. They are related to the Stoneys of Portland.[257] He's married to an old acquaintance of mine. When I joined in Newry Lieutenant Ormond was acting paymaster. He was a nice little fellow and used to ask me to tea with him and his wife and daughter in the evenings and we'd play cards. Stoney joined while I was out in the West Indies and began courting Ormond's daughter. When Mrs Stoney got the letter from young Stoney asking for her consent to marry Miss Ormond she didn't know what to do. She used to be at my brother William's and he told her to write out to me to find out the Ormond's character. And so she did and I told her they were a nice proper couple and Miss Ormond a nice little girl. She withdrew her restriction when she got my letter and they were married. Lieutenant Ormond was made full paymaster when he memorialled government for it and he came out to the regiment in the West Indies. He was paymaster after Grant.'

I told Mr W that a son of Stoney's was going to Weir one time and his name was George Ormond Stoney. 'Doesn't that show I'm right!' says Mr W.

We talked of the christening today of Maxwell's child, Elinor. She had only one Godmother and one Godfather. This did not please Mr W who said there should have been more Godparents than that.

Some time before this I asked Mr W could an officer talk to a private and now he said to me 'I think you could if you wanted to and I'll tell you why. It's a thing that concerned me very much. We had a young sergeant', (I

---

256   Pitons, old volcanic peaks on the south of the island 2,619 feet high. Source: Hunter Davies, *A walk around the West Indies*. (2001), p. 287.

257   Probably the Stoneys of Portland Park, Co. Tipperary.

think Mr W said in Gosport WD) 'of the name of Tremble. He was a son of Sergeant Tremble of Kinnitty who was in the militia. There was a goodfull little scoundrel of the name of Smith and he met Sergeant Tremble drunk one night. 'Sergeant Tremble' says he, 'you're drunk.' Tremble told him he wasn't and Smith told him to go home to barracks. He said he would when he liked, that it was nothing to Smith. Smith was in coloured clothes and Tremble thought there would be nothing about it but Smith reported him. Tremble was put in the guard room to wait for a court-martial. I went to see him and he started to cry. I was going home and asked him had he any message for his family. He said he had no good message and didn't like to send a bad one. It'd make you cry to see him there. He was transported after. It was a pity. They had a right to give him three or four days imprisonment or reduce him to the ranks. There was wrong on both sides. Smith had a right to walk on by and not mind him and Tremble had a right to walk on and not stand and talk, if he did he could do nothing to him. If I had seen Tremble I would have passed him by. When I went back out he had been transported. I says to Galloway 'Ye transported Tremble.'
'Yes Whit' says he 'but not with my consent.'

'We had another sergeant in Jamaica, Sergeant Donaldson and he done some foo-faa and was reduced to the ranks. He very wisely memorialised the Colonel to let him join the New Foundland Veteran Company. He knew he'd have a better chance to rise again there.'   About here in the discourse a tinker's wife came (from Frankford I suppose WD) with a gallon which was given to be bottomed. She charged five pence for it and Beck came into the parlour to tell Mr W. He had only a shilling and I took it out to our house for change but there was none there. Beck met me in the hall as I came back in and took the shilling. By and by she came into the parlour and told Mr W she sent to another place for change although I heard her say afterwards that she went and dug five pence worth of potatoes and gave them in payment. I can't tell whether Mr W got his shilling.

It was in today's *Warder* that one of the McCauslands was home from his regiment in India. He had an ensigncy in a highland regiment. He served in India all through the mutiny and consequently his bad health. Mr W suggested I go up and ask him about the examination.

Shortly after this Mr Gill's brother Haslam from near Roscrea came in to the parlour with a girl - I suppose his sister. They were on a visit to James Gill. Mr W wanted to sell him some hay but Haslam said it was too far to draw it. By and by James Gill came in and we drank some punch, I had two glasses. It was a happy hour of my life for I drank it in Mr W's presence in his parlour. Beck made the punch and gave it round. I sat at the window near the door of Mr W's room. It was dark by this time and the candle was lit. Beck's sister Frances gave round some apples from the apple room. Haslam wanted the hay at thirty-five shillings a ton but Mr W wouldn't give it for less than forty shillings a ton and no agreement was made.

It was on this day generally known that Francis Whitfield of Harvest Lodge was preparing to go to church on last Sunday and cut his throat dangerously with a razor. I never heard the particulars of it. It is enough to record that I do not think he did it intentionally. His wife (my aunt Sally WD) was so shocked by it that she some day since last Sunday went out of her mind.

Birr, Monday, September 12th 1859.

Was wet from near eleven in the morning till night. On my way to Birr near Ballynaguilsha big hill I saw my uncle Richard over in the fields and went over to talk to him. I was not in Birr till after ten and did not trouble myself to go to school.

Birr, Tuesday, September 13th 1859.

It was raining this morning so that I think this rain is connected with that of yesterday and that it rained all night and did not stop until this evening.

I saw Captain Young, the battalion paymaster, passing with an umbrella over his head. I stopped him at the chapel and told him my friends were about to purchase me a commission and I wanted to know what examinations I had to pass. He asked me who I was, where I was from and if I was educated. Then he told me my friends should apply to the Commander in Chief's military secretary. I would have to pass a classical and mathematical examination. He told me to call to his house at fifteen, The Mall, after two o'clock when he would give me every information he could.

I went to the house a little after two and a girl let me in. She went in to a room on the left and Captain Young came out, I think he was at his dinner. 'I came for the instructions.'
'I'll give you the best information I can, come upstairs.' I followed him to a beautiful carpeted room - the drawing room. He handed me a chair saying, 'Take a chair.' He wrote a few lines which he then read to me. He said it would be better to get Major Warburton's recommendation than Colonel Bernard's. (Major Warburton is a son of Dr. Warburton's WD). I should fall into chat with young McCausland about the examinations as he was preparing to pass. Captain Young did not know much about the examinations as he was promoted from the ranks. Here is a copy of the paper he wrote for me. 'Write to the Commander in Chief's military secretary to have your name placed on the Commander in Chief's list of candidates for commission. Get it recommended by at least two persons of some note - if in the service the better. When this is done and you are ready to pass the examination (they take place periodically) go up to London having first signified your intention in writing to the military secretary and having passed you will shortly after be gazetted to a regiment.'

Davistown, Thursday, September 15th 1859.

Some wet. I got up at four and walked home to show Mr W the paper Captain Young gave me. When I came as far as Nanny Reilly's I went by the Ballincard and Clontyglass old road and Cash's field. It was raining all the time.

My mother was at Harvest Lodge for my aunt Sally was then in a sad state of madness. My mother stopped up last night with a few other women minding her. Francis Whitfield is getting better of his wound and she worse. When mother came home I asked her when was she first noticed to be mad. She said she was raving mad since last Tuesday week. Sometimes she enquires 'Did the devil take my old mother yet?' And when Richard Davis's wife goes near her in her mourning dress she tells them 'Hunt away the black lady, don't let the black lady near me!' She is able to hear the lowest whisper given in the room. She says 'They have me starved; I never eat a bit since I was in the Holy city of Jerusalem. Ye stole all my gold and wouldn't give me time to make my will." She begins to rhyme some times and at others she thinks the police are come to shoot all her children and she will say 'O, my new born babe!' She often softly tells those in the room to go down now and leave the window open, that there's no fear of her. Then she strives to get to the window to throw herself out. Other times she says 'John Davis if you have any brotherly love in you come and take these handcuffs off me' (the bands tying her). She craves of those around her to put their hands to her mouth. Gret Cleary (daughter of Brian Cleary, a neighbour of theirs WD) to try her, put her apron to aunt Sally's mouth and that instant she snapped at it and left in it the marks of her teeth. She then ground her teeth, shut her eyes and distorted her face with vexation that it was not Gret Cleary's finger.

I went out to Mr W's in the evening and stayed in the kitchen till he went to his punch. I told him that it was talked of in Birr that the Chinese fired at some English vessels sinking them and killing some officers. 'O', said Mr W 'that'll be another war.' I showed him the letter Captain Young gave me. Mr W thinks that if I study well I should be ready for the examination in two or three months – 'Stay up till twelve every night studying; you'll have nights enough to sleep.' He advises me to get one of the sergeants to teach me drill for a few shillings. The £450 must be lodged when I send in my name. I will get two per cent interest in Birr - that's nine pounds a year. The money can be left in the bank till I get my commission. Mr W said hereabouts of the examination 'They had as good officers at Waterloo as ever they'll have and most of them hardly knew how to write their name. The examination is only a rigmarole, a humbug.' I said I hoped they would do away with it.

Mr W remarked that it was Wellington (when he was Commander in Chief) who got him back on full pay. 'I was on half pay because the regiment was disembodied. That was the time I was sent home from the 8th West Indian on half pay, three shillings a day. I wrote to the Duke of Wellington to say that I wished to be restored to full pay and he wrote me an answer that my claim would be attended to. After a time I wrote again and got an answer that I would get the next vacancy. Five months after I was gazetted to an ensigncy in the 86th in place of a fellow of the name of Selway who died in the West Indies.'

Before I came in Mr W urged me to go to McCausland about the examination.

Birr, Friday, September 16th 1859.

Was fine. Today I walked to Birr against seven o'clock. Tiger came with me almost all the way. At Pensioner's Hill I threw him into a drain on the left but he followed me still. A little further on I came to Tom Connor's and there I thought to set him at a cock that was on the road. He stood till I was out of sight and then went off home. I was not at school for I heard that Weir was gone to Limerick since yesterday evening. Today was the second fair day of Banagher - the horse fair - and a great many went there from Birr without any business and I was one of them. I left Birr by Oxmantown Mall at about half past ten taking the direct road to the right of the castle gate till I came to the church of Banagher which is just at the entrance to the town. I stood there for a minute looking at the lightning conductor of the church from the road and then walked back to Birr without ever entering the fair. I met William Smallman not far from Banagher. He always took great pleasure in going to the horse fair. I was back to Birr a while before three o'clock.

Davistown, Saturday, September 17th 1859.

Weir was not home so I did not attend school. At about half past nine James and I went up to the barracks where there was an inspection. (James brought my mother in this morning WD.) After some little parleying with the sentry (a private of the 21st in side arms WD) we were admitted. Lieutenant General T. F. Love a Waterloo veteran and his Aide de Camp inspected. It was beautiful to look at.

This evening Richard went home first and afterwards James, mother, Margaret and Charlotte went in the ass's car. I waited in Birr to get money from James Davis to pay Wallace and Jude Mulrooney but he broke his promise and did not come. I left Birr at half past six and it was dark a little after that.

Davistown, Sunday, September 18th 1859.

Morning hazy, evening some smart wet. I was not at church. When I went out Mr W was reading the paper. 'O', he said, 'the war's up, the Chinese'll pay for it.'

I had seen an account in the paper in June last that the British were proceeding up the Peiho[258] River which was barred against them when the Chinese fired on them. They sank three of the ships and killed and wounded near five hundred men. Our troops - officers and men - were obliged to wade through mud and mire where all of the scaling ladders save one were lost. It is supposed that the Chinese were assisted by the Russians for within the walls people were heard calling for powder in Russian. It is further reported that some of the wounds on the men were rifle wounds and the Chinese had no rifles. By this massacre the Chinese have broken the treaty with England, France and America.

'Part of the treaty' (says Mr W) 'was that the English ambassadors should be permitted to live in the city of Peking. They were going up the river when they opened their batteries and fired on us. We have an island there called Chu San and all we wanted was free trade and honest dealings.' The *Warder* says France is preparing to send out 12,000 men to China and the British government 8,000 (at least).

Dooley who bought some hay from Mr W came and gave him some pence he owed him. Mr W brought him into the kitchen to tell him how the markets rated and while talking on this subject Mr W said, 'I never saw such potatoes as are on the hill, every one of them nearly a pound weight. But I don't like to see the great price of them and all the poor people in the cities having to buy them by the stone.'

After my dinner I returned to Mr W's parlour where he told me to pull near the fire as it was no way warm. I told him that I had been talking to the pedant[259] Gaynor, a Catholic. He had prepared McCausland the last time he went to London. Weir prepared him the first time when he did not pass. Gaynor told me he would have me ready to pass in three months. McCausland had to learn three books of Virgil[260], French, three books of Euclid, Algebra, Arithmetic and English.

'What use in you going to Birr in the morning without seeing James Davis? If I were you I'd go up to Curraghmore in the morning and I'd tell him that there was a man in Birr that'd prepare me for the examination in two months - you needn't say three months.'

I told Mr W that I had walked to Banagher on Friday. He wanted to know did I see the bridge but I did not go that far. He said the school was there somewhere outside the town.

About here I asked Mr W about several of his officers and what became of

---

258   25th June.'The English and French forces accompanying the English and French ambassadors to the emperor of China being obstructed in their passage up the Peiho River on their way to Peking attempted to force their way, but were repulsed with the loss of about 450 men and were compelled to withdraw'. Source: Roger Vaughan's internet history pages.

259   Schoolmaster or teacher.

260   Renowned Roman poet 70-19 BC. Source: *Collins English dictionary*.

them. Mr W said that poor Creagh, an old 'chip' of his, was gone home and I afterwards saw in the Gazette '86 foot Lieutenant Colonel & Brevet full pay Colonel James Creagh[261] has been permitted to retire on under the provisions of the 37th clause of the Royal Warrant of Oct 14th 1858, Sept 16th.' (NB The date of his retirement Friday 16th WD.)

'Poor Jimmy', says Mr W 'he's very old now, about seventy. It's a long time now since I seen him. I seen him in'29. I shook hands with him when he was going from Tobago to Trinidad.' (I think it was Trinidad and Tobago WD.)'He had small brown eyes and about five foot nine in height. I think he was from County Limerick or Clare. It's likely he's living now in the clubs if he's not married. He'll have all the news and every attention paid to him. Creagh stuck by the 86th all along but nearly all the old hands are gone now. He may be a relative of Pearse Creagh. Warnell was another chip of mine. He's living at one of the clubs in London and every time he sees George Whitfield he does be asking about me. Johnston stuck by the 33rd. He lost an arm in the Russian War.'

He never heard what became of Hatwell or Captain Westmore (with whom he was never on intimate terms). He thought Captain Stuart of the 86th went home shortly after him (Mr W). He had a large family in Scotland in the Isle of Sky. His son Willy was also in the army but was a wild fellow. Mr W had much occasion to speak to him and threatened him once with a court-martial for all his tricks. His father had little influence over him.

Galloway was Mr W's favourite. Says he 'I wouldn't give Galloway for the whole of them - we spent too many days together. He was very fond of pipes and would buy every handsome one he'd see. He'd come to me and say "Here, take a smoke out of this pipe, never fear you'll like this pipe." We used to lodge together when we were on the march but he'd as soon fight at Waterloo as to go take lodgings and I would always do that. I think he was from Chatham or Woolich. One time he came to me in the middle of the night to say his father was dead. He needed money to go home and settle his affairs and I gladly gave him what I could. I looked after his wife while he was away. We were in Newry that time. I never heard of Thene or Lowe after. Sergeant Thomson got to be paymaster the time of the Russian War. There was a vacancy for it and my friend Warnell in the club thought to get it for George Whitfield but the officers had sent in Thomson's name and he got it.' (I afterwards saw in the army list the name of John Thomson paymaster of the 33rd. His commission was dated 25th May '55 WD.)

'Warnell was always discontented' (says Mr W). 'Every officer that fought at Waterloo had a 'w' before their name - a small w in italics. He had been in

---

261   'A Colonel's rank at a Major's pay. Brevet rank is permanent army rank, as regards precedence, but with the regimental pay of the rank next below that indicated by the Brevet (commission). It is conferred for long or special services'. Source: Ottley Lane Perry, *Rank and badges* etc. (1888) p. 84. Information supplied by Royal Ulster Rifles Museum Research.

charge of the baggage guard and he had ne'er a w to his name and he was discontented. Sure someone should be in charge of the baggage!

'McGrath was another paymaster we had. Then there was Grant of the 86th. He was paymaster for four years. If you put the pen between your toes and dipped it in the ink you'd write as well as Grant. He had a terrible bad hand but he kept the accounts correct and honest. I vexed him one day - says I 'Begad Grant if I dipped my little finger in the ink I think I'd write as well as that.' He never said a word but I made it up to him afterwards.... I had no right to say anything to him. He paid the men honest and correct; I had no right to say anything to him. He was the fellow that was always turning pot sticks and the like. He couldn't keep himself from getting fat, seventeen stone weight he was. One morning when we were at St. Anne's barracks in Barbados he got a terrible pain in his head and that's the first symptom of fever. Halliday told him to go down to the beach and fire a few shots, that it would do him good. We took Halliday's fowling piece down and it wasn't long before Grant began to sweat and recover. I had my big Panama hat on me to keep off the sun.'

Here I told Mr W that I met young officer Hazlebrick (Arthur) of the 21st going to Banagher fair on a car. He had his legs crossed and the whole side of the car to himself. He was singing as loud as he could. I asked Mr W would he approve of such conduct. He did not. He said 'When you go in there don't talk much for a week only sit at the mess and if they ask you to take a glass of wine take it and you needn't say much. You'll know what every one of them is in a week. Don't make an acquaintance of any of them young fellows at all.'

Shortly after this I came off. Mr W again advised me to go up to Curraghmore in the morning to see the lame fellow. My aunt Sally being still bad I was telling him of her this evening and he said to the effect 'She'll be apt to recover, I hope she may recover.'

Birr, Monday, September 19th 1859.

Was fine. I went to Curraghmore for Wallace's money by Mr W's hill. There I learned that Jas. Davis was gone to our house. On my return I met him near Mr W's lodge. He gave me a sovereign and bid me give Margaret £0-2-6 out of it. When I came home I went out to Mr W's with the supplement. I asked him if he was going to the fair of Frankford on Friday would he speak to Colonel Bernard about giving me an ensigncy in the militia.[262] 'Sure there's not a word in the paper about them being called in,' says Mr W. 'If I were you I'd go up to Curraghmore and see about a commission in the army.'

---

262   See *King's County Chronicle*, 3 August 1859 where it was reported that the King's County Royal Rifles (Militia) under the command of Lieutenant-Colonel Bernard, were inspected by Colonel Smith, C.B., commander of the depot battalion in the garrison at Crinkle, Birr. The regiment was under the control of local officers including Major Warburton and was called in for twenty-one days of training and manoeuvres.

Later we all set off for Birr. Richard and I walked but near the Fivealley Richard got a carry with Brian Connors in an ass's car. I went into Jude's and paid her the one shilling and five and a half pence that I owed her saying I should pay her sooner. She said it was no matter.

After school Dick walked home to spend his thirteenth birthday there.

Davistown, Wednesday, September 21st 1859.

Some wet. James came in this morning with some provisions. Anderson the photographer - or likeness taker by chemical process - that was in Birr lately is gone to Frankford and James heard he would stay no longer than Saturday. I had some money remaining out of the sovereign James Davis gave me and I wished to have my likeness taken so I had James wait for me till after school. We got some wet coming home. Onny (our servant girl) told me that after I leaving on Monday Mr W came to the pond calling for me.

View House, Parsonstown.

KING'S COUNTY.

AUCTION.

FATTENING FARM—155 ACRES.

FEE FARM GRANT.

JAMES CONNOLLY & SON are instructed by Mr. JAMES DAVIS, to dispose of by public AUCTION, On the Lands, On THURSDAY, the 19th JUNE, 1879, His Farm, Known as CURRAGHMORE, Containing 155 Statue Acres or thereabouts, of very Superior FATTENING LAND, situate within 2 miles of Frankford, and 7 of Parsonstown, which he holds under fee-farm grant, dated the 14th day of April, 1859, at the annual rent of £103 7s 8d.

The Land is all under grass, with the exception of about 4½ acres, which is highly manured and cropped with Potatoes, Turnips, and Mangolds. There is a most comfortable Dwelling House on the Lands. Also Barn, Coach-house, Stabling for 7 Horses, Cow-house to hold 20 head, large Garden, Yard, and Pump. The Lands are well Watered, Sheltered and Divided. The premises are in first-class order, not requiring any outlay. A 3 Horse Power Threshing Machine, etc.

The Farm must be seen to be appreciated, the Vendor or his Herd will show the bounds.

Terms and Conditions at Sale, which will commence at 12 o'clock.

For further particulars apply to the Owner, Mr. JAMES DAVIS, Curraghmore, Frankford ; or to JAMES CONNOLLY & SON, Auctioneers & Valuators, Parsonstown.

VALUE OF LAND IN KING'S COUNTY.—On Thursday last Mr James Connolly, auctioneer, Parsonstown, conducted the sale of the fee-farm-grant of Mr James Davis's farm in Curraghmore, principally under grass, containing 155 statute acres, or about 96 Irish measure, on which there are dwelling-house, offices, &c., all subject to the yearly rent of £103 7s 8d. There was a good attendance and most spirited bidding. Mr M'Grane, Cloghan, bid £800, £900, £1,050, £1,250, and £1,460. Mr Barrett, Temora, bid £850. Mr Gerald Foley, Aghancon, bid £1,150 and £1,200. Mr Thomas Slattery, Parsonstown, bid £1,525, £1,600, and £1,720. Mr Colclough, solicitor, Dublin, bid £1,310, £1,670, £1,750, £1,780, and £1,800. And Mr Adam Mitchell, solicitor, Parsonstown, bid £1,300, £1,450, £1,550, £1,575, £1,620, £1,680, £1,710, £1,730, £1,760, £1,790, and £1,810. This being the highest offer, the farm was knocked down to Mr Mitchell for £1,810 and auctioneer's fees. It appeared to be the prevailing impression that the farm brought a long price considering the depressed state of farming at the present time.

A NEGRO BISHOP IN TULLAMORE.—On Tuesday evening Bishop Hillary, of the American Wesleyan Communion, gave an interesting address in the Town House, Tullamore. The circulars announced a "Gospel address," and the large audience were treated besides to an able disquisition on the state of the American Negroes, both before and after the late civil war which led to their emancipation. In many respects the Bishop did not think the war did much to improve the negroes' condition, principally owing to the rooted aversion of white people to mix with them, but the attitude of the Roman Catholics and Quakers admitting them to their churches and communion was worthy of all praise. The Bishop is a man of commanding appearance, and there is very little in his accent or style of speaking to indicate his race. At the close of the lecture a collection in aid of the Church and schools over which he presides in San Francisco was made, and over £5 subscribed. Had the circulars contained an intimation that a collection would be made, the sum would have been larger.

(G)   Notice and report of the sale of the Davis, Curraghmore farm, in June 1879 from the King's County Chronicle

Davistown, Thursday, September 22nd 1859.

Was fine. Early in the day I went to Frankford by the ancient, lonely and beautiful old road to get my likeness taken. Anderson took all the likenesses in the old yard of the second house in the turf market. He stops at Delany's Hotel. I got mine in a case for £0-2-6, one shilling of my own, one shilling of my mother's and the six pence was Margaret's. Anderson was a gentleman-like fellow about thirty three years of age. I heard he was at church in Ballyboy the Sunday before, I think he is a Scotchman. Lizzy and Mary Anne Davis had their likenesses taken also. I think Lizzy's is better than mine. It is in a case and cost three shillings.

Birr, Friday, September 23rd 1859.

Day fine, evening showery. James got up very early in order to get ready to go to the fair of Frankford. I eat my breakfast of the stirabout he had done and we were at Jack Brien's before daylight. James waited there for Jack and I continued to Birr. Before school I went to Wallace's house and paid him his bill of £0-15-9. Later Phil Robinson told me that McCausland got word that he did not pass his examination in London.

Davistown, Saturday, September 24th 1859.

There was very hard wet in the morning, the day was fine. No one but James came in this morning. After school we all left Birr together, Richard and I walking, the other three in the car. About a quarter of a mile outside the town William Hernon, the carpenter's son, overtook us with a horse and cart and gave us a carrying as far as his house.

I went out to Mr W who was in the parlour at his punch to tell him that McCausland was cast in his examination. I had also heard that McCausland was now intending to study for the medical profession but it was my opinion that he did not have the taste for it. Mr W said 'I knew a man that was educated in Maynooth four years. It was his parents wish that he be a priest. Well, when he went to be ordained he dressed himself up like a dandy and when the bishop saw him he told him to go home. Neither his father or mother would speak to him for a week. At the end of the week he asked his father for twenty pounds and set off for Edinburgh where he passed an examination for the medical department. He was put on board a ship as assistant surgeon in the navy.' I said to Mr W that it was a wonder he passed the examination when he was educated to be a priest. 'I mistrust' (says Mr W), 'that while he was at Maynooth he paid more attention to that than to anything else.'

I said I should go in to show Margaret Mrs Murray's[263] (so I used to call her) likeness. She got it taken yesterday. My likeness and Lizzy's were sent

263   Beck.

out to Mr W's yesterday. Mr W said he thought Lizzy's likeness the best. 'Rebecca'd laugh at me if I said that to her' says Mr W, (NB that Lizzy's was the best WD). Shortly after this I came in bringing Beck's likeness with me. Lizzy was gone to Harvest Lodge to mind aunt Sally. Later I sent back the likeness by Nell Carroll who came out to our house on some message (a little girl then living at Mr W's WD).

Davistown, Sunday, September 25th 1859.

Some showers. I was not at Eglish or my boots needed mending. A little after one I went out to Mr W's. He was in the kitchen with Tim Stapleton (the mason that built our house WD) and an old man that looked to be a pensioner. Mr W said to me 'They found out what became of Sir John Franklin.'[264] (A navigator, WD.) He gave me the *Warder* and supplement and I read that Captain McClintock had returned from his search for John Franklin and his companions, bringing relics of them and tidings of how they perished of cold &c.

After my dinner when I returned to Mr W's I found the kitchen door bolted and I entered by the hall door. In a few minutes he came in with a whip in his hand saying he was herding the cattle as there was no one else at home. He remained outside the hall door walking up and down and I with him. I said I had a geranium since it was an inch high and now it was more than a foot. He showed me a plant with a little yellow flower that was growing opposite the kitchen, but he did not know its name. He brought me to the end of the little enclosure next the orchard to show me the Colt's Foot saying it was a queer plant that did not blossom till January. He told me that when the Woods daughters were there they used to be sowing many things.

It was from the haycocks Mr W was minding the cattle. As I had the paper with me I said I would mind them and for him to go in to his punch. There was a heavy shower while I was watching them and I got under a bush. In a while after Mr W sent Wm. Rigney out to let me in. He had been to Broughal to tell Willy Welsh (formerly a National School master) to come to Mr W's tomorrow to survey potatoes and meadow.

Mr W asked me how they were getting on at Harvest Lodge. I told him that Francis Whitfield was getting better and my aunt Sally was a little better too, that she usen't say so many strange things. I told him some of her sayings about the holy city of Jerusalem. He said 'She made good haste to be there', and that she ought to get a shower bath. I asked him did he ever see a mad person. 'I did, I knew a man that was mad and he used always be cursing and swearing. 'Jack' says my father to him one day, 'what makes you always be cursing and swearing?'

---

264 Artic explorer, 1786-1847. He died with all his companions on an expedition to discover the North West Passage. Source: *NE* vol. 6, p. 94.

'I don't be cursing and swearing' says he. 'To curse is to kneel down and give one your curse and to swear is to take up a book and take your oath. I do neither of them.'

She ought to get a shower bath. Madness is a great affliction in England. I knew a beautiful asylum near Stafford. It was kept by Doctor Garret, a nice man. He was a doctor in the army and used to invite us to his house to dine. The first thing that'd be done with a patient that'd come in was he'd dip every bit of them in the well. When they'd be recovering they'd be let walk a bit every day three or four of them together, but a man would go with them to mind them. They used to keep the women in the top storey and there was one girl there who had a lovely singing voice. She'd never begin to sing until the sun would be setting, then you'd hear her all over the country. Sure aren't them that go out hunting mad. They spend all day endangering their lives and for what - to catch a fox?'

Here I told Mr W what my mother told me James Davis said to Tedy Digan on the fifteenth last. They were sorting sheep that came from Banagher and he cursed Tedy's crooked soul to a certain bad place. 'O, the pot talking to the kettle' (says Mr W). 'They are lifeless that are faultless. No one should ever upbraid another with his failings.'

Mr W said he thought the old road to Frankford was a nice road. (The Clontyglass and Balincloghan old road. In Ireland the time of the wars between William and James that was the road from Birr to Frankford WD.)[265] I asked Mr W where did the old road go long ago where it ends now at the end of Ballincard. He said it went out at Billy Hanlon's across from the bridge of Eglish by my grandfather's door and up by George Fagan's (the sexton) and out on the present road near Thomas Guinan's and on to Birr. There was no road that time from Hanlon's to Frankford.

About here Mr W said our house was built in a bad position facing the south westerly wind in the front and the north wind in the back door. It was built that way to face the road. He said he could have his hall door open all year round with ne'er a bit of wind in the house.

He bought the best stripper cow ever he saw in Frankford on Friday from Gaff of Ballincloghan. She cost only three pounds and gives eight quarts of milk a day.

Birr, Monday, September 26th 1859.

Some showers. Margaret went to Frankford to get her likeness taken. Richard walked in to Birr followed by James, mother and Charlotte in the ass's car. I was in against half past eleven o'clock. Grandfather was in and eat his dinner with us. I did not go to school. I sent home to Mr W five

---

265   See OS sheet 117 for this road north west of Kilcormac, from Barnaboy to Ballykealy house via Davistown and Ballincard.

volumes of Wesley's works containing chiefly his journals.

When I could not get an army list at the *Chronicle* office Fred Lloyd lent me a copy. Upon turning to the 70th regiment I saw the name of poor Galloway: Thomas James Galloway, c 22 Dec 48 (c meaning Brevet Colonel WD). He was the first of two Lieutenant Colonels, the other was Trevor Chute. On looking at the 86th I saw Creagh's name: Lieutenant Colonel James Creagh c 30 April 52 (the date of his commission WD) so that he only got two steps since Mr W left the 86th. This army list was for the then present month but was dated August 29th which was before Creagh's retirement. I also saw Willy Stuart's name on the 86th: Major William Kier Stuart, Lc 29th September 54 (Lc = Brevet Lieut. Col. WD). Captain in the 86th was John Jerome[266] 28 March 54 son of the Jerome[267] Mr W brought to the mess table when he (Jerome) was promoted from sergeant. In the 33rd was Lieut. Col. J.D. Johnston cbc 9 March 55 at the Russian War.

Birr, Tuesday, September 27th 1859.

Some wet. Margaret came in this morning and brought her likeness which was faithful enough but not so much as Lizzy's. She was coming in last night but mother met her as she went home with James and made her stop at grandmother's for the night.

Davistown, Wednesday, September 28th 1859.

Evening wet. I got out of school at twelve and wrote till Margaret &c came. After I dined I walked home. It rained terribly on me and I got as great a wetting as I got for a long time before. James was in Birr today with provisions and grandmother came to our house with him to see our likenesses. She could not go home for the wet and slept at our house.

Davistown, Thursday, September 29th 1859.

Some wet. I went out to Mr W's early in the morning just as he was about to go to his breakfast. I said Galloway was alive yet and gave him the army list to look over for the day. James went home with grandmother.

This evening I went out to Mr W when he was at his punch and Beck gave me a tumbler of ale which I drank in Mr W's presence. He had at that time a half or quarter barrel of Egan's Kilbeggan ale which he got a short time before at Jude Mulrooney's. It was Mr W's opinion that Galloway had enough time served to retire on full pay. 'He's about fifty five years old now'

---

266 'Ensign 9-4-1842, retired as Hon. Maj. Gen. 23-5-1877'. From Lt. Col. G.B. Laurie, *History of Royal Irish Rifles*, p. 469. Source: Royal Ulster Rifles Museum Research

267. 'Joseph Jerome Quartermaster 23-3-1826 - 17-3-1854 to half pay'. Source: ibid.

(says Mr W). 'Jerome is getting on better than Willy Stuart. He was a little fellow about the size of Albert when I left him. I brought his father to the mess table where he never was before. One day I was lolling on a sofa in my room' (in Barbados WD), 'and Jerome came in with the servants pay. Well in the course of chat I discovered that he never went to mess. He had been promoted from sergeant to quartermaster and I think he felt out of place among the other officers. That day I made him come to mess with me and we had a glass of wine together. Before long he was drinking with the rest of them. Well he would do anything for me after that. When a cask of pork or beef'd be opened he'd send me the prime part of it. I think he lives now in the county Meath near Trim where his wife is from.'

Mr W again told me tonight to pursue James Davis about the commission. If he refuses I am to say I'll list[268] and he daren't hinder me then. It was after nightfall when I came in.

---

268   To enlist.

CHAPTER 12

October 1859

An American circus comes to Birr, Mr Whitfield meets the governor of Barbados, black soldiers in the army, a Canadian walks on water?, Wesley's visit to Offaly, John Philpot Curran and the Emmets, brother Richard's schooling ends abruptly, William tracks down Mr Whitfield's old army comrade.

Davistown, Saturday, October 1st 1859.

Morning some rain. Howes and Cushing's United States Circus exhibited in the Fair Green today. I was not at it but saw a free exhibition of theirs which was given to attract the people. A very strange procession of horses and men curiously dressed passed through the town representing the Court of Spain going to a Spanish bullfight. In the evening when Richard and I were walking home we were overtaken by Mr W's pony and car at Dan Molloy's of Ballindown. A little fellow from Clontyglass was driving with Bid Neal and Frances (Beck's sister WD) also in the car. They had been to Birr with cabbage and brought us as far as the piers.

Davistown, Sunday, October 2nd 1859.

Morning wet. I was not at church. About twelve I went out to Mr W's but Wm. Rigney was gone to second mass and the paper wasn't come.

Later I went out again to read the paper. Mr W told me this evening about Colonel Mallet who was made Governor General of St. Lucia. He made a great speech to the members of the House of Assembly and put himself into such a sweat that he took a fever and died a few days later. Mr W continued, 'Sir James Lyons lived in the beautiful Government House in Barbados. He had a military secretary that used to do nothing only tell stories to make Sir James laugh. One day I was invited to the house and my brother lent me a gig to go. Sir James was very fond of bottled porter and says he to me 'Mister Whitfield, will you drink bottled porter out of an old leaden quart after the good old English fashion?' And so we did while the rest drank out of glasses.

'One day Sir James, his military secretary and his Aide de Camp - a Lieutenant - were riding to Bridgetown when they met a black man who made a great bow to them. Sir James gave a great military salute and the other two laughed heartily. 'What are you laughing at?' says he.

'Begad we're laughing at the great salute you gave the black.'

'Do you think' says Sir James 'that I'll be outdone in politeness by a black man?'

'One time General Lord Hill[269] the Commander in Chief inspected us after we coming from Jamaica to Gosport. He came up to all the officers asking them their names and saluting them. He saluted me 'How are you Mister Whitfield?'

'Well, your lordship.'

'Do you want for anything?'

'Nothing.'

The other fellows were asking me after 'What did you say to Lord Hill?'

'I told him' says I 'to pass on and let the sun shine on me'.

About here Mr W said of the black soldiers 'They're a very well conducted body of men and they'll do as well as white soldiers but leave them where they are. When they're worn out in the service they're kept there in a big house and they have nothing to do only cook their food and they're as happy as the day is long. There's a white officer over them from the next garrison. Black pensioners they're called. When they first come to the West Indies from being recruited in Africa there's a bit of board tied round their necks and their names written on it - Peter, Tom or John. Every time an officer or sergeant meets them he'll rise up the board and tell them their name.'

I asked him did he ever see Daniel O'Connell. 'I did not. He was a talented fellow if he turned his talents to the good of the country. But he might as well strive to get up to the moon as try to get the repeal of the Union.

'Now Washington was a clever man and it was by his cleverness that he got the independence of America. He knew that our army was able for him and we beat them every time he offered us battle but then he would not fight with us. He brought us up to where we could neither go on or turn back and we surrendered at discretion. When he offered us battle at Bunker's Hill[270] we beat them, and at the battle of Brandy Wine'.[271]

About here I asked Mr W did he ever drink any sugar in its liquid state as it came from the tree. He said he saw it one time. All you have to do when you are in the West Indies is ask the Colonel at mess may you be absent from parade in the morning. Then you can get up early to walk off to the

---

269   Commanded a division at Waterloo where his horse was shot from under him. Succeeded
       the duke of Wellington as commander in chief of the army in 1828, died 1842. Source:
       NE, vol. 7, p. 172.

270   Battle occurred 17 June 1775 near Boston Harbor. Source: Bryan Perret, *The Battle book*
       (1992), p. 60.

271   Battle occurred 11 September 1777 near Philadelphia. Source: as above, p. 53.

next sugar plantation. They will show you the whole of it and you will get as good a breakfast as you ever got in your whole life.

'The steamers go out there (West Indies WD) twice a fortnight now' says Mr W. 'When I was there the packet would go out once a month. A ship going to the West Indies comes in sight first at Moncreef about ten miles from the barracks on Barbados. The very minute a sail is sighted at Moncreef they signal down to the barracks 'A sail in sight'. Then we would be standing out on the veranda waiting for the next signal saying what type of ship it was. If it be a transport she'll put up a blue peter, if it be the packet she'll put up a white peter.'

Mr W had come looking for me last Monday to suggest I write a letter to my uncle asking him to buy me a commission. He said I must write tonight. I said he was to be at the fair of Ballinasloe. 'That's no matter; you can send it up to him before he goes. Write him a plain letter of facts and tell him to answer it in writing.' I said James Davis was no fool to answer me in writing. 'It's no folly at all. It's worse for him not to answer, its roguery and ignorance. Keep a copy of the letter you send him and a copy of his reply. You say he hates you but what need you care about his hatred. Let you do your part and have it on at once. What use you asking me what to do if you don't do what I tell you? If he refuses you can strike out on another course.'

Davistown, Monday, October 3rd 1859.

Was wintery but fine. Margaret &c returned to Birr to school. I remained at home as my boots wanted to be mended and I sent them into Birr by James.

Early in the day I went up to Parker's Grove opposite Mr W's lodge and waited for James Davis. But when I saw that he had Davy in the car with him I did not go near him. I was wrong in not taking Mr W's advice. What need I have cared for the hatred of James Davis? I was not at Mr W's today.

Davistown, Friday, October 7th 1859.

There was some wet. Being barefooted I have not been at school all week. I was not at Mr W's. I heard that Francis Whitfield's wife was in her right mind again and was in Curraghmore yesterday.

Davistown, Saturday, October 8th 1859.

Was fine. My mother and James went to Birr but my boots weren't mended. I went in my bare feet to James Davis and told him I had no feetware but he drove off. I confess that I am ashamed that I did not follow him to speak plainly and boldly to him.

Davistown, Sunday, October 9th 1859.

Was fine. Not being at church today I fixed old shoes on my feet and went out to Mr W's about noon. He was in the parlour and Beck or some of them brought out the *Warder* to the kitchen for me. Later Mr W gave me the supplement saying 'Read that, it'll give you some insight.' It read "The next examination of candidates for first army commissions will take place on the twenty- first of November and subsequent days. This is rather earlier than intended: but out of the last batch of candidates nearly sixty were, it is said, sent back ('plucked' the wise call it) and there is consequently an insufficiency of youth to supply the numerous vacancies. Only one young gentleman passed for the cavalry."

After my dinner I returned to Mr W's bringing with me a pencil to note down the heads of the discourse as they occurred and three volumes of Wesley's journal. I told him my aunt Sally was as well as ever only a little silly. 'O, that'll wear away.' After this we were reading, Mr W the supplement and I the *Warder* till he stood up to light his pipe at the fire.

I asked him did he read in the *Warder* where the fellow in Canada walked on the water. He had read it and wondered if it was true. I thought it was. 'But how did he balance himself, he must have had some artificial means?' I told him he had some kind of shoes three feet long and a boat beside him. He is going to get a patent for it. Mr W got up and went outside the hall door remarking as he went that the like of that was never heard of since our Saviour walked on the water.

When he came back in he put his pipe on the chimney piece and walked about the parlour from time to time putting some deal on the fire. Here I asked him had he read that book pointing to *The Holy War made by Shaddai upon Diabolus for the regaining of the metropolis of the World: or the losing and taking again of the town of Mansoul*[272] by John Bunyan, author of *Pilgrim's Progress*. (This was an old book of William Smallman's that I had brought to Mr W's a few months before this and remains there to this day WD). He said he had and that Bunyan was a clever fellow. He had also read *Pilgrim's Progress* - a book of my uncle Wm's I brought him some time before. (It was not until the sad morning of 22nd of February that I brought in the *Pilgrim's Progress*. Beck had it till then in the pretence of

---

272   An allegorical work published in 1682. Source: Drabble, Margaret. *Oxford companion to English literature*, p. 470.

reading it WD.) [273] Mr W then sat down to read over Wesley's journal while I looked at *The Holy War*. After a short time he brought out from his own room a tumbler full of ale and ate with it some white bread and butter. This was his evening meal. He used to dine late on weekdays and early on Sundays. He then prepared for his punch by putting the kettle on the fire and brought out a little glass jug of ale from his own room to mix with it. When the punch was made he took off his cap (a brown tweed one), and his shoes, and sat down to his punch at the corner of the table next the fire and the apple room. I then moved my chair from the inside of the parlour door to my usual place at the corner of the table next Mr W's room door.

'It's surprising all the escapes Wesley had' (says Mr W). 'He says they gave him a bad egg in Birr that made him sick.' (NB In Wesley's journal of 1748 I find he was in Birr on May 3rd and in Clara on the 4th. I find the following on Thurs 5th 'Though my flux continually increased - which was caused by my eating a bad egg at Birr - yet I was unwilling to break my word and so made shift to ride in the afternoon to Mountmellick'.) Shortly after in reply to a question of Mr W's I told him that sometimes there would be about forty people at the Methodist chapel in Birr. Sometimes Shields and Fayle, (John Shields Deceased WD) would address them. Mr W remarked that there were no papists in Bandon, that they were all hunted out of it in the wars between William and James. Someone wrote on the gate of Bandon 'A Turk or a Jew or an Atheist may come in here but not a Papist.' The reply to that was 'He that wrote it wrote it well for the same is written on the gates to hell.'

Shortly after this Mr W said 'O what cruelties they will practice in wartime. In the wars between William and James in 1641 James's army thought to besiege the city of Derry, a walled city. There's lots of fellows called apprentice boys there and they shut the gates of the city and wouldn't let James' army in. He surrounded the city and placed a boom across the river the way no ship could come with provisions to the besieged. They went and got all the Protestants they could gather and placed them outside the gates. They had to give them something from within for they were half starved. Then they had only a meal a day to live on.... then only half a meal. They began to eat rats and dogs and everything they could find. At last a ship came up the river breaking the boom to pieces and the siege was lifted. And I was wrong about the date, it was 1690.'[274]

'Did you ever hear of John Philpot Curran[275] William, oh he was a clever counsellor. He got a great deal to do the time of the rebellion defending state prisoners like Tandy, Wolfe Tone and the Shearses. He was on a trial

---

273   Whitfield died on 22 February 1860, see *KCC*, 22 February 1859 for his death notice - a lieutenant in the 33rd regiment and formerly of the 86th he died aged 63.

274   Siege of Derry was in 1689.

275   A famous wit and orator. Born near Cork in July, 1750. Died in London, 1817. Source: *NE*, vol. 4, p. 394.

one day in Dublin defending one of them and there was a little fellow from England sitting beside the judge by the name of Tenpenny. He was interrupting Curran all the time. "Your Lordship" says Curran, "I can't plead here if you allow Mr Tenpenny to interrupt me".

"Well, Mr Tenpenny you can't be interrupting counsellor Curran. If you interrupt him again I'll put you out of the court."

"I thank your Lordship" says Curran "for nailing that rap to the counter."

Well, the judge and the whole court was in shouts of laughter.

'Emmet (says Mr W), got him into trouble six years after, in 1804[sic]. William Addis Emmet.[276] He was courting Miss Curran' (Mr W pronounced it like currant fruit WD), 'and when he was taken up for rebellion Curran's papers were ordered to be seized. He was real great with Curran before that and it's likely there was something about it for says he 'I'll plead guilty if counsellor Curran's papers are returned.' Miss Curran visited him in prison the night before he was executed and stayed with him for an hour' (or it might have been more than an hour Mr W said WD). 'O it would make you cry to read of the way they parted. Her father never let her into his house after. One night at a ball she met a Captain and they were married.[277] She said to him 'I'll give you my hand but my heart is dead in the grave with Emmet.' He had a brother Thomas Addis Emmet.[278] He done very well in America, I think he was a counsellor.

'The judge that time was a fellow of the name of Norbury.[279] He used to hang everyone that he'd try and he was called the hanging judge. He lived below Tullamore at _____' (Mr W told me the name of the place but I forget it WD).[280] 'He was at dinner one day and asked the fellow next to him what was in his dish.

"It's beef" said the fellow.

"Is it hanged beef?" says Norbury.

"No, but if your Lordship'd try some of it it'd be hanged beef" says he!

O the Irish are a very shrewd people. There was a very nice fellow out in Barbados, a Captain in the 19th. He hated nothing as much as cabbage water, and so it is very ugly. At any rate he told us he was travelling in a

---

276   Mr Whitfield has confused the names of both brothers. This should be Robert Emmet, 1778-1803.

277   Sarah Curran married Captain Henry Sturgeon on 24 November 1805. Source: Michael Barry, *The romance of Sarah Curran.* (1985).

278   Thomas Addis Emmet 1764-1827. Leading counsel for the United Irishmen. Departed for America in 1804, joined the New York Bar where he built a large practice, specialising in pleading for escaped slaves. Source: R. F. Foster, *Modern Ireland 1600 – 1972*, Penguin, 1988.

279   Lord Norbury. 'Toler, John, First Earl of Norbury. 1745-1831. Chief Justice. Born at Beechwood, Tipperary, 1745. Notorious on the Bench for his scanty knowledge of the law and his callousness, while his buffoonery often had the court in an uproar......he was induced to resign in 1827....he died in Dublin in 1831.' Source: Boylan (ed), *Dictionary of Irish biography* (1998).

280   Norbury purchased the Durrow estate near Tullamore in 1815 and died in 1831.

poste chaise one day in Clare (I think it was Clare Mr W said. WD) 'and the horses stopped and wouldn't go on. The driver got down, opened the door and gave it a great bang shut. When he got back up the horses went on. They opened the skylight next the driver to speak with him. "What did you do that for" says the Captain.

"O", says the driver "they thought I let down the load, see how well they go on now."

'One time there was a priest above in Kinnitty of the name De Wire from Birr. He was telling us he had a parishioner of the name Pat Ryan, otherwise Pat the rake. A snug farmer's son Pat always had a shilling in his pocket. One day he went to confession. "I came to make my confishin your reverence", (Mr W pronouncing confishin in imitation of Pat WD). "'Well come in, it's a while since you were here, you must have a long story to tell." When he had given his confession... "Well such a black catalogue of crime I never heard. Can you remember one good turn ever you did all your life to come again this?"

He thought for a time, "I can your reverence; I have a minister's daughter in the family way."

'James Kenny has a brother in the police at Dolla near Limerick. He wrote home the other day to say that a priest down there has a farmer's daughter big with child and he's gone to Australia.'

After Mr W had paused for a long time he asked me would I be going to school tomorrow. I said no, that Margaret and Charlotte would go with James who would bring home my boots. Richard was to go to Frankford to leave his measure for clothes. I told him there was shortly to be an opera at Shields' to be held in a large room over his new printing office. (It lately appeared in the *Warder* WD).[281]

Here again Mr W paused for some time and at last I broke the silence by saying the Queen was very much liked by her subjects. This prompted Mr W to say 'It's a queer custom but in England when a woman has three children at a birth she has a claim on the Queen for three pounds. She might be very charitable if she wished. She pays a man one hundred pounds a year for settling her hair. If that was expended in charity....'. I said she might be good enough to settle her own hair. 'Or if her servants done it, O God knows she has servants enough to do it. I think her income is £40,000 a year. But what does Albert do with his? He has £30,000 a year and £5,000 a year out of Germany, What must he do with it all? I think they have a sad account to give what they done with their talents. Dear me if I had £40,000 a year I think I'd put every poor person in the country farmers. What explanation will that man give by and by what he done with his riches and there so many poor people in the world. I agree with Wesley, while you live you must give

---

281   The *Chronicle* reported that the holding of an opera as an event that rarely occurs in a provincial town but that one had been held in the town of Birr in 1858 – *King's County Chronicle*, 22 June 1859 and 10 August 1859.

whatever money you have in charity as it comes in.'

Here Mr W turned his chair to the fire and began to smoke again. Albert Murray came in from the kitchen to lie down on the sofa beyond Mr W near the door of the apple room at the wall opposite the parlour window. Mr W stood up to cover him and as he returned to the fire he told me I should not smoke at all if I could help it. I asked him what made himself smoke and he said 'Custom, what else. I don't like snuffing at all. It gives you a dirty nose all the time.' He got up again going to the hall door saying 'I must look out, William's gone to Frankford.' (This was to see if the cattle were at the hay WD.) I brought home five books from Mr W's this evening, the *Arminian Magazine*[282] for 1807, Wesley's *journals* and the *Holy War* by Bunyan.

This day's journal proves Mr W beyond a doubt to be a sincere Christian and not as it has been too often represented - a heathen. He prayed for Albert and he declared his love for the poor and his agreement with Wesley's doctrine. This at once confutes all that his enemies have said of him.

Davistown, Monday, October 10th 1859.

Was gloomy but fine. James brought home my boots that were mended. This evening when I went out to Mr W's he was walking back and forward between the kitchen and the hall door with a whip in his hand minding the cattle.

He asked would anyone be going and coming from Birr tomorrow, that he wanted some supplement (sublimate for dressing sheep WD). When he was about at his punch I went into the parlour and took my old seat opposite to Mr W at the corner of the table.

'O, Port Royal is a queer place', says Mr W. 'It's built on a sandbank as far as from this to Frankford from the sea. The town's about twice as big as Frankford. I slept a night in it when I went out there first. Half the town was swallowed up in an earthquake just the same as if you chopped it in two with a hatchet. I thought I'd die with the heat in Jamaica at first. They have no glass in the windows, they have them green things', (Mr W told me the name of them but I forget WD). 'You have to keep a net all over your bed like a curtain the way the mosquitoes can't get at you. They're a sort of fly. They'd bite the life out of you if they got at you and when you're going to bed you raise up the net and get in under it. Another thing you must have in Jamaica is what they call a safe hung up out of the ceiling. You put everything in it the way the ants can't get at it.' (Mr W also told me something about oil in some way or other attached to the safe ... that it's full of ants and only for the oil they'd creep down and get into the safe WD.)

'There's what's called cockroaches there too, they're about the size of a

---

282   This refers to Arminianism, the doctrine of James Arminius who died 1609. He was a
       Dutch Protestant theologian. Source: Margaret Drabble, *Oxford companion to English
       literature.* (1985).

beetle. Another little animal you'd see is the crab and if one of them came into your room at night you'd think it was twenty men tramping about. The people make butter there in some parts of the Blue Mountains. The nicest thing you'd see in Jamaica is the Humming Bird. You'd stop for an hour looking at them. They're just about the size of a bee and they suck the honey out of flowers. Another bird there is called the Plover. One day I saw a flock of them coming over and I had a shot of Galloway's gun at them. I thought I'd die of the heat before I had them all picked up - about fourteen of them.

'O dear me what strange things you'll see in the army. There was a sloop of war cruising about Port Royal and the Captain kept a cow on the ship. Captain Cotton grew tired of the cow and made a present of it to Johny Forbes. The cow stayed a day and a night and then made off with herself out of the barrack yard. A planter lent Johny a horse and gig and we two would go off every day to look for the cow. The horse went so easy we used to call him "Bright". We had him most killed looking for that cow. Galloway had a great laugh at us. She was sent back to the barracks about a month or two after and Johny very wisely sold her for ten pounds.

'Poor Forbes went to the bad. He was ten years younger than Galloway and me. When he came home from Jamaica some rich friends of his in London purchased his company for him. He was promoted to the 92nd Highlanders and had to buy a new outfit. They were stationed in Cork that time. He didn't like the 92nd and went to the 64th and had to buy another new outfit. But he didn't like the 64th and when the regiment was ordered out to Jamaica he would not go. He rose kibbeldy with the Colonel but the Colonel insisted that he go. Johny went into the orderly room, wrote down the sale of his commission and off with him to France that minute. Galloway would never tell me why he did it - Galloway and Forbes were married to two sisters. Mrs Forbes was in Ireland that time on a visit to her father's in Sligo and she came into my room crying. "Ah Mr Whitfield" says she "it's little I thought I'd ever meet you in this way". She knew that he'd never do as well anywhere else as in the army. A Captain has ten shillings and six pence a day and he has two shillings non-effective and two shillings contingent, that's 14/6. He has the two shillings contingent and the two shillings non-effective for keeping the men's firearms in repair. If there be a bad nut or screw the sergeant will tell him but if they wear out or are injured or broken he hasn't to pay for them. Galloway was married in Castlebar. He and Johny were married to the two daughters of the Reverend Doctor Garret rector of Ballymote. I think Sligo is on the sea coast and Ballymote is between Sligo and Castlebar. When the regiment came to Ireland Dr Garret sent Galloway a present of a beautiful horse. When I was in the North I lent my horse to Mrs Galloway. She'd put on her side saddle and off she'd go with Tommy trying to keep up. She was the best horse-woman I ever saw. Her whole delight was being on horseback but she wasn't more than seven stone in weight.

'Mrs Galloway,' I'd say 'you may get my horse to ride.'

'Now Mr Whitfield,' she'd say 'I'm too troublesome getting your horse every day.'

'O that's all he has to do Mrs Galloway. There'll be horses Mrs Galloway when you and I are in heaven.'

She'd trot and Tommy'd walk. He didn't like a horse, he'd sooner be smoking a pipe. Four or five of them went out to ride with her one day. She went trotting on in front of them a great piece. They couldn't overtake her and they didn't like to gallop. 'Mr Whitfield, I beat out the whole of the fellows today with your horse' says she to me when they came back.

Says Tommy 'Begad we had the races today, and Lizzy run away from the whole of us'.

Poor Mrs Galloway, she used to tell me everything. I think she's dead now - she was delicate. O what I'd give to see Galloway now. If he walked in now I think I'd go mad. I'd write to him if I had his address. William, will you write to the Adjutant at Canterbury for Galloway's address. Ask is Colonel Galloway with the service companies or where is he. Direct it to the Adjutant, Depot 70th Regiment, Canterbury, England .' I said I would get him to send the answer to our house in Birr as the door is numbered there.

About here I said to Mr W that I did not like weasels, that I was afraid of them. Out of this he told me that he once had a bitch of the name of Fury who would take any cow or bull by the nose but she would not go near a weasel's nest. I came in shortly after.

Birr, Tuesday, October 11th 1859.

Gloomy but fine. I got up early and walked to Birr against daybreak - about six o'clock. I think I was not at school. I sent the following letter and directed it on the cover as Mr W had told me.

"30 Cumberland Street, Parsonstown, King's County, Ireland.

Sir, as I am interested in your regiment I request that you will have the goodness to inform me by return of post whether Colonel Galloway is with the service companies of his regiment or where he is. Also where in Bengal are the headquarters of the 70th and in what year the regiment embarked for India and how long it has yet to remain there.

I am Sir faithfully yours

William Davis."

Birr, Thursday, October 13th 1859.

Fine. James came in for the first time with an ass load of turf, we not being able to buy any.

Birr, Saturday, October 15th.

We had a holiday on account of the horse fair of Birr. Dick who had gone home yesterday came in with the young ass to bring Margaret and Charlotte home. I remained in Birr expecting to get a reply to my letter in the morning.

Davistown, Sunday, October 16th 1859.

Fine. Not getting any letter this morning I left Birr before eight o'clock and walked home. I met Dick, James, mother and Margaret going to church.

At about one o'clock I went out to Mr W's. He had got two newspapers from America one of which he thought the nicest paper he ever saw. This was *The New York Ledger*, vol xv no 29 Sep 24th 1859, P. Bonner Proprietor and editor, no 44 Anne St. It had mostly stories in it. The other was *The Daily Missouri Republican* by George Knapp & Co, St Louis, Monday, September 12th 1859. Both of these were from Mr W's nephews the McBrides at St. Charles.

Some time after the traitorous wretch Rigney came from Frankford with the paper. Charles Coughlan and James Gill were in the kitchen waiting to hear the rates of the markets. Mr W told them out of the paper, there was six pence of a rise on wheat. Coughlan was saying that he heard they could have an account in Ireland of the London markets the same day they were held by means of the Telegraph and wasn't it a queer thing. 'I believe they work it the same way as they play a piano' (says Mr W). 'Half a crown for so many words and they play on the wires and the message is from Birr to Cork that minute. Sure a hundred years ago if you told anyone that the coaches'd go along the roads without horses they'd laugh at you. The first steamer that came out to the West Indies came to Trinidad. The wind was blowing against her and when the black fellows saw her puffing they run off into the woods and wouldn't go near her at all. They said it was the Devil, that no ship could come in that wind.

'The first time I was going out to the West Indies when we got as far as Liverpool we had to give in seven pounds a piece for our mess and they should find you in everything. If it was for seven months or seven days it was all the same. Our captain - a nice little Scotchman   bid me go to the ship's Captain and ask him what had he put in for our mess. Captain Cannon said 'Tell him there's live sheep and creels of fowl on board and there's plenty of bottled cider, porter and ale and preserved tripes. Tell him if he likes he can bathe in brandy every morning.'

'It's a wonderful thing to say that for seven or eight weeks you'll see nothing but sky and water. One evening we were asking would we soon see land. 'If my chronometer be right I'll see land at twelve o'clock tonight. I'll rap on the deck over your cabin if I see land.' At twelve o'clock the Captain rapped and there we were the next morning drawn up beside the island. Another time we were sailing down by the Scilly Isles. There's a terrible rock down there of the name of Wolf Rock. You could just see the top of it sometimes when a wave would break over it. O the Captain would never go down to dinner till we had passed it by.'

Coughlan told Mr W he wanted ink. Mr W gave it to him telling him to bring it back tonight, that he wanted to write a note. 'The pen' (says Mr W) 'is too soft, I like a hard pen. It destroys a quill pen to leave it in the ink and it rusts a steel pen. I don't like a steel pen at all.' Gill and Coughlan went away shortly after. Later Rigney came in to tell Mr W that there was a whole lot of soldiers billeted in Frankford. Says Mr W, 'I was billeted one time in Rugby. It's a great place for schools. One day I walked out and not one of the men could I see. I strolled down as far as the school and there was every one of the men playing leap frog with the scholars.'

After I had my dinner when it was near dusk I went out again to Mr W. He asked me did I read in the paper (an extract from a London paper in the *Warder* WD), where MacMahon[283] (NB A Hibernian-French General WD) was to be king of Ireland. I said I did but that he'd be very old against his reign'd commence. All Mr W said was 'There let him!'

Later I joined Mr W in the parlour where he was at his punch. He told me to write to him from Birr if I got word about Galloway and he would send me the paper to send to him. I am to write Mr W's name on the top of it with his address. The paper will go to India via Southampton for a penny and via Marseilles overland for 3d. 'There was a paper here last Sunday with the Post Office accounts in it but they tore it up.' (NB The paper referred to was the second last supplement. It was dirty round meat but I procured it and saw in it that letters and newspapers can be posted at the General Post Office Dublin for India (Calcutta) via Marseilles till 6pm Oct 25th. I cut out the Post Office account and here subjoin it WD).

[It is still attached to the page in the original diary. SR.]

During the course of our private conversation in the parlour this evening Mr W said 'You never saw such a hand as Galloway writes' (Little I then thought I would ever see his writing WD). 'You could hardly read it. He'd go over a sheet of paper in a few minutes. 'O then Galloway, 'I'd say, 'Why don't you write plainer, sure no one can read that.' 'If they don't read it then let them not - let them leave it there. I'd sooner be smoking a pipe of tabacky.' 'Poor Galloway, another thing he never cared about was what he had for mess; he left it all to Mrs Galloway. If I was in the market and came

---

283   A French commander of Irish stock. Following his victorious command of the Franco-Piedmontese army at Magenta he was made Marshall of France and Duke of Magenta. Magenta was hailed as 'A celtic victory' and he received a favourable press in Irish newspapers. Some saw him as a possible leader of a French force of liberation of Ireland. The MacMahon Sword, designed and crafted from subscriptions raised in Ireland, was presented to him in 1860. He never became actively involved in the Irish liberation movement. Source: Comerford, Richard V. 'Anglo - French tension and the origins of Fenianism' *in* Lyons, F.S.L. & Hawkins, R.A.J., *Ireland under the Union.* (1980).

on any delicacy I'd give some to his cook - a bit of celery or anything.'

Charles Coughlan did not send home the ink as he promised to do. Mr W sent Rigney for it and wrote a letter to Tom Manifold for £9-2-6d to pay Saunderson's agent (Co. Cavan) the head rent of Ballincloghan for George Whitfield. Mr W wrote the letter in the parlour by candlelight. He signed this note yours truly but I wish Tom Manifold had been true with him and not carried two ways with him, the smooth sweet way of the hypocrite today and the foul tongue of the slanderer tomorrow. Mr W said he had great trouble twice a year sending for the head rent of Ballincloghan. By and by Rigney sent in Albert to know would he (Rigney) go to Heath Lodge in the morning. Mr W said he would and I gave Albert the letter off the chimney piece to give Rigney. Shortly after this I came in.

Birr, Monday, October 17th 1859.

Was very fine for the season of the year. This was the last day of the fair - the cattle day. The others left home and were into Birr before me. There was no school at Weir's for he was gone to Limerick. Today Richard was nine months going to Brady.

Margaret told James Davis that Richard needed money for a school book. He sent for him and told him he was doing no good at Brady's. He ordered him to get his books in the morning and go home. Thus ended Richard's schooling.

Birr, Tuesday, October 18th 1859.

Was dark and wintery. This morning Richard went to Brady's for his copy book and left for home about seven. Harbourne the postman gave me a letter from Canterbury. It was postmarked October 15th although it was dated two days earlier.

"13th October 1859

Sir, I beg to acknowledge the receipt of your letter of the 11th inst. and to inform you that Colonel Galloway is at present Brigadier Comg at Peshawur[sic]. The 70th regiment are now stationed at Royal Pinder[sic].[284] The regiment embarked for India at Cork in the year 1849. When the regiment may come home is quite uncertain.

I have the honour to be Sir, yours obediently

J. A. O. Rutherford Captain 70 Comg Depot."

I was not at school today although Weir was home from Limerick. Near 3pm I left Birr for home to show Mr W the letter.

After I read it to him I asked Mr W was Galloway fond of sport. "No,"

284   Rawalpindi.

(says Mr W). 'He had only a wild spaniel in Jamaica that was never trained. His whole delight was in letting her out about the barrack yard and to see her running about looking for birds. When he came to Liverpool Mrs Galloway got a little Fido. It'd nearly fit into a bottle - it'd fit in that glass', (meaning the tumbler he was drinking his punch out of WD). 'Whenever she'd be going any place she'd surely tell me to mind Fido. One evening I took Fido out to walk with me. Well, not a door she'd see open but she'd run in through it and when you'd have her out of that she'd be in some other place. She was so small a crowd would always gather about you. I never brought her out again after that.'

During the evening I read for Mr W a scrap that I cut from some old paper. It was thus - "Colonel James Creagh, brother of Major General Sir Micheal Creagh of Limerick city has retired from the command of the 86th regiment on full pay. This distinguished officer was engaged in every action with his regiment in India and his departure from the corps is much regretted."

After hearing this Mr W said, 'Michael must be very old now. He was in charge of the depot in Newry when I was there. He was in India for ten years and when he came home the cholera broke out in England.' (Or it might be Ireland Mr W told me WD.)   'He was consulted about it and I suppose he gave his opinion so well he was knighted.'[285]

This evening I told Mr W that if I could pay my passage out to India I should go out as a volunteer.

Birr, Thursday, October 20th 1859.

Was fine. Shortly after four this morning Richard was in with an ass's load of turf for us.

Davistown, Saturday, October 22nd 1859.

Morning frost, day cold, some hailstones. I did not mind going to school today. Dick and mother came to Birr this morning in the ass's car. Rigney was in with Mr W's pony and carried Margaret home. James Davis gave me six pence to get my hair cut and told me he would carry me home by Kingsboro, that he wanted me to write a notice.

I paid Finally [sic] (an old pensioner and barber WD), three pence and with the remainder I got pen, ink and a penny stamp. I folded up the *Warder* and put the stamp on it as the postmaster Kennedy had told me to do. It will go to India via Marseilles. Shortly after James Davis called for me and we

---

285   Sir Michael Creagh assumed the civil government of the island of Saint Lucia in 1832
       in place of Lieutenant Colonel Mallet C.B. who had recently died. Protocol would have
       required him to have a title. This was probably the cause of his knighthood. Source:
       From information supplied by The Royal Ulster Rifles Museum Research, 5 Waring
       Street, Belfast, Northern Ireland.

went to Madden's. There he said he would not go home by Kingsboro at all and went off down the town for a long time. When he returned he put the pony under the car as it was his custom to get the pony ready and out in the street for an hour or more before he'd go. It fell to me to stand in Madden's yard holding the pony. Later he told me to bring the pony out on to the street, that he was going home. Then the wretched liar and Dyass of Frankford stayed in eating and drinking for I suppose an hour and a half. I would leave the pony there and go home but he would not stand. Weir had been talking to James Davis about some situations to be got by competition in the registry of deeds office and he was stammering something to Dyass about me going to try for it. When at last I left him at the piers he told me to go up to him in the morning.

The daily diary entries cease abruptly at this point in William's journal. Underneath he has written 'To be continued in another book'. I know he did continue with other journals but none of these has survived.

51.   *James Davis (brother of the diarist William) and his wife Ann nee McBride c. 1915.*

Epilogue

The diary of William Davis was continued in other journals, but these have regrettably not survived. Research has established an outline of the subsequent lives of William and some of his contemporaries, but many gaps remain. Particularly frustrating is the fact that it has proved impossible for me to trace William Davis between October 1859 and August 1872. In August 1872 he was in Davistown but it is unclear if he was living there or visiting. He does appear to have spent time in Liverpool and appears to have lived there between 1870 and 1905, perhaps even longer. William was appointed an overseer at the post office in Liverpool in 1876 which would suggest that he had taken up work there in the previous ten years.[286] He made his plans for burial at least thirty years before he died and purchased a plot in Mount Jerome cemetery, Dublin while still having an address at 18 Ashgrove, Seaforth, Liverpool. Some ten years later his address was 25 Beechgrove, Seaforth, Liverpool. Probably some time between 1905 and 1911 William returned to Ireland and went to live with his sister Charlotte in Dublin.

William's sisters Charlotte and Margaret, and his mother Jane, moved to Rathmines in Dublin some time before 1893. Charlotte worked in Dublin in the clothing trade as a draper. One can only wonder at their change in circumstance. How, why and when did the women decamp to Dublin?

It seems likely that the marriage of William's brother Richard in 1878 precipitated a move out of the family home for Jane and any of her remaining offspring.[287] Perhaps Charlotte and Margaret were already in Dublin and Jane chose to go there rather than remain in Davistown where she would have to share her kitchen with her new daughter-in-law. In any event the Davis women seem to have made good despite a very uncertain future stretching ahead of them at the diary's end in 1859. William's youngest brother, Thomas, died at Windsor, Melbourne, Australia in his 32nd year in 1884.[288]

Charlotte played an important part in the lives of the children of her brother James (my great grandfather). James and his family lived in Offaly but most of his children lived with Charlotte at one time or another. Gretta, born 1888, went to live with Charlotte in Dublin as a young child and was reared by her. Gretta's brother Henry and sisters Charlotte, Matilda, and Kathleen also spent time with their aunt Charlotte. They all trained in the drapery trade, either at Charlotte's shop or in Pim's large store in Dublin city.

---

286   William's progress was reported in the *King's County Chronicle* for 29 June 1876.

287   Richard married Sarah Ellen Rorke of Ballinagar House, Tullamore. See *King's County Chronicle*, 17 October 1878.

288   *King's County Chronicle*, 16 October 1884.

52.   *The Davis family Dublin home at 14 Rathgar Road, Dublin (courtesy of Ms Natalie Voorheis)*

In 1893, William's sister Margaret, died of tuberculosis in Dublin aged forty-nine and was buried in Mount Jerome cemetery.

 In 1905 Charlotte, Gretta and Jane were living at 14 Rathgar Road where they had a shop and some workrooms. Charlotte's business specialised in making bridal trousseaus and underwear for the wives of army officers serving abroad.

Jane died there on 3rd June 1905 aged eighty-three. She had a heart condition and died of heart failure.[289]   Charlotte continued with the drapery business assisted by Gretta and a number of staff.

The 1911 census return for 14 Rathgar Road makes for very interesting reading. As usual in this story it throws up more questions than it answers. By that time William was living with Gretta and Charlotte. However he had changed his religion and had become a Roman Catholic. This must have caused quite a stir amongst the family, but unfortunately I have been unable to discover when and in what circumstances his conversion occurred. Not a whisper of it has come down through the family. All that was ever said which could refer to this was that "He was a bit of a Republican you know". Another interesting detail from the 1911 census return is that Charlotte's religion is noted as being Christian instead of one of the usual abbreviations for a particular denomination. This leads me to believe that a great deal of

---

289   *King's County Chronicle*, 3 June 1905

thought and discussion about religion had gone on between William and Charlotte. If one could only have been a fly on the wall. She is also recorded as the 'Head of Household' although this was a time when it would have been customary to record the resident male as Head of Household.

William was with Charlotte when she died of pneumonia in April 1915 aged sixty- four. Charlotte, probably with the memory of her father's disastrous will in her mind, left very specific instructions in her own will.[290] Her estate which was valued at £717 (Approximately €60,603 in 2003 figures) was to be divided amongst her five nieces and her two remaining brothers, William and James. The value of her estate was to be realised with half the resulting sum of money to be divided equally amongst her five nieces. The other half of the money was to be invested with the interest being divided equally between James and William. Perhaps she didn't have much faith in her brothers' spending habits. No mention is made in the will of her only nephew, William Henry Davis who was at that time living in Canada.

William's death in 1921 aged seventy-nine leaves us with another mystery. He died on 21 August at the Mercer's Hospital, Dublin, from shock and internal injuries, including broken ribs. Contemporary death notices state this was the result of an accident but there are no further details.[291] We don't know if his injuries resulted from some form of traffic accident or an accident at home in 14 Rathgar Road. It is sad to think that his life came to an end prematurely in this way. Had he gone on to be as long lived as his beloved grandfather Watkins perhaps more of his life story would have been absorbed by the youngsters of the extended family and we would be better able to tie up some of the loose ends.

It was a surprise to discover that he died intestate. I thought that after the debacle of his father's will he would have been sure to have his affairs taken care of. However, William had taken care of one significant item, the erection of a magnificent headstone[292] at the grave of his mother and sisters in Mount Jerome Cemetery. The first person commemorated on the stone is his father who had been buried in Aghancon in County Offaly. Maybe he had at last come to some understanding of his father's actions and accepted what had happened. When the Letters of Administration were granted to his brother James later in 1921 the value of William's estate was estimated to be ninety-seven pounds and sixteen shillings (worth approximately €3,930 in 2003 figures).

Gretta then ran the drapery business with a Miss Bannon till the mid 1920s when she returned to Offaly to be with her widowed mother whose sight was failing. Miss Bannon took over the shop at Rathgar Road.

Mr Whitfield lived for only another four months after the diary ended. He

---

290   *King's County Chronicle*, 22 April 1915

291   *King's County Chronicle*, 21 August 1921

292   See appendix 8.

died at Davistown on 22 February 1860 aged sixty-four. This must have been a sad loss for William and left him once again without the father figure he craved.

Frances Sarah Davis, whom I believe to be grandmother Davis, died at Curraghmore in April 1865 at eighty years of age. When her will was proved the value of her effects was under £100.

Lizzy the eldest sister remained unmarried and living at Davistown. She died there of tuberculosis in 1870 aged thirty.

William's grandparents James and Sarah Watkins were living with their son Richard who had remained at home in Ballynaguilsha. Richard had converted to Roman Catholicism and in April 1858 he married Catherine Quirke in the Roman Catholic Church in Eglish. Richard and Catherine went on to have at least ten children. Their grandson Dick Watkins lives in the house at Ballynaguilsha today. Unfortunately the grandparents Watkins lived out their days in poor circumstances.[293] Sarah Watkins was still alive in 1872. James died in April of the following year at the great age of ninety-eight.

The much-maligned 'lame fellow' (uncle James Davis) continued as collector of the poor rates and the county cess for many years after the diary ends. I don't think he deserved all the scorn poured upon him by his nephew. William had a very poor grasp of money matters. Egged on as he was by his hero Mr Whitfield in his pursuit of an ensigncy, his youth and naivety blinded him to the financial difficulties involved in becoming an officer. A family which hadn't the wherewithal to keep adequate boots on their feet is not going to be able to launch a young man on a glittering officer career. William seems to have viewed the option of enlisting as a private soldier to be beneath his dignity. Uncle James Davis died on 24 July 1888 aged seventy-four. His address at the time of death was Ballincarrig, Kilcormac. He was buried in Aghancon.[294] Following on his retirement in December 1879 his solicitor and the purchaser of the farm at Curraghmore, Adam Mitchell, persuaded the board of the poor law union to allow James a pension of £15 per year – or about half of his annual salary. On a vote this was agreed to.[295]

William Davis's brother Richard stayed at Davistown where he took over the farm. He married Sarah Ellen Rourke in 1878. They had eight children, five of whom emigrated to Canada. Two others died in their youth. Elsie, who was the eldest and the only one to remain in Ireland married twice. Her first husband was Mr Gorman. After his death she married Sam Watson. She went on to have a Mourning Ware business, Davis & Co, at No 45 Grafton Street, in Dublin. This business had no connection with Charlotte's

---

293   See Appendix 7.

294   For death notice see *KCC*, 2 August 1888.

295   *KCC*, 5 February 1880.

shop in Rathgar.

The tuberculosis, which had blighted the family for some generations, dealt another blow in 1899 when Richard died at only fifty-two years of age. His widow Sarah was left to run the farm with the help of her eldest children who had not yet emigrated. Richard's will[296], made only eight days before his death, is a moving document in which he takes great pains to ensure his wife, Sarah, is left provided for and in control of the farm. He was clearly anxious that she should not be left helpless as his mother had been.

James, my great grandfather, went on to have a number of jobs including farming, collection of the rates and acting as a land steward. He had been appointed as rate collector in succession to his uncle James in January 1880 by the board of guardians of the Birr poor law union.[297] For a time he lived at Davistown, then in Frankford (Kilcormac). The family also lived at Killygally near Belmont, later in Banagher, and finally in Manor House, Acontha, near Durrow outside Tullamore. In 1882 he married Anne McBride of Hundred Acres, Kinnitty. They had six children - Matilda, Henry, Charlotte (Lotte), Kathleen, Margaret (Gretta) and Aileen Mary (Nellie). All of them, except perhaps Nellie, lived with their aunt Charlotte in Dublin at one time or another.

Lotte later went to Canada before returning to Tullamore in the 1920s to marry Alfred Joughin of Ballyduff, Tullamore. Their son Henry still runs a grain business there.

Kathleen went to live in Manorhamilton, Co. Leitrim after her marriage to Alan Stephenson.

Matilda had a mental disability and spent much of her life in St Fintan's hospital, Portlaoise.

Henry emigrated to Canada where he entered the Church and later joined the 4th Canadian Mounted Rifles as pastor during the First World War. He served on the Western Front where he received an MC. He was killed by shellfire in August 1918 while helping to bring in wounded from No Man's Land.

His father James Davis died on 13 April 1924 at Manor House, Durrow, Tullamore aged seventy-six.

---

296   See appendix 5.

297   *KCC*, 8 January 1880. The other candidate, Thomas Darmody of Cloncarbon was defeated by 31 votes to 15. The suggestion of anti-Catholic bias was dismissed by Adam Mitchell, solicitor to the uncle of the new appointee.

Thomas, the youngest of William's siblings, died in Melbourne, Australia, on 19 August 1884. He was only thirty-two years of age. The cause of death is unknown but perhaps he was yet another family member to die of tuberculosis.

When Gretta Davis moved to Manor House, Tullamore from Rathgar to look after her mother Ann in the mid 1920s she brought William's diary with her. The two women ran a small farm adjoining the house and when Ann died in 1947 Gretta continued alone. Over the next twenty-five years the house fell into a bad state of disrepair until it was demolished in the early 1970s.[298] Gretta died shortly after going to live with her sister Nellie in Belmont, Co. Offaly. Nellie (my grandmother), died in 1980. During the demolition of Manor House the diary as earlier mentioned was rescued from a bonfire. It was later given to my uncle Ron Robinson. He passed it on to me some years later.

---

298   Houses were built on the land near the Tullamore Road to Kilbeggan for John and Thady Spollen.

Appendix *One*

Letter from Robert Healy, curate, Church of Ireland, Eglish, to The Secretary of the Central Relief Committee of The Society of Friends in 57 William Street, Dublin in March 1847

From *The land by the River of God: a history of Ferbane parish from ancient times to c 1900*, by Brendan Ryan (Ferbane 1994). Published by St Mel's Diocesan Trust.

> Eglish Lodge
> Fivealley
> King's Co.
> May 13th 1847

Dear Sir,

I beg to enclose the list of queries filled up, which you required to have answered and trust the answers satisfactory. I took particular care to answer them as correctly as possible. The rice you were so good as to send me has been of the most immense advantage to my parishes. In fact it has benefited thousands. We have had no boilers in either of the parishes and in order to ensure the distribution of the rice according to the wishes of your committee I sent one bag each to some ladies in these two parishes who undertook to administer it in a cooked state to those most in want. By this means I was sure of equal distribution of it through the immense district of which I have the care.

I now humbly ask, can I reasonably expect any more from you? I solemnly assure you, when what I now have is gone, and it cannot last much longer, I know not what to do. Fever is alarmingly prevalent all around me and I could not attempt describing the innumerable cases of violent dysentery that are presenting themselves before me daily. Being the curate and sole minister of these two parishes and having had your generous aid to distribute to the poor sufferers, almost all flock to me, and from an early hour in the morning until late at night I am occupied (except when duty calls me away) giving out medicine or food. I implore you if you can at all, grant me a little more help. If you do it shall be most cautiously distributed and particularly accounted for.

Meanwhile, for your past kindness, I offer my most grateful thanks and most earnestly pray the Lord may restore it "fourfold unto your bosoms"

Your very grateful servant

R. Healy, Clk.,

Eglish and Drumcullen.

Appendix *Two*

William Davis's Accident in 1851

King's County Chronicle, 12 February 1851

Two young men yesterday afternoon while labouring under the influence of drink jumped into a car which was on the street and drove through the Cumberland Square [Birr] into Green Street. The horse took fright, the two persons were thrown out and the horse returned at a furious pace through the square where the efforts of the police and others to stop its flight were ineffectual. The horse ran as far as Mrs Egan's corner where it fell.

We regret to say that a child belonging to Mr William Davis of Eglish was knocked down and severely hurt but not dangerously. A woman was also knocked down and one or two cars overturned. Owing to the crowded states of the streets at the time it is astounding that lives were not lost. One of the fine windows in Messers Paxton and Muirisson's shop in Duke Street narrowly escaped demolition. The two persons who were the cause of the accident are in custody and will be tried this day.

Appendix *Three*

Record of Mr Whitfield's service

16/11/1815 - 24/6/1816. Ensign in the 8th West Indian on full pay and without purchase.

24/6/1816 - 24/10/27. Ensign in the 8th West Indian on half pay and by reduction.

24/10/1827 - 24/12/1829. Ensign 86th Regt on full pay and without the difference.

24/12/1829 - 17/3/1836. Lieutenant. 33rd Regt. On full pay and without purchase.

In 1827 he joined the 86th at Newry. He sailed to Barbados in the *Brig Robert* and returned in the *William Harris*. He was abroad with the 86th in Barbados from 22/4/1828 - 29/5/1830. He received his promotion to Lieutenant while in Barbados and returned to Britain to join the 33rd in Burnley, Lancashire.

He was in Jamaica with the 33rd from 30/11/1830 - 30/5/1832. He sailed to Jamaica with the 33rd in *Stephen's Ship* and returned in the *Roslin Castle*.

He retired 17 March 1836.

Appendix *Four*

Accident involving James Davis

King's County Chronicle, 31 March 1858, p. 3

Dangerous accident to Mr James Davis

On Monday evening last Mr James Davis, Barony Cess Collector, was employed at his residence, Curraghmore, near Frankford, superintending the working of a threshing machine, which was driven by three horses: a shaft of about fifteen-feet projected from the centre machinery, which moves round it horizontally at a distance of little more than a foot off the ground, part of this shaft is covered by a metal case for its protection, and this was becoming chocked[sic] by straw, to remove which Mr Davis introduced his hand, the sleeve of his coat became entangled in it and the machinery being in motion, he was dragged down and round with the shaft, which several times passing over his body heavily squeezing and bruising him against the ground, his exclamations attracted the attention of the workmen by whom he was extricated, after an interval of about a minute or more; he was suffering much when released having evidently received severe injuries. So violent was the pressure which he underwent that his watch was flattened in his pocket and several silver shillings were bent, and it is believed that it was only to the softness and yielding of the floor that he owes his escape of being more seriously if not fatally injured. Medical assistance was promptly procured and it was ascertained that no very serious injury had been sustained by him although much bruised.

Appendix *Five*

Richard Davis's Will

28 February 1899

Will of Richard Davis of Davistown, Frankford (brother of the diarist)

This is the last will of me Richard Davis of Davistown, Frankford in the county of King's I leave everything I possess including my two farms of Davistown and Countyglass to my wife Sarah Davis for her use and benefit and the use and benefit of my children who are to live with her until such times as they are otherwise provided for and further, I wish my eldest son William to live with his mother and manage everything for her, and if his mother finds him steady and obedient, kind and considerate she has my authority to hand over to my said son the said farms if she chooses to do so or if she prefers to hold them for the natural term of her life she can do so. If however on the other hand she finds that farming or stockraising does not pay and that to hold possession of the said farms is most inconvenient to her she has my full authority to sell the said farms and all they may contain and invest the money for the good of herself and our children. And I revoke all former wills and codicils dated this twenty- eighth day of February 1899 (one thousand eight hundred and ninety nine)

Signed Richard Davis

Signed by the testator in the presence of us both present at the same time who in his presence and in the presence of each other have hereunto set our names as witnesses,

J. Wybrants Johnston, [Rector Ballyboy, *Slater's Directory* 1894].

John William Smith, Kilmurry, Tullamore."

(This will was made only eight days before his death on 8 March 1899).

Appendix *Six*

Table of landholding in Eglish district from the 1851 census

Number of holdings consisting of 0 - 300 acres											
	Total Area Acres	←1 Acre	← 10	← 20	←30	←40	←50	←100	←200	←300	Other
Aghagoogy	451	0	17	11	1		1	1 1bog			
Balincard	391	0	4	1	1	1 bog	0	1	0	1	
Ballynacurra	217	1	1 4 bog	11 bog	2	1		0 1 bog, turbary[299]			
Broughal	3785	10	25	16	7	3	4	6 1 bog	3	1	1796 acres of red bog
Curraghmore	697	2	8	3	0 1 bog	1	3	1	1	1	
Davistown	210		1 1 bog					1	1		
Derry, Lr.	184			0 1 bog				1 1 red bog/ turbary			
Derry Upr.	66		3					1			
Dovehill	500	1	3 1 bog	1	1 1red bog	1			1	1	
Kiladrown	157	0	2	1			1	1			

299   Turbary, bog where turf is cut.

Appendix *Seven*

Transcription of letter to William Davis from his grandfather James Watkins, Eglish, 21 September 1872

My Dearest granchild and good Benefactor. I take the Liberty to Address you in This Critical Time when I am Lying on my Bed and Does not Ever Expect Too walk out any more. You Know the Poverty of this House. A little from you would be a Great Relief at this Critical Time you wont........ it (unreadable) the Lord will give again.

Do not let your mother know I addressed you. If you send anything in a Post Office order send in your granmamy's name as she is still able to go to Birr.

Perhaps I wont be an Inhabitant of this world when it comes.

My Kindest Love to you

your Poor old Granfather

James Watkins.

Transcription of letter to William from his grandfather James Watkins Eglish, 27 September 1872

"My Dr and Blesed granchild. I Recd your great supply for my Earthly wants and your blessed and Heavenly advice to Look to the one [think]. Needful which is all that is worth a thought in this Weary World Below. But I'm Looking to Jesus the Author & Finisher of our faith in whose Blood and ritousness alone we Trust for salvation & may we all set our Hearts and Thoughts on Things above where Tru Joys alone are to be found. I sit on my Bed side While I write These few lines and now Farewell and may we all meet where there will Be no more Farewells. May the Lord of Heaven and Earth give The Holy angels Charge over you By day and night and give you Every Blessings is the Praye of your old granfather and granmother.

James and Sarah Watkins"

On another scrap of paper in what appears to be James Watkins's writing is the following.

If it was the Lords will to call me Today They Could not Buy my Coffin

On the reverse, perhaps in a different hand is

Direct

James Watkins, Eglish, Fiveally P.O., King's County Ireland

53.   *The Davis memorial in Mount Jerome cemetery, Dublin (courtesy of Ms Natalie Voorheis)*

Appendix *Eight*

Davis Grave, Mount Jerome Cemetery, Harold's Cross, Dublin

Grave No 6, Section 299, No 9026

Enter Main Gate, right at Chapel, along Hawthorn Walk, straight through cross roads, take left fork into Neville's Walk, left into North Walk, large grey grave stone on the right hand side.

An exact transcription taken by Glynis Robinson, 13 April 2004

IHS

Gloria in excelsis Deo

SACRED TO THE MEMORY
OF
WILLIAM DAVIS
OF DAVISTOWN FRANKFORD (KILCORMIC) KINGS COUNTY
WHO DIED ON FEBRUARY 27TH 1854 AGED 48 YEARS
AND IS INTERRED IN AGHANCON KINGS COUNTY
AND OF HIS WIFE
JANE DAVIS
ELDEST CHILD OF JAMES WATKINS EGLISH BIRR
WHO WAS BORN ON FEBRUARY 2ND 1822
AND DIED ON JUNE 3RD 1905 AND IS HERE INTERRED
IN SACRED MEMORY ALSO OF THEIR CHILDREN
ELIZABETH JANE DAVIS
BORN MARCH 19TH 1840 DIED MAY 7TH 1870
AND IS INTERRED IN AGHANCON
THOMAS DAVIS
BORN NOVEMBER 15TH 1852 DIED AUGUST 19TH 1884
AND IS INTERRED IN ST KILDA MELBOURNE AUSTRALIA
MARGARET DAVIS
BORN AUGUST 4TH 1844 DIED JUNE 7TH 1893
AND IS HERE INTERRED
RICHARD DAVIS
BORN SEPTEMBER 19TH 1846 DIED MARCH 8TH 1899
INTERRED IN EGLISH BIRR
CHARLOTTE DAVIS
BORN OCTOBER 20TH 1850 DIED APRIL 15TH 1915
AND IS HERE INTERRED

In filial and fraternal love

Erected by William Davis

Appendix *Nine*

Money comparisons

In 1862 an Irish agricultural worker with nine months work per year earned £12-10-0[300]. This converted to €1,249 [301] approximately in 2003 (the latest year for which comparisons can be made).

In 1862 the same worker with a full year's employment – which would be unusual - earned £18 approx. This would be worth €1,799 approximately in 2003.

Teacher's salary, 1853. The annual salary for a male teacher at Frankford National School in 1853 was £25-10-0.[302]

James Davis earned a total of £47-8-0 from the cess and poor rate collection in 1859.

In 1860 he earned a total of £62-13-9 from cess and poor rate collection. The former would have been worth €4,855 in 2003 and the latter would convert to €6,198 approximately.

The sum of £450 necessary for the purchase of an ensigncy, which Mr Whitfield constantly urges William to lodge in the bank for that purpose, was completely beyond the finances of James Davis. It was equivalent to more than seven year's income at that time. It would convert to €46,487.

300   Arthur Bowley, *Wages in the United Kingdom*. (1900), reprinted in 1972.

301   These conversions were calculated using Table 1, Composite Price Index 1750 to 2003 from the Office of National Statistics, U.K.

302   From the *22nd Report of Commissioners of National Education*.

Appendix *Ten*

Family Trees

Family tree of William Davis, b 1842, the diarist.

Bold text denotes further details below.

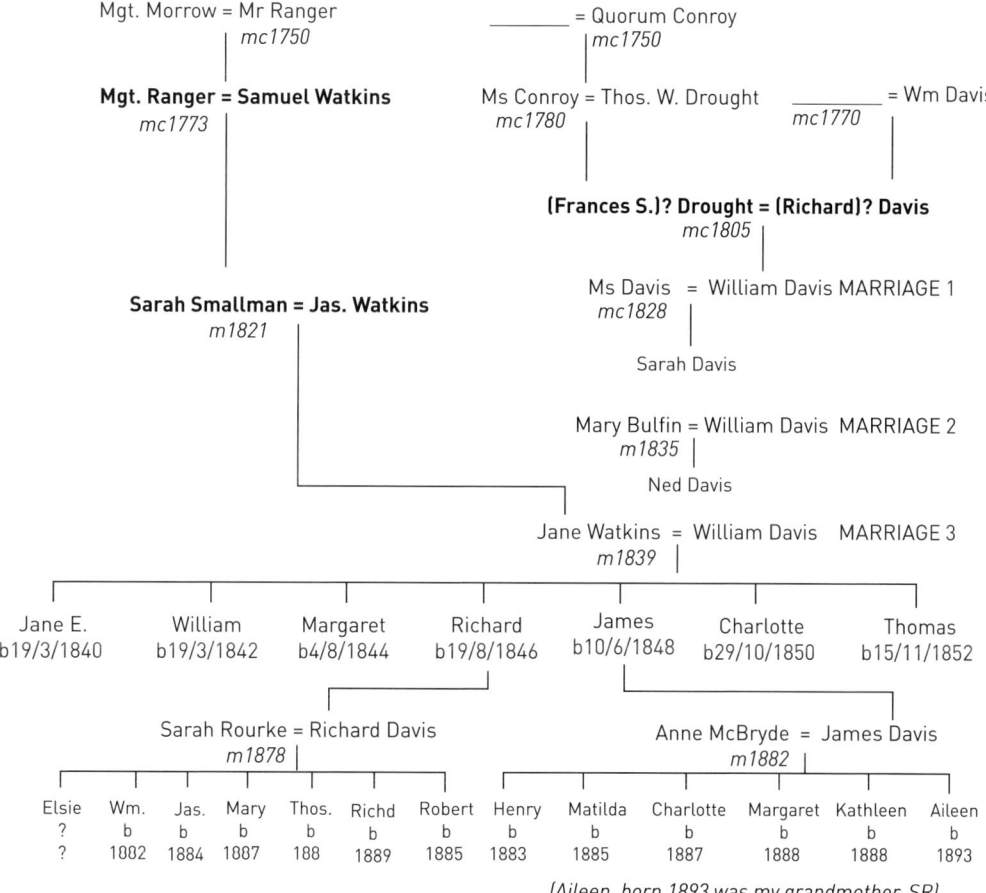

Mgt. Morrow = Mr Ranger
mc1750

_____ = Quorum Conroy
mc1750

Mgt. Ranger = Samuel Watkins
mc1773

Ms Conroy = Thos. W. Drought
mc1780

_____ = Wm Davis
mc1770

(Frances S.)? Drought = (Richard)? Davis
mc1805

Sarah Smallman = Jas. Watkins
m1821

Ms Davis = William Davis MARRIAGE 1
mc1828

Sarah Davis

Mary Bulfin = William Davis MARRIAGE 2
m1835

Ned Davis

Jane Watkins = William Davis MARRIAGE 3
m1839

| Jane E. b19/3/1840 | William b19/3/1842 | Margaret b4/8/1844 | Richard b19/8/1846 | James b10/6/1848 | Charlotte b29/10/1850 | Thomas b15/11/1852 |

Sarah Rourke = Richard Davis
m1878

Anne McBryde = James Davis
m1882

| Elsie ? ? | Wm. b 1882 | Jas. b 1884 | Mary b 1887 | Thos. b 188 | Richd b 1889 | Robert b 1885 | Henry b 1883 | Matilda b 1885 | Charlotte b 1887 | Margaret b 1888 | Kathleen b 1888 | Aileen b 1893 |

(Aileen, born 1893 was my grandmother. SR)

mc = married circa.   m = married.   bc = born circa.   b = born.

Family of Margaret and Samuel Watkins of Eglish, great grandparents of William Davis.

Order of births may not have been as shown below.

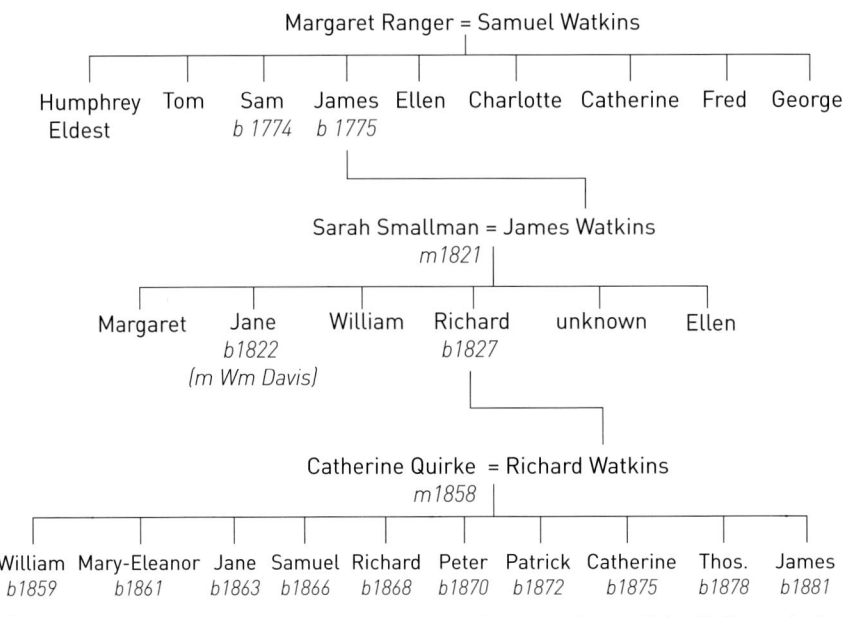

Margaret Ranger = Samuel Watkins

| Humphrey | Tom | Sam | James | Ellen | Charlotte | Catherine | Fred | George |
| Eldest | | b 1774 | b 1775 | | | | | |

Sarah Smallman = James Watkins
m1821

Margaret	Jane	William	Richard	unknown	Ellen
	b1822		b1827		
	(m Wm Davis)				

Catherine Quirke = Richard Watkins
m1858

| William | Mary-Eleanor | Jane | Samuel | Richard | Peter | Patrick | Catherine | Thos. | James |
| b1859 | b1861 | b1863 | b1866 | b1868 | b1870 | b1872 | b1875 | b1878 | b1881 |

(Thomas, born 1878 was father of Dick Watkins who lives at Ballynaguilsha, Eglish, today.)

Family of (Richard?) Davis and wife (Frances?) of Curraghmore, William's grandparents.

Not necessarily in correct order of birth.

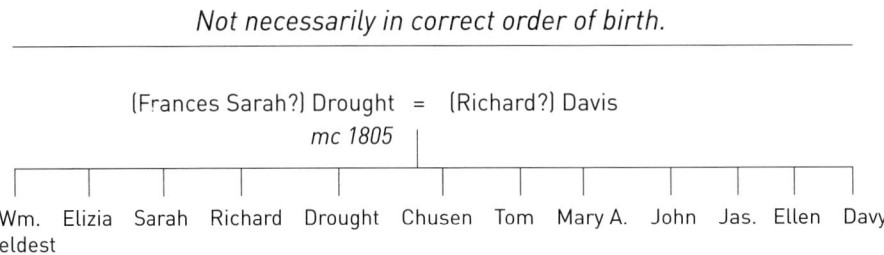

(Frances Sarah?) Drought = (Richard?) Davis
mc 1805

| Wm. | Elizia | Sarah | Richard | Drought | Chusen | Tom | Mary A. | John | Jas. | Ellen | Davy |
| eldest | | | | | | | | | | | |

Family of Jane and Thomas Smallman of Birr, William's great grandparents.

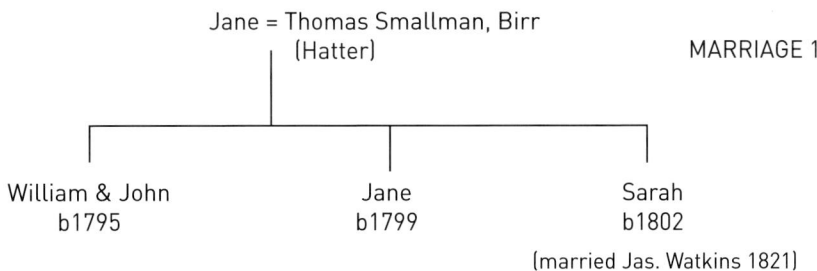

Jane = Thomas Smallman, Birr
(Hatter)   MARRIAGE 1

William & John	Jane	Sarah
b1795	b1799	b1802

(married Jas. Watkins 1821)

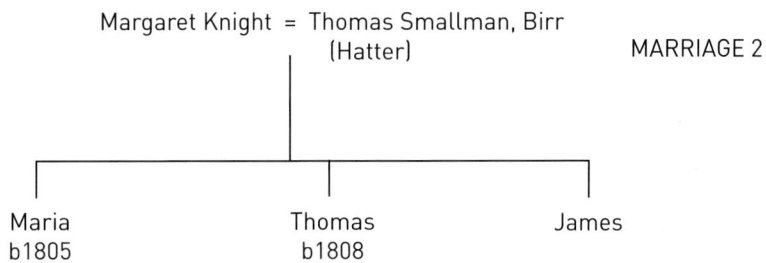

Margaret Knight = Thomas Smallman, Birr
(Hatter)   MARRIAGE 2

Maria	Thomas	James
b1805	b1808	

Index